FILM, FASHION, AND THE 1960s

FILM, FASHION, AND THE 1960s

Edited by Eugenia Paulicelli,
Drake Stutesman, and Louise Wallenberg

Indiana University Press

This book is a publication of

Indiana University Press
Office of Scholarly Publishing
Herman B Wells Library 350
1320 East 10th Street
Bloomington, Indiana 47405 USA

iupress.indiana.edu

∞ The paper used in this publication meets the minimum requirements of the American National Standard for Information Sciences—Permanence of Paper for Printed Library Materials, ANSI Z39.48-1992.

Manufactured in the United States of America

Cataloging information is available from the Library of Congress.

ISBN 978-0-253-02559-3 (hdbk.)
ISBN 978-0-253-02610-1 (pbk.)
ISBN 978-0-253-02641-5 (ebk.)

1 2 3 4 5 22 21 20 19 18 17

The editors would like to dedicate this collection to the spirit of the 1960s.

Contents

Acknowledgments

The first seeds for this volume were planted in March 2010 at an international one-day symposium initiated by Louise Wallenberg and Eugenia Paulicelli and coorganized by the Centre for Fashion Studies at Stockholm University and the Fashion Studies programs at the Graduate Center of the City University of New York.[1] The uniqueness and importance of this international gathering of film and fashion scholars lay in its exploration of the rapport between film, clothing, costume, and identity by way of an open dialogue between scholars and practitioners.[2] The intent of the symposium was to revisit the pioneering and iconic era of the 1960s through fashion and film on the occasion of the era's fiftieth anniversary. The symposium was accompanied by a multimedia exhibition curated by Eugenia Paulicelli and entitled *Fashion + Film: the 1960s Revisited*, which included photographs, stills, costume sketches, and actual costumes from the 1960s.

The symposium also opened up a dialogue with scholars who had not taken part in the conference but were later contacted in order to add their voices to the topics we discussed and to give a more multinational dimension to the volume. In the process of editing the anthology and creating a coherent structure, Drake Stutesman was invited in 2013 to join the team to share the work, reenergize the collection, and refine its content.

This book would not have been possible without the enthusiasm of the staff at Indiana University Press, particularly the editors Raina Nadine Polivka and Janice Frisch and their close attention, and the detailed, thorough comments from the anonymous external readers of the proposal and manuscript. As editors and authors, we have been very grateful for the support, attention, and guidance we have enjoyed throughout this long process of sharing and dialogue, particularly important for a volume of collected essays containing different voices and edited by those who live and work in different continents. Our heartfelt thanks go out to all the contributors for their hard work and the patience they have shown throughout the different stages.

In particular, the editors would like to thank: the Center for the Humanities, the Fashion Studies (MALS and PhD Concentration) and the PhD program in Comparative Literature, and the Women's Studies Certificate program at the Graduate Center of the City University of New York; the students at Queens College and the Graduate Center; the graduate students and colleagues at the Center for Fashion Studies at Stockholm University; the Costume Design in Film students in the Cinema Studies program at New York University; Stiftelsen Bergmangårdarna on Fårö, Sweden; Adriana Berselli; Patrizia Calefato; Nancy Deihl; Jane Gaines; and Torkild Thanem, David Ward, and Anna Ward for their unwavering support.

Notes

1. The symposium received generous funds from Stockholm University and from the Center for the Humanities at the City University of New York Graduate Center, and for this, we are grateful.

2. Our invited speakers covered topics that ranged from the collaboration between Jean-Luc Godard and costume designer Christiane Fageol in Paris in the 1960s to the outspoken fashion nationalism in romantic American 1960s films and the role of fabric in the texture of cinematic *mise-en-abyme* of identity in Alfred Hitchcock's work.

FILM, FASHION, AND THE 1960s

Introduction

Eugenia Paulicelli and Louise Wallenberg

Thomas, the photographer in Michelangelo Antonioni's film *Blow-up*, played by David Hemmings, epitomizes the spirit of the 1960s. He wears narrow white jeans and a tight shirt as he wanders restlessly through London parks or streets documenting the lives of homeless people, while also working on a fashion shoot in his studio with the glamorous real-life model Veruschka. By blurring the boundaries of photographic genres with other arts and ways of seeing, as well as engaging with the way fashion and youth culture revolutionized social, personal, and political hierarchies, *Blow-up* remains *the* film of the period of transformations in society, culture, and media that was the 1960s. Indeed, it was in the 1960s that, against the background of political unrest and protest, the youth became a new protagonist of social change.

The decade of the 1960s was marked by the culmination of the Marshall Plan, also known as the European Recovery Program, a program that provided aid to a continent wreaked by the havoc of World War II. This plan for economic aid, proposed by the US Secretary of State, General George C. Marshall, contributed massively to the reconstruction of Europe's economies and brought with it a more general Americanization and hybridization of European societies. Against such a background of political change and unrest, this volume seeks to explore some of the important cultural phenomena that impacted film, music, fashion, and other manifestations of culture in the 1960s, especially the shift in boundaries between popular and high cultures. The blurring of boundaries was apparent not only in a number of institutions, including the family, schools, the workplace, but also in gender relations. This cultural shift was also borne out through the emergence of industries that catered to the new tastes of the era, such as ready-to-wear clothing and street styles. These changes in fashion were often linked to the youth rebellions, protest movements, and pop music of the 1960s and are now considered iconic markers of the period.

At the core of this volume is the question of how and why the year 1960 was so foundational for Western and Eastern aesthetics, politics, and culture. The groundbreaking films of the decade—such as *La Dolce Vita, À bout de souffle, L'Avventura, Persona, Cléo de 5 à 7, Breakfast at Tiffany's,* and *Psycho*—brought with them a revolution in cinematic language and representation that reconfigured time and space and transformed perceptions of reality. Hand in hand with this new kind of filmmaking and film representation that changed the world of cinema, the fashion of the 1960s offered a break with that which came before—both as a hierarchical economic system and as an aesthetic expression. Interestingly, not all of the must-see films mentioned above have been "revisited" through the critical lens of fashion, a perspective that, we argue, allows us to see the cinematic innovations of the period in a new way. It was out of innovation in both fashion and film that a new aesthetic and politics of style were born, redefining cultural and social class boundaries and age hierarchies in an urban environment that was undergoing huge economic and political transformations. Fashion materialized these changes in society and addressed them cinematically.

The goals of this volume are threefold. First, we examine the role of youth culture and sexual liberation in the fashion and films of the 1960s. Parallel to the socioeconomic and political changes in the decade, fashion underwent a revolution that launched youth styles and street styles and revolutionized gender appearance and performance in dress and body types, such as long hair for men and the influence of the Beatles' haircuts. Second, we explore the role of fashion in a large number of urban, modern, and "auteuresque" films made during the 1960s, examining how fashion helps us to understand narratives of modernity in the films. The chapters in this volume analyze fashion in film as it appears on the international stage during the decade, with case studies that range from India to England and from France to the United States. Third and finally, the volume as a whole focuses on the key role gender played in lifestyle revolutions of the 1960s. Gender norms and definitions were completely rethought during the decade, laying the groundwork for a much more fluid notion of gender that undermined binary opposition. Men and women could literally and symbolically enter each other's wardrobes and appropriate and experiment with color, shape, fabric, and accessories that had not, until then, been shared by the two sexes. This also meant that the 1960s saw important moments of convergence and dialogue between women and the feminist and gay liberation movements.

Fashion, Film, and the Youth Culture of the 1960s

Revisiting the 1960s through cinema, the contributors in this volume all deal with a time and era that was a breaking point in many ways: politically, socially, and culturally. One significant break or change that the time embraced and made possible was the expansion of youth culture, a culture that cherished, advocated, and liberated—as well as commercialized—the desires and needs of the young. The 1950s had already given ground to a burgeoning youth culture that, in its most visible (and audible) materialization, was expressed through a new pop music targeting younger audiences. It was the youth culture of the 1950s that laid the foundation for the expansive, powerful youth culture of the following decade, which gradually became more and more politically inclined. In the 1960s, young people not only became protagonists in society but also created a completely new way of being in the world through music, fashion, and popular culture in general.

One example of the impact of pop music and youth culture on fashion and film is the phenomenon of the Beatles, which is explored in detail in Ronald Gregg's chapter on their film *A Hard Day's Night*. The Beatles were indeed a revelation. Never before had a pop or rock band had such a huge impact on young people from all races, genders, and walks of life. Ron Howard's 2016 documentary *Eight Days a Week* offers further testimony of the unprecedented impact youth and popular culture had in the development of new ways of behaving and interacting in public and private, dressing, thinking, and consuming in the early and mid-1960s. Howard offers insights into how Beatlemania and live concerts offered opportunities and space for young people to express their rebellion against old hierarchies of class, generation, and race. Not only whites were enthusiastic about the Beatles, but also African Americans, Asians, and people across the globe. The film shows very clearly the complexity and contradictions of the 1960s, a period of crisis and political unrest characterized by the emergence of youth culture, civil rights and feminist movements, as well as by tragic events in American and world history such as the assassinations of John F. Kennedy, Martin Luther King and Robert Kennedy, and the Vietnam War.

In the wake of the youth revolution, the establishment began to pay more attention to and take into consideration the opinions of young people on a variety of matters, not only those concerning style and music. An example of how this shift continues to impact media today can be seen in the recently released television series *Good Girls Revolt* (2015–), in which we see the struggles of young female journalists to be recognized at the same levels as their male counterparts in the world of a fictionalized weekly magazine called *News of the Week*. Along with the gender and political struggles, this series brings to the fore the variety of lifestyles, sexual behaviors, consumption choices, fashion and ideas that percolated in the life of young women who were trying to make their voices heard within the establishment in the 1960s, a struggle that continues to resonate today. As the series progresses and as the fictional magazine seeks a new readership, the policy pursued by its editor is to pay far more attention to youth culture, taste, language, and political ideas. *Good Girls Revolt*, while bringing to the fore the emergence of youth and feminist struggles in the 60s, also points to the shadows and darkness of a period marked not only by rebellion and creativity but also by violence, war, and unrest.

This crossing of boundaries and barriers in youth cultures was a global phenomenon in the 1960s. As several chapters in the volume show, this permeability also had a profound impact on cinematic language. Federico Fellini's landmark film, *La Dolce Vita* (1960) illustrates the impact of youth cultures, music, and fashion in the rapidly changing landscape of Rome and of urban areas in general during the decade. In the film, Fellini includes both the Italian singer Adriano Celentano, who was well-known and very popular in Italy for his Italianized version of Elvis's rock 'n' roll, and Christa Päffgen, a well-known model who had worked for *Vogue* and other fashion magazines. After playing herself in Fellini's film, the latter left for New York, where she eventually joined Andy Warhol's factory and Lou Reed's band The Velvet Underground under the name of Nico. The inclusion of figures such as Celentano and Päffgen, and of popular culture in general, points to the mass media's cinematic awareness of this important transformation in Italy and the West brought about by the process of modernization.

Fashion, Modernity, and the City

The contributors to this volume also revisit and reexamine the cinema of the 1960s in terms of its representations and engagements with fashion, modernity, and the city. Already in the literature of the second half of the nineteenth and the beginning of the twentieth centuries, fashion was considered a crucial manifestation of modernity directly linked to urban life and transformation. In his seminal essay of 1863, "The Painter of Modern Life," Charles Baudelaire identified fashion's fleetingness as one of the quintessential manifestations of modern life.[1] Similarly, for the philosopher and sociologist Georg Simmel, the new rhythms of modern urban life led to restless and nervous behavior, not unlike the movement of bodies in the 1960 film *À bout de souffle* (*Breathless*), directed by Jean-Luc Godard.[2]

Film, then, as the chapters in this volume show, offers a unique platform for observing fashion in the city and its role in the processes of modernization. In the 1960s in particular, the crumbling of old hierarchies and the interconnectivity of once separate domains brought with them the crisis of credibility in Western thought and narratives of progress that has been examined by postmodern philosophers such as François Lyotard.[3] This crisis of modernity can be observed in 1960s culture and in films such as *La Notte* (Michelangelo, 1961) and *Cléo de 5 à 7* (Varda, 1962), which show the emerging conflict between tradition and modernity and the alienation yet freedom that the modern city provides its inhabitants. The authors in this volume have set themselves the task of gauging such different faces of modernity as seen in fashion and film, exploring how they intersected with and affected viewers, consumers, and bodies and, ultimately, how they contributed to creating a new film aesthetic.

Cinema is a privileged lens through which to gain an understanding of the spirit of different cultures and historical epochs. In the films from the 1960s, the representation of the modern, contemporary city is a central theme, inspiring in viewers a desire to "wear the city." In this context, fashion acts as a prismatic and kaleidoscopic lens that does not simply mirror reality but continually invents it. Representations of urbanity on screen offer real and imaginary images of places in which different realities take shape (see chapters 5, 6, and 7).

The cinema of the 1960s also turned to fashion as the ultimate expression of urbanity, youth, and political (un)awareness in its representations of life in Western and non-Western cities. Via a range of accounts of the central role fashion had in various national cinemas from the decade—beyond just the major centers of Paris, New York, and London—we argue that fashion and cinema were intrinsically connected in the various cultural, social, economic, and political situations found around the world at the time. While fashion and film have been linked from the early days of cinema, fashion came to play an especially paramount role in the films of the 1960s, where it was instrumental in negotiating and expressing modern life in the context of mass-market society and the development of other media forms. Norm-breaking and trailblazing representations and stories dealing with the spirit of the 1960s as a transformative and highly political époque were shown and told on the screen, and for these representations and stories, fashion (and costume) were absolutely fundamental.

Fashion, Film, and Gender

The chapters in this volume demonstrate the conscious relationship that cinema of the 1960s had with fashion as an industry, as spectacle and aesthetic, and as a means for performing gender. While earlier fashions had served to solidify and naturalize a gender status quo that was taken for granted, marking women as feminine and men as masculine, the fashions of the 1960s were in tune with new political and social movements and a new sexual liberation for women and would upset and question that very status quo. Unlike Dior's effeminate new look, which had held a firm grip on Western fashion and had strongly inspired non-Western looks since 1947—1960s fashions were not about elegance and effeminacy. Instead, they were young and carefree, made from new materials, and combined colors and patterns in brave, innovative ways that at times transgressed the gender binary.

This was the decade when the traditional correlation between fashion and haute couture was broken (i.e., between fashion and Paris), with the new fashion of the 1960s taking its inspiration from youth culture, art, music, and street fashion and from playful (yet dystopian) notions of what the future may be like. Competing with old, established fashion houses, designers such as Mary Quant, Sighsten Herrgård, and Courrèges broke with old bourgeois notions of fashionability and style, becoming advocates and creators of a new kind of fashion. The style can be referred to as "geometric" in terms of its cut: short A-shaped skirts and dresses, tight tops, cutout low-heeled shoes or high boots. Inspiration from men's fashion (ties and jackets) was common and added to the geometric style, and most often, these male-inspired accessories or garments came in bright colors and in "new," modern materials such as polyesters and easy-care acrylics. The apparent desire to challenge conventional notions of gender through a blurring of the boundaries between male and female opened up a kind of "unisex" fashion that was aligned with both the feminist and gay movements of the period. Fashion went from expressing and fortifying a rigid, dualistic, and heteronormative gender constellation, to communicating and signifying a playful jumbling of both gender and sexuality, dismantling the normative standard through its aesthetics, cuts, colors, and materials.

In tandem with the changing fashion industry and its new, playful, and frequently unisex fashions, was the new kind of cinema. A vast number of the films produced in this era, like the fashion of the decade, confront issues of gender and sexuality in humorous and serious ways. Here, the films of directors such as Federico Fellini, John Schlesinger, Mai Zetterling, Blake Edwards, and Ingmar Bergman serve as obvious illustrations of this connection between fashion, film, and gender. In Schlesinger sensitive drama *Midnight Cowboy* (1969), for example, conventional masculinity and male heterosexuality are under scrutiny through the depiction of a growing friendship between two social outsiders in late-capitalist America, and in Bergman's *The Silence* (1963), female sexuality is portrayed in complex, direct and—for the time—intrusive ways. In the third section of our book, these issues of gender representation through fashion and film take a central position.

Film and Costume

In many of the films discussed in the chapters that follow, fashion occupies center stage, highlighting film costume both as a handicraft and as a specific, yet integrated, part of the overall film text. Film costume is also a visual representation of a film's zeitgeist, and it is in this capacity that fashion and film costume must be understood as intrinsically and intimately linked. As a representation of the immediate "newness" of an era, the line between fashion and film costume is often blurry, and as part of their analysis, the authors in this collection frequently question the borders between the two.

The relationship between film and costume has gone through many different stages and processes of transformation that have paralleled the changes in the landscape of the fashion industry and its relationship to the media as a whole. Indeed, it is not possible to think of cinema and fashion without considering their intermediality. There are two different ways of understanding the meanings of film costume: from the standpoint of production and from that of reception. The former is shaped by the making, the process in which many parts work together to create a whole (the finished film), while the latter is shaped by the reception, the reading of the finished film as a complex, collective, and multilayered text. Although they occupy two different moments, these perspectives are related if we consider the film as a whole and as a spectacle for the senses.

The art of creating a costume or readapting one for film is kept alive today thanks to the incredible skills of artisans like those in Italian costume houses such as *Tirelli Costumi* or *Annamode*. Besides being valuable clothing and costume archives, they are also laboratories where younger and older generations of artisans make the magic of costume and spectacle happen on the screen. The legendary costume designer Piero Tosi, while he was visiting a 2016 exhibition held in Rome at Palazzo Braschi in Piazza Navona (*I vestiti dei sogni/The Clothing of Dreams*), noted that the interpretation of historic costumes is not a static act. Rather, it is a dynamic process informed by knowledge and events that define the present in which the past is revisited.[4] Tosi is noting the importance of exploring the present through the past, a technique that we use as we look at and revisit films from the 1960s and their continuing impact on today's cinema.

Fashion and the Future: The Timeless Nature of the 1960s

Feminist scholar Nancy K. Miller adapts the title of Godard's *Breathless* for her 2013 memoir, which is a testimony not only to the continuous reinvention and remaking of the lived reality of the 1960s but also to its timeless return in our present.[5] Indeed, the tempo of Miller's book and the important shifts in the protagonist's thoughts and behavior while she lived in Paris during the 1960s all follow a cinematic rhythm inspired by the film. For the protagonist of Miller's memoir, Godard's work was the quintessential representation of modernity and rebellion against bourgeois standards in the 1960s.

The way that Godard, Antonioni, Fellini, Bergman, and other filmmakers of the decade were able to visualize and verbalize the restless spirit of the rebellions and experimentations of the 1960s ensures that these auteurs, their films, and their costumes never seem to be out of fashion. In the words of Stefano Tonchi, Editor in Chief of *W* magazine, "The 1960s never left us."[6] Our global supermarket of style contains a constant return of details, prints, colors of different decades, or "past fashions." Indeed, as Walter Benjamin stated in his philosophical concept of *Tigersprung*, fashion is never completely new.[7] Rather, it is a reinvention and redressing of *newness*. The impeccable dresses worn by Anouk Aime in Fellini's *La dolce Vita* or the exquisite coats worn by Monica Vitti in Antonioni's *Il deserto rosso* (1964) could be worn today and still seen as fashionable without any alteration.

It is not surprising that the films that were made during the 1960s continue to be referenced and reused for inspiration in fashion design. Their influence can be seen in many a theatrical performance on the catwalks of fashion weeks, in television shows, and in music videos. Indeed, the popularity of the decade and its eternal return has been a constant feature in the 2010s. For example, the success of Matthew Weiner's television series *Mad Men* illustrates the allure and nostalgia that the 1960s provoke, not just for older generations but also for younger consumers of fashion and popular culture. Indeed, one of the distinctive features of the show is its fashion and set design. Among other things, *Mad Men* is a continuous fashion catwalk that feeds the fantasy of millennial fashionistas and consumers who perceive the coolness of the costumes on display as the ideal coolness and glamour of the advertising industry in the 1960s.

The 1960s was a period of many political movements, including the beginnings of activism in the sphere of sexual freedom and of a wave of transnational student uproar. The era has also come to be seen as the epitome of the Cold War, which had a large impact on the countries and cultures of the West and which continues to echo through the present day. Fashion and cinema allow us to revisit this period and provide further interpretations of the tensions, desires, economics, and cultural and political transformations currently found in various cities around the globe. By examining case studies of fashion and film from different cities, contributors to this volume illustrate how the real and imaginary spaces and identities of these locales have been shaped in and by cinematic representation. Besides an overall emphasis on the meaning of fashion and costume in specific films made by prolific auteurs such as Ingmar Bergman, Federico Fellini, Andy Warhol, Jean-Luc Godard, Blake Edwards—the various chapters address issues of style, race, gender, and identity, including: the tensions between tradition and modernity (chapters 9 and 10); youth counterculture (chapters 1 and 4); the impact cinematic fashion has on tourism, consumption and national identity (chapter 6); and dress, art, and politics (chapter 2).

Fashion and film also share a highly interactive quality. As two of the most popular and widespread commercial industries to grow out of modernity, cinema and fashion have always had a synergetic relationship, both using the technology of the camera and that of the body and performance. Costume is integral both to the actor's performance and to the whole of the cinematic rendition of visual narratives and experience. Since the birth of cinema in the late nineteenth century, the film scene has constituted a virtual shopping window, exhibiting and making desirable the newest fashions and goods available at the department stores.[8] Film costume has not only borrowed from fashion and haute couture; it has also inspired the production of the newest fashions. Costumes in cinema have also been used as narrative tools for telling stories on screen that emphasize character identity and development while also attracting a larger audience. More recently, the digital genre of "fashion film" became a widespread advertising and storytelling tool of fashion luxury brands such as Prada, Louis Vuitton, and Dior, amongst others.[9]

Researching Fashion and Film

Although fashion and film costume have always been vital to the totality of the cinema industry, they did not greatly attract the attention of scholars until the 1990s.[10] US-based film scholars Jane Gaines and Charlotte Herzog edited their important collection *Fabrications* in 1990, and in 1996 and 1997, UK-based film scholars Pam Cook and Stella Bruzzi published monographs on fashion in British national cinema (Cook) and on film, gender, and identity (Bruzzi). These monographs were two of the earliest scholarly works to read film through the lens of fashion and costume and focus on important issues related to national identity and the performance of identity and gender on the screen. These seminal books, while offering a reflection on methodology and histories (of gender and nation), paved the way for new interpretations of film, body and performance, masculinities, fashion, popular culture, and stardom and, at the same time, challenged age-old hierarchies in the humanities.

The intersection between fashion and film and the growing scholarship dedicated to it are now becoming a very fertile terrain for analysis.[11] Nevertheless, the combined study of fashion and film is still at an early stage of development within film studies and other related areas and disciplines. The present anthology is a contribution to further the dialogue among scholars and showcase how the study of fashion, costume, and cinema can reveal links between historical transformations in the West and East, gauge the role of spectatorship and viewers, and help us to understand the different stages and complex processes of making a film. It is thus gratifying to see that more academic publications on the relation between fashion and film continue to appear, and it is just as gratifying to see that a journal completely dedicated to fashion, film, and consumption has also been created.[12]

And yet, as happens with new disciplinary configurations and reconfigurations where domains become more porous, we are still faced with a void and a concomitant demand for more scholarly work on this subject by academics from an array of backgrounds, disciplines, and areas. The thrust of this volume is the intersection of these domains that are typically considered separate in academic disciplines. The study of dress and objects does not pertain solely to museum curators or dress historians, but also to those in other disciplines in the humanities, sciences, and social sciences. Fashion, dress, and costumes are now used not only in fashion schools but also in a variety of pedagogical manners to study history, culture, and technology in colleges and universities across the United States and Europe. This development necessitates further consideration of the configuration of courses of studies and interaction of the arts and humanities with the sciences and social sciences.

Structure of the Book

This book is divided into three overlapping sections: "The 1960s: Youth, Culture, and Sexual Liberation"; "Wearing the City"; and "Gender: Modernity and Tradition." The chapters in the first section discuss more specifically the influence of popular culture, music, and youth cultures on the fashion and films of the 1960s. In Ronald Gregg's opening chapter, "Sanitizing the Beatles for Revolution," he explores how fashion and style open up cultural change through an examination of how the Beatles were being standardized and polished in the movie *A Hard Day's Night* (1964), a film that was at first produced merely in order to sell the soundtrack album but which turned out to be a mega success on both sides of the Atlantic. The four wild rock 'n' roll lads from Liverpool were made safe—from rough to nice—so as to present the Beatles as a safe brand, encouraging merchandising companies to sell all kinds of Beatles gadgets, such as soaps, bracelets, and dolls. Fashion, represented by what became known as the "Beatle suit," was one of the major elements that transformed the band and sold its members as nice lads. Yet, as Gregg argues, their new stylishness may in fact have influenced a broader cultural revolution in the fluidity of gender identity.

The experimental cinema of Andy Warhol, the influence of urban culture, and the politics of affect are the center of Amy Herzog's chapter, "The Art of Undressing." Focusing on Warhol's portrait films, such as *Poor Little Rich Girl* (1965) and *Screen Tests* (made between 1964 and 1966), and reading them alongside the more typical pornographic peep show loops produced in the mid-1960s, Herzog explores the modalities that these films employ. These modalities, she argues, inform each other and suggest new provocative ways of rethinking questions regarding labor, spectatorship, and politics in cinema.

In the chapter "Pasolini's *Teorema*: The Eroticism of the Visitor's Discarded Clothes," Stella Bruzzi explores the 1960s ideals of sexual liberation and the disappointment of a failed revolution as expressed in the odd yet masterly film *Teorema* (1968). While she emphasizes the meaning of costumes in the film, some of which were designed by Roberto Capucci and Marcella de Marchi, Bruzzi's sensitive and perceptive reading helps to pinpoint the inherent fragility and ultimate disappointment of a dreamed 1960s sexual and bourgeois liberation.

Drake Stutesman's chapter "Rite of Passage: The Hat that Wouldn't Disappear in the 1960s," concludes the first part of the book. Focusing on two narrative films about the fashion industry, *A New Kind of Love* (1963) and *Puzzle of a Downfall Child* (1970), Stutesman discusses the importance of the hat, a fashion and a status object that, despite its decline in popularity in the industrial world after the 1950s, was still an object that would harbor many different meanings in the 1960s. As she shows in her reading of the two films, the hat is used as a symbol that represents the pre-1960s' cultural stability as seen from the more volatile decade that followed.

The chapters in the second section all focus on fashion and film in relation to the urban setting—the modern city—and to nationality. They discuss the metropolis as a springboard or a setting for negotiations and explorations of modernity, politics, gender and sexuality, and social and personal realities in a number of 1960s films. In "Fashion Apart: Godard and Fageol in 1960s Paris," Astrid Söderbergh Widding looks at the relations between the "New Wave" in Parisian cinema, fashion, and urban space in the 1960s with a specific focus on *Vivre sa Vie* (1962) and *Bande à part* (1964). In her discussion, she highlights how new cinema, new fashion, and new urban life appear as closely interrelated and goes on to argue that this particular period's new cinema and new fashion opened up a novel way of conceptualizing urban spaces altogether.

Eugenia Paulicelli's chapter, "Fashion, Film, and Rome," explores the crucial role of the city of Rome, the presence of the Cinecittà studios, and the massive presence of American filmmakers, actors, and crews in the post-war years. "Hollywood on the Tiber" was a phenomenon of the 1950s and 1960s during Italy's reconstruction that resulted in an economic boom that was largely fuelled by the marriage of fashion and film. Together, the fashion and film industries helped to construct an attractive idea of Italy, turning a nation in ruins at the end of World War II into one of the world's most desirable tourist destinations. In particular, the chapter focuses, first, on how fashion took a central role in the process of the hybridization of Italian and American cultures and, second, on how fashion developed connections with the film industry and the multilayered history of Rome.

In "Contexts, Contradictions, Couture, and Clothing," Pat Kirkham and Marilyn Cohen use the film *An American in Paris* (1951) as a lens to explore how *Breakfast at Tiffany's* (1961) and *That Touch of Mink* (1962) raise issues regarding Frenchness, Americanness, age, class, sexual mores, star personae, morality, and heterosexual coupling. These various themes are expressed in all three films through the use of costume and fashion. In addition, the authors discuss how, in both films, fur and its many varied connotations play a central role and function as a sort of microcosm of these issues.

The chapters in the third and last section of this volume analyze representations of fashion, gender and (to a lesser extent) sexuality and sexual liberation, within four different national contexts. In "The Fashioning of Julie Christie and the Mythologizing of 'Swinging London,'" Pamela Church Gibson explores how images of femininity came to change in the 1960s. Church Gibson focuses her study though an exploration of London as a vibrant fashion capital and of one of the era's most famous female stars, Christie. Two of Christie's early films are at the center of Church Gibson's vivid discussion: *Billy Liar* (1963) and *Darling* (1965), both directed by John Schlesinger.

Gender is also very much at the center of Anupama Kapse's chapter, "Women in white: Femininity and Female Desire in the 60s Bombay." Through a reading of Bombay cinema in the 1960s and of the (white) khadi, Kapse explores representations of femininity and female desire, arguing that Bombay cinema of the time was melodramatic in its unfailing reliance on costume and that costume and performance were intimately connected in this cinema. Bombay cinema, she writes, mobilized clothing as a "primary sign of dramatic communication in highly coded and spectacular ways." She goes on to detail how the white cotton khadi, as worn by female protagonists in 1960s Bombay cinema, came to hold political and ideological meanings, signifying desire, female agency, and social mobility.

In the chapter "Mago's Magic," Louise Wallenberg discusses the long and intense working relationship between queer costume maker Mago and iconic Swedish film director Ingmar Bergman. Identifying the crucial role that Mago played in the making of most of Bergman's 1960s films, Wallenberg offers a reading of *Persona* (1966) that brings out many queer and lesbian implications and desires that are supported and made visible through Mago's magical costumes.

Discussing the symbolic place that the 1960s occupy in layering past styles in our own era, Nick Rees-Robert's chapter "Single Men" examines the reliance of current fashion and film on revisiting 1960s cinema and style. The iconographic hold that 1960s cinema has on contemporary filmmaking, he argues, raises important critical questions of adaptation, lineage, and heritage. Through readings of *Reprise* (2006) and *Oslo August 31st* (2011), two contemporary films made by Norwegian director Joachim Trier that are both heavily influenced by 1960s cinema, Rees-Roberts offers a rich analysis of the handling of cinematic memory in relation to the aesthetics of masculinity.

The book's three sections are closely linked to each other and overlap in many ways. Gender, for example, occupies a central role in most of the contributions as does the concept of modernity and its relationship to tradition. A short memoir by Italian costume designer Adriana Berselli titled "Souvenir of A Costume Designer," accompanied by a short introductory chapter by Eugenia Paulicelli, concludes the volume. Berselli was a costume designer in the 1960s in both theater and television, who worked with directors such as Antonioni. Her story offers a practitioner's perspective on film costume and underscores the importance of the dialogue between the director and the costume designer. She also reveals the complexity involved in the task of character construction during the cinematic process and how the creation of character involves many factors and individuals, from the actor to the director of photography and so forth. In film, dress not only reveals but also hides, sometimes masquerading or playing tricks on the audience and on a monolithic view of identity.

As the chapters that follow will demonstrate, the 1960s were a watershed period in fashion and film just as they were in many other areas, such as sexuality, artistic experimentation, morality, the rise of prosperity and a culture of consumerism, and technical progress. While the twentieth century offers endlessly rich approaches to and possibilities for the study of the relations between cinema and fashion, the 1960s have proven to be a distinct decade in terms of both: it is one of the most experimental and volatile decades of the century, both artistically and politically. And, in the cinema and fashion industry alike, this decade was groundbreaking. Cinema prior to the 1960s had constituted a dream factory, selling and promoting popular and hegemonic representations of the lifestyle of the white, hetero-normative, upper middle class. Similarly, the fashion industry of the 1950s and preceding decades had been structured as a top-to-bottom, trickle-down industry, with Parisian haute couture dominating and dictating what was to count as fashion. But, in the 1960s, cinema and fashion offered a clear break with these traditions and, in doing so, became a critical part of what constitutes the spirit of the 1960s, not only as commercial industries, but also as cultural and political representations, as actual material artifacts, and as artistic expressions.

New York and Stockholm
June 2017

EUGENIA PAULICELLI is Professor of Italian, Comparative Literature, and Women's Studies at Queens College and The Graduate Center of the City University of New York (CUNY). She is author of *Fashion under Fascism. Beyond the Black Shirt; Writing Fashion in Early Modern Italy: From Sprezzatura to Satire*; *Fashion is a Serious Business: Rosa Genoni, Milan Expo 1906 and the Great War*; and *Italian Style: Fashion & Film from Early Cinema to the Digital Age.*

LOUISE WALLENBERG is Associate Professor in Film and Fashion studies and former Director of The Centre for Fashion Studies at Stockholm University. She is also coeditor of *Nordic Fashion Studies, Modernism och mode; Harry bit för bit;* and has published extensively on film and fashion.

Notes

1. Charles Baudelaire, *The Painter of Modern Life and Other Essays* (New York: Phaidon Press, 1995; originally published 1893).
2. Georg Simmel, "Fashion," *American Journal of Sociology* 62 no. 6 (May 1957): 541–58.
3. François Lyotard, *The Postmodern Condition: A Report on Knowledge*, vol. 10, *Theory and History of Literature* (Manchester, UK: University of Manchester Press, 1984).
4. Eugenia Paulicelli, *Italian Style: Fashion & Film from Early Cinema to the Digital Age* (London: Bloomsbury Academics: 2016), 13.
5. Nancy K. Miller, *Breathless: An American Girl in Paris* (Berkeley, CA: Seal, 2013).
6. Stefano Tonchi, "Editorial," *W* magazine, April 2015, p. 34.
7. Walter Benjamin, *The Arcades Project* (Cambridge, MA: Belknap, 1999).
8. See, e.g., Charles Eckert, "The Carol Lombard in Macy's Window," *Quarterly Review of Film Studies*, 3.1 (Winter, 1978), and Anne Friedberg, *Window Shopping: Cinema and the Postmodern* (Los Angeles: University of California Press, 1994).
9. For a discussion on fashion films, see, e.g., Natalie Khan, "Cutting the Fashion Body: Why the Fashion Image Is No Longer Still," *Fashion Theory* 16 no. 2 (2012): 235–50, and Marketa Uhlirova, "100 Years of the Fashion Film: Frameworks and Histories," *Fashion Theory* 17 no. 2 (2013): 137–58.
10. That is not to say that the topic was neglected, however, as one of the first books on the relationship between fashion and cinema, *La moda e il costume nel film*, was published in 1950 in Italy and edited by the university professor and critic Mario Verdone, the father of actor Carlo Verdone. The book contains a homage to the costume designer Gino Carlo Sensani, who was praised by Antonioni. Costume design began to be recognized as a profession in the world of Italian cinema at this time but was viewed strictly in relation to fashion, especially during the contemporaneous launch of Italian fashion (Paulicelli, *Italian Style*, 116).
11. See these 1990s pioneering works in English: *Fabrications: Costumes and the Female Body*, ed. Jane Gaines and Charlotte Herzog (London and New York: Routledge, 1990); Pam Cook, *Fashioning the Nation: Costume and Identity in British Cinema* (London: BFI, 1996); and Stella Bruzzi, *Undressing Cinema: Clothing and Identity in the Movies* (London: Routledge, 1997). There has been considerable growth in publishing since 2000: Sarah Berry, *Screen Style in 1930s Hollywood* (Minneapolis: University of Minnesota Press, 2000); Sarah Street, *Costume and Cinema: Dress Codes in Popular Film* (London: Wallflower Press, 2001); Julianne Pidduck, *Contemporary Costume Film: Space, Place and the Past* (London: BFI, 2004); *Fashioning Film Stars: Dress, Culture, Identity*, ed. Rachel Moseley (London: BFI, 2005); Deborah Nadoolman Landis, *Dressed: A Century of Hollywood Costume Design* (New York: Harper Design, 2007); Nadoolman Landis, *Hollywood Costume* (New York: Abrams, 2013); Michelle Tolini Finnamore, *Hollywood before Glamour: Fashion in American Silent Film* (New York: Palgrave, 2013); *If Looks could Kill*, ed. Marketa Uhlirova (London: Koening Books, 2008); *Fashion in Film*, ed. Adrienne Munich (Indianapolis: Indiana University Press, 2012); *Birds of Paradise: Costume as Cinematic Spectacle*, ed. Marketa Ulhirova (London: Koenig Books, 2013); and Paulicelli, *Italian Style*.
12. The journal *Fashion, Film and Consumption* is edited by Pamela Church Gibson and published by Intellect.

PART I

The 1960s: Youth, Culture, and Sexual Liberation

1 Sanitizing the Beatles for Revolution: Music, Film, and Fashion in the 1960s and *A Hard Day's Night*

Ronald Gregg

The Beatles' highly acclaimed and financially successful first feature film *A Hard Day's Night* (Richard Lester, 1964) went into production following the group's emergence as rock stars not only in their home country of Great Britain but in the United States as well. Beatlemania arrived in the United States in February 1964 with tremendously successful live performances on television's *The Ed Sullivan Show* and sold-out concerts at the Washington Coliseum in Washington, DC, and New York City's Carnegie Hall. The production company United Artists had been primarily interested in using the film to sell the soundtrack, but with the Beatles incredible success in the United States, all parties involved realized that the film would receive more attention than initially envisioned. As film scholar Stephen Glynn recounts, "While the film was still in its frantic post-production phase, United Artists informed the media that, during August and September of 1964, *A Hard Day's Night* would be shown on a saturation basis in every available market around the world, with 'more prints in circulation than for any other pic in history.'"[1] The Beatles had become mega rock stars almost overnight and were poised to be film superstars as well.

In the making of the film, the Beatles were surrounded by a creative team, including their manager Brian Epstein, music producer George Martin, the film's producer Walter Shenson, director Richard Lester, screenwriter Alun Owen, and clothing designer Dougie Millings. The film turned out to be more than the conventional "pop" commodity, and the artful, amusing results pleasantly surprised critics. For instance, Arthur Knight, film critic for the *Saturday Review*, expressed his unexpected pleasure at the time:

> The Beatles are, of course, England's most controversial export since tea, and in the normal course of events such phenomena are generally "packaged" in a sleazy, indifferently made exploitation picture that goes into hundreds of theaters simultaneously, on what is known as a saturation booking, so that the producers can get their money out of it before the public learns that it is being robbed. Since everything about *A Hard Day's Night*—posters, advertising,

> mass bookings—suggested just such a picture, I skipped the press screening. I was wrong. On the advice of friends and breaking the critics' protocol, I went to a local theater, bought a ticket, and thoroughly enjoyed every minute of my first exposure to John, Paul, George, and Ringo.[2]

Most critics agreed with Knight in commending the film and likewise found the Beatles to be witty, playful, and talented lads.

Beatles scholars applaud the abundance of original, innovative songs by John Lennon and Paul McCartney for the soundtrack, which captured a new direction for both the group and pop music. Film scholars have praised the film equally for its documentary-like structure, active camerawork and editing, slapstick elements, "music video" interludes, and for capturing the band's youthful energy and polite rebellion against their elders that signaled the rise of a 1960s youth-based counterculture. In his detailed, thorough study of the production and reception of the film, Glynn exemplifies this admiration, writing, "The enduring appeal of *A Hard Day's Night* lies predominantly in the ageless charm of its protagonists, four lads from Liverpool who changed forever the style, the content, and the significance of popular music around the world."[3] Neil Sinyard agrees, boldly claiming, "Rather than the Citizen Kane of the juke-box musical, I would call Hard Day's Night its Battleship Potemkin. The message is in the montage and the music, and the message is one of social revolution."[4]

On the other hand, with a hindsight that Knight did not possess, many Beatles experts disparage the group's polished image at this time, which was used to sell not only record albums, but also schlocky merchandise. While the film's form and style and the Beatles' music encapsulate their transition to a more creative future, such critiques view the fashion and performance style as devices that papered over the quartet's more rebellious rock 'n' roll past. The standardized performance and chic dress of the film present the Beatles as a safe brand to merchandize soap, charm bracelets, dolls, wigs, and other products.

Glynn attributes the repackaging from rough to nice to the band's manager Brian Epstein, pointing out that fashion was a significant part of this shift. Glynn writes, "Before signing with Epstein the group wore rock'n'roll leather jackets and blue jeans. . . . Conscious of the associations of such dress with juvenile delinquency—with sexual and violent excess—Epstein had persuaded the boys to wear the newly designed Beatle suit, the epitome of 'smart casual.'"[5] Ian Inglis points out that Epstein also cleaned up the boys' behavior: "[He] prohibited certain forms of behavior, including smoking, drinking, eating, and swearing on stage."[6] Media scholar Michael R. Frontani sees Epstein as the major force behind "sanitizing" their image:

> He exerted great control over the image of the band throughout the touring years, particularly during the years of the band's rise first to national prominence in England and then to international stardom. He "cleaned them up,

> sanitizing the rougher, more rebellious image that had been developed in Liverpool's Cavern Club and on Hamburg's Reeperbahn. . . . Rather, Epstein marketed the Beatles as clean, wholesome entertainment. Well-coifed and donning suits and ties, the new Beatles were cheeky and at time irreverent, but never vulgar.[7]

These accounts suggest a dominant narrative in Beatles scholarship that blames Epstein for taming and cleaning up the more unruly and authentic group through acceptable, tailored fashion and a good-mannered, robotic performance style for the entertainment and commercial industries. Since Epstein had a taste in smart menswear, fashion became a weapon for criticizing how he suppressed the Beatles' individuality and taste. Clearly, Epstein fostered a new dressed up look and professional performance style for the band, but they were also ready to expand their audience and, so, actively participated in developing the new image. Labeling this simply as a "sanitizing" process erases the possibilities of creative transition offered by this new image. "Cleaned up" implicitly marks the new image as conventional, conformist, and commercial. In *The Conquest of Cool*, a study of how the cultural revolution in the 1960s impacted American business, Thomas Frank challenges this facile dismissal of fashion and commercial culture:

> Advertising and men's wear . . . were deeply caught up in both the corporate and cultural change that defined the sixties. . . . Both industries underwent "revolutions" in their own right during the 1960s, with vast changes in corporate practice, in productive flexibility, and especially in that intangible phenomenon known as "creativity"—and in both cases well before the counterculture appeared on the mass-media scene. . . . Seeking a single metaphor by which to characterize the accelerated obsolescence and enhanced consumer friendliness to change which were their goals, leaders in both fields had already settled on "youth" and "youthfulness" several years before saturation TV and print coverage of the "Summer of Love" introduced middle America to the fabulous new lifestyles of the young generation.[8]

Could it be that, along with *A Hard Day's Night*'s loose narrative structure, film style, and musical track, the Beatles' haircuts and stylish suits influenced a broader cultural revolution—that this new look was actually a modern turn through which not only the Beatles but also corporate culture, and individuals could embody and announce change?

A few possible reasons stand out for this critical dismissal and implicit demonization of Epstein's taste and impact on the Beatles. One is that fashion is implicitly understood as a frivolous, less creative space. As fashion theorist Gilles Lipovetsky notes: "The question of fashion is not a fashionable one among intellectuals. . . . Seen as an ontologically and socially inferior domain, it is unproblematic and underserving of investigation; seen as a superficial issue, it discourages conceptual approaches. The topic of fashion arouses critical reflexes even before it is examined objectively: critics invoke it chiefly in order to castigate it, to set it apart, to deplore human stupidity and the corrupt nature of business."[9] Beatles scholars seem to venerate the rebellious and self-fashioned pre-Epstein Beatles, asserting connections with the iconoclastic images of Marlon Brando in *The Wild One* (1953) and James Dean in *Rebel Without a Cause* (1955), as well as with the self-made fashions of the "teddy boys." Thus, they implicitly dismiss the shift into sleeker, suited attire and the more androgynous "moptop" haircut.

Many ignore this "cleaned up" look and make little or no attempt to historicize the new styles in men's fashion that mark the Beatles' look at the time of *A Hard Day's Night*. To critics unversed in fashion, jeans and leather jackets emblematize the rebellious, independent aspects of rock 'n' roll music, while the casual, tailored suits suggests a clone-like pop style, selling out to commercial music, and the marketing of junk. But as Glynn notes, the rebel look was also associated with troubled, often dangerous, juvenile delinquents as seen in the 1950s films *The Wild One* and *The Blackboard Jungle* (Richard Brooks, 1955). The new styles embraced by the Beatles, under the tutelage of Epstein, moved them away from the cultural references of youthful volatility suggested by "delinquent" fashion and toward the evolving, innovative space of coolness and cutting-edge taste associated with the new men's fashions. These new fashions were not the conformist suits worn in *The Man in the Grey Flannel Suit*. They suggested, rather, rebellion against conformity and an embrace of youth, as suggested by Frank.

Moreover, Epstein's refashioning of the Beatles is implicitly read as a queer action, moving them out of their rebellious, masculine image in Liverpool and Hamburg and into dressier, effeminate couture as they broke into the mainstream. As Paolo Hewitt notes, "many American males sneered at The Beatles. The band wore long hair and pretty suits. American fashion was much more masculine, based on jeans, Chino trousers, Bass Weejun shoes, button-down shirts and Harrington-style jackets. This was the all-American preppy look, and no way was a bunch of prissy Brits going to change that which was sacred in the US."[10] Many scholars seem to sympathize with this contemporary young male response, regretting the loss of the more rebellious roots, and are implicitly troubled by this effeminization. Drawing attention to and confronting this implicit dismissal of Epstein and his makeover of the Beatles, Steven D. Stark, in his revisionist history *Meet the Beatles*, argues, "The Beatles also challenged the definition that existed during their time of what it meant to be a man. This ultimately allowed them to help change the way men feel, the way men look, and the way men think about the way they look. Brian Epstein, their gay manager, influenced the group in many ways, but his most lasting contribution was to help design an image for the group that explored the fluidity of gender."[11] As Frank and Stark suggest, Epstein's remaking may have begun (and certainly at least abetted), a revolutionary transition for both the Beatles and the large culture to the later more outrageous, colorful, androgynous men's styles associated with the release of the band's 1967 album *Sgt. Pepper's Lonely Hearts Club Band* and to the youth-based countercultural phenomenon known as the "summer of love." Both the album and the phenomenon made a total break from rock 'n' roll's tougher, juvenile delinquent image.

The Beatles in Transition: Original Compositions, Studio Recording, and the New Sound in *A Hard Day's Night*

Elvis Presley is credited with unleashing repressed desires and physical energy through his style of singing and performing, but he did not write his own songs, and by the beginning of the 1960s, he was less of a spokesperson for the youth-driven market. The original music composed and arranged for *A Hard Day's Night* signals a new direction for rock 'n' roll performers, which is immediately announced by the film's opening theme song. As the Beatles flee a group of hysterical fans in the opening montage, the soundtrack begins with a single guitar strum, followed by a beat of silence, and then Lennon's voice exuberantly exclaiming the opening lyrics, "it's been a hard day's night," accompanied by high-spirited music. The innovative song's musical construction and lyrics, written by Lennon and McCartney, move from the exhaustion of work to the promise of sexual pleasure. According to Sinyard, Lennon and McCartney's song "had a gritty down-to-earth quality . . . and was hailed by the poet Thom Gunn as a major breakthrough in pop realism: 'Where, by comparison, in a Frank Sinatra ballad is there any suggestion that he works for a living?'"[12]

A few years before the film's inception, Epstein had looked for a record deal with a number of companies, including Decca and Columbia, all of which declined to sign the young unpolished rock group. He finally approached Martin at EMI's label Parlophone who gave the Beatles a chance in 1962. While suspicious of their ability to appeal to a larger public, Martin heard something in the harmonies, later claiming, "And it suddenly hit me, right between the eyes. This was a group I was listening to. . . . That distinctive harmony, that unique blend of sound—that was the selling point."[13] In their first sessions, the Beatles convinced Martin to feature Lennon and McCartney's original compositions instead of following the usual practice of recording the work of other established composers. Martin helped arrange their compositions with creative suggestions, along with smoothing out and creatively mixing their sound with the help of multitrack recording. According to Martin, his "job was to make sure recordings were artistically exceptional and commercially appealing, maximizing the qualities of artists and songs."[14] Music journalist Marc Myers explains, "Martin's early magic can be heard in the 'hooks' that kick off many of the Beatles' hit singles. These hooks include the opening drum roll on 'She Loves You,' the initial ringing guitar chord on 'A Hard Day's Night' and the first yelp on 'Help!'"[15] Martin's assistance shifted the group's recordings into a technologically flawless sound and experimental approach to rock 'n' roll, influencing their future interest and creative use of multitrack, studio-based music over live performance, as epitomized by the later *Sgt. Pepper's Lonely Hearts Club Band*. As music critic Tim Riley points out, the soundtrack for *A Hard Day's Night* "begins to show how the Beatles' music and the recording medium were meant for each other. George's double-tracked guitar solo on 'Can't Buy Me Love' talks to itself across the left and right channels; he answers his own melodic question with an echoing response, countering Paul's rampant affability with stereo dialogue."[16] While originally schooled in the rock 'n' roll music of the 1950s that inspired their Liverpool and Hamburg performance and earliest compositions, the Beatles continued their schooling through Martin's knowledge of recording technology and ingenious suggestions on how to develop their sound.

The song "A Hard Day's Night" and other recordings for the film signal a turn for the Beatles towards innovation, as they made the shift from doing knockoffs of earlier rock 'n' roll standards to composing, performing, and recording their own material. And in their future music, they began to synthesize the energy from a variety of musical styles, including rock 'n 'roll, British music hall, classical music, and psychedelia. The film thus captures this transitional moment for particularly Lennon and McCartney, who continued to develop their songwriting craft and take the standard pop song into a more creative and musically layered direction.

A Hard Day's Night, Modern Filmmaking, and the Liberation of Youth in the Pop Musical

While the film is an imaginative, energetic romp in itself, United Artists financed *A Hard Day's Night* solely as a vehicle to sell its soundtrack, as was thought to be the case by Knight in his review at the time. Producer Walter Shenson acknowledged as much, claiming that United Artists was more interested in producing an album than a film, asking him to deliver a film "with enough new songs by the Beatles for a new album."[17] Thus, United Artists budgeted for a standard rock 'n' roll exploitation film. But, working within that budget, the creative talent involved made history by amazingly redefining the pop musical film genre.

Shenson admired the director Richard Lester's previous pop film *It's Trad, Dad!* (1962), and had worked with him on the successful comedy *The Mouse on the Moon* (1963) before moving to the production of *A Hard Day's Night*. For *It's Trad, Dad!*, Lester had innovated the approach to shooting and editing musical numbers in the pop musical, stylistically drawing on the use of multiple cameras in live television. For their part, the Beatles loved Lester's 1960 short, surrealistic slapstick comedy *The Running Jumping Standing Still Film* (codirected by and featuring Peter Sellers), making Lester an easy sell to the band. The director did not disappoint, drawing upon an imaginative range of new filmmaking approaches, including the surrealistic staging and editing he used in *The Running Jumping Standing Still Film* and the creative approach to editing musical performance as developed in *It's Trad, Dad!* Lester also drew on the looser structure and style developed by French "new wave" filmmakers and the new approaches to realism in documentary filmmaking. Similar to Martin's innovative suggestions in the recording studio, Lester's rejection of conventional cinema positioned the four Beatles as modern actors in these freshly evolved cinematic approaches.

The Beatles also approved of the hiring of Welsh playwright Alun Owen to write the screenplay. According to biographer Barry Miles, McCartney suggested Owen because of his successful British television kitchen-sink drama *No Trams to Lime Street* (1959), which had impressed McCartney for its hard-edged, social realistic depiction of Liverpool.[18] Owen spent a few days with the band and decided to structure the screenplay like a loose, fictionalized "day-in-the-life" documentary based on their grueling schedule. Working to bring realism into the profile, he focused on including characteristics of their personalities that he had observed, including their youthful energy and humorous banter, their camaraderie, and the impact of their tightly orchestrated touring schedule on their personal lives. The film therefore focuses on showing them traveling to gigs, practicing, answering fan mail, engaging with the press, and performing, although by the end of the film, viewers are made to believe that the Beatles need no real practice, since the prerecorded music never sounds deficient.

Through the energetic collage of styles, lively performances, youthful good looks, and anarchic wit, the film seduces viewers to desire the Beatles, but it also equally entices them into the group's utopian space of unrestricted playfulness and rebellion against older authority. For instance, Lester's playful camerawork and editing, used to visually construct the song "Can't Buy Me Love," moves the viewer from an objective, voyeuristic position to a more subjective, kinetic position, inducing viewer participation. This song in particular is credited with influencing the music video form that premiered on MTV in the 1980s. Through handheld camera techniques, unusual camera placement, fast- and slow-motion, jump cuts, and quick edits in this sequence, Lester releases both the Beatles and the viewer from the laws of physics, conveying a joyous, liberating escape from adult supervision. In his study of the British and American pop films of the 1950s and 60s, Andrew Caine extols Lester's unique approach here, asserting, "The fast-cutting, jump cuts and hand-held camera work because they match the youthful spontaneity of the protagonists, best indicated by the 'Can't Buy Me Love' escape sequence," which "convey(s) a feeling of effervescence: the immediate thrills obtained in that moment of freedom from the constraints of adult authority."[19] Through the style of this sequence, which embodies this "effervescence" and "freedom," Lester's filmmaking allows the viewer to experience what it means to let oneself go, physically breaking free from adult supervision and decorum.

This challenge to adult authority is a theme that runs throughout the film. The Beatles constantly laugh at and challenge the uptight, self-important representatives of the older generation. For instance, when traveling by train, they encounter a pompous, conservatively dressed, bowler-hatted gentleman who enters their train compartment and proceeds to order them around. He belligerently demands that they close the open window in their carriage and turn down their transistor radio, claiming authority over the group by being their elder and a veteran of World War II. But the Beatles mock his patriarchal pomposity through sarcasm and childish slapstick. John, for one, responds to his demand to close the window by claiming that the four Beatles have rights and then batting his eyes girlishly. Later, as the gentleman lectures them and proclaims his right to control the dynamics in the compartment, John disrupts the man's seriousness by declaring, "Give us a kiss." The boys then leave the compartment, but childishly disturb and taunt the gentleman through a series of slapstick gags performed outside the door and the window.

Other authorities are equally mocked. For instance, later in the film, George is asked by a corporate trendsetter to comment on the new style in clothing that he plans to market to youth in the future. Without hesitation, George summarily dismisses the new style as "dead grotty." Tim Riley connects these various scenes of playfulness and polite mocking of the conservative establishment to the music, explaining, "Before they play in front of a live audience they cut up together, mock their agent, put on the press, put down fashion experts, baffle the Victorian-costumed extras, ridicule their elders, cavort on an empty soccer field, flirt with women—in short, enact the music's flair and impulsiveness—before hopping on stage to deliver a set of such power and excitement that they themselves find renewal in playing it."[20] As Riley notes, in addition to capturing the excitement of their musical performances, the film's form, style, and attitude emblematize a modern shift in how the Beatles, avatars of the younger generation, mock authority and entice their fans into a more direct, uninhibited dismissal of the conservative values of the older generation.

Finally, by choosing the "day-in-the-life" structure for the film, Owen constructs little romantic space for the Beatles, implicitly rejecting the emphasis on monogamous heterosexual romance that is dominant in the musical film genre. While they flirt with female fans along the way, they begin and end the film single; at no point do they acknowledge that one single girl could satisfy their romantic needs. Instead, they are there for all their fans, seducing both male and female listeners at the final concert through their music and performance, although the film particularly focuses on the young female listeners, who scream, jump up and down, and cry, suggesting an unleashing of their adolescent sexual energy. The film also starts with these uninhibited, screaming fans, again both male and female, chasing after their idols. Through the band's music and behavior, the youthful mob is led to reject reticence, properness, and respect for the values of their elders, indicating a move towards the sexual revolution of the 1960s. Moreover, similar to this youthful rebellion against proper behavior, the film challenges the conservative film, television, and marketing apparatuses with new forms, styles, and behaviors.

Coolness and Modern Fashion in *A Hard Day's Night*

While Martin fine-tuned the Beatles' sound and Lester surrounded them with the energy of new cinematic forms and styles, their tailor, Dougie Millings, dressed them in a confident, solid palate and attractive, tailored shape that signified their cool, seductive stance on stage and in *A Hard Day's Night*. Epstein knew that fashion would take the Beatles into the corridors of mainstream culture, but he might not have realized that fashion would eventually surpass and lead that culture.

As with the music and film, fashion is a sign of the Beatles' openness to change at this time. From the group's beginning, they were known for using fashion to set themselves apart. Hewitt notes that the band had a "thirst for the new, the future. . . to use clothes to differentiate themselves from the rest of the world—to tell everyone, in the late 60s phrase, 'I am not a number.'"[21] The Beatles not only had to sound and perform modern on stage and off; they had to look it as well, and they constantly constructed a look that corresponded to their music. *A Hard Day's Night* stands as a snapshot of the look that brought them their first taste of success: the Beatle haircut, the form fitting, tailored suits, the skinny ties, boots with Cuban heels and zip-up ankles, and other aspects of fashion that signified the unified group but also allowed each Beatle to express distinctiveness. But this was only one look in their seven years as a band.

Before starring in *A Hard Day's Night*, the Beatles experimented with several looks to signal difference from other British rock groups of the day. When in Hamburg in 1960, for example, they remade themselves into what Hewitt called the most "radical-looking band in the UK."[22] Influenced by the dark existentialist look of German art students, the band shifted from a Liverpudlian look of velvet jackets, black jeans, modish winklepicker shoes, and teddy boy haircuts to black leather jackets and pants, flat caps, longer (often unkempt) hair, and cowboy boots. The group returned to Liverpool presenting themselves as the most distinct group in Britain. But in a relatively short period of time, they were to encounter Epstein and change again.

The "Beatle-cut" was also introduced to them through their German acquaintances. Initially, the Beatles styled their hair in the longer hairstyle worn

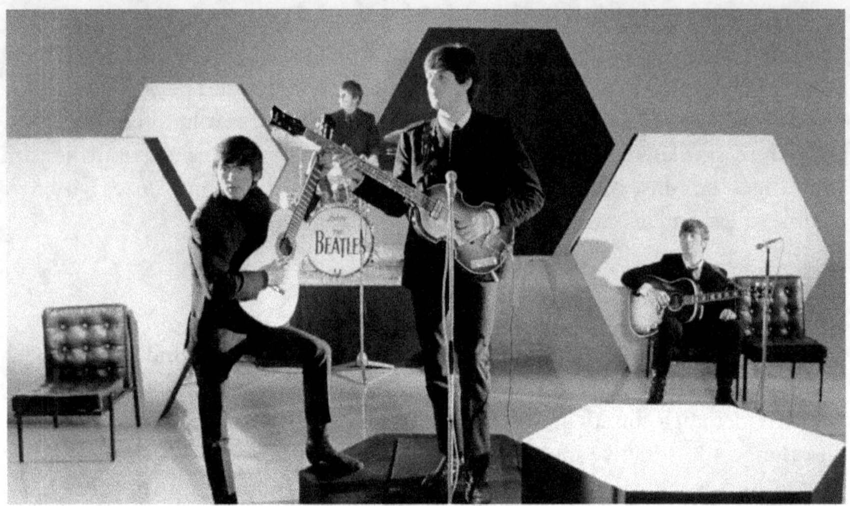

Fig. 1.1 The Beatles as cool, seductive models for a new generation in *A Hard Day's Night.*

by the teddy boys, with the hair shaped in the front with grease such as Vaseline or Brylcreem and parted in the back, like a "duck's arse." For the Beatle-cut, the hair was combed forward and allowed a new freedom instead of the more sculptured teddy boy look. (There might be more daring, queerer roots for the look; Beatles acquaintance and photographer Astrid Kirchherr claims that the idea for the haircut in Germany was influenced by Jean Cocteau's 1950 film *Orpheus.*) Back in Liverpool, the style was thought to be original to the Beatles and caught on, again, marking them as trendsetters.

The Beatle-cut became the most identifiable and, for many, the most radical aspect of their physical look as the foursome conquered the United States and produced and released *A Hard Day's Night.* Their hair became a major obsession for the press, which Lester restages in the film. The popular press seemed bemused by their hair, unable to figure out whether it was a publicity stunt or the sign of a troubling contemporary turn to a more androgynous look. In interviews, the group deflected the implicit challenges to their look through lighthearted, jocular responses. For instance, in an interview on October 16, 1963, the questioner asked, "But your funny haircuts aren't natural?" to which John replied, in what reads like a James Cagney gangster style, "We don't' think they're funny, ya see . . . cobber?"[23]

The film restages the press's probing curiosity with similar humorous responses. During a fictional meet and greet with the press, a reporter asks Ringo, "Do you think these haircuts have come to stay?" Ringo replies, "Well this one has. You know, it's stuck on good and proper now." As Hewitt reminds us, long hair suggested effeminacy at this time and initially upset many young men and parents by its bold challenge to traditional masculine presentation. John's queer mocking of the bowler-hatted gentleman seemed to flout these concerns about whether the band had embraced effeminacy and were possibly queer themselves. In both real interviews and those restaged in the film's, however, they never acknowledge this possible subversion of gender norms, merely suggesting that the haircuts might be harmless and "have come to stay." But the haircuts were only one part of the new "pretty" image that made American males "sneer" at the Beatles during their first American tour, as noted by Hewitt. Along with the haircuts, their new skintight, polished suits turned them into desirable pinups.

Upon first seeing the Beatles at Liverpool's Cavern Club, Epstein noted, "They were not very tidy and not very clean. . . . They smoked as they played and they ate and talked and pretended to hit each other. They turned their backs on the audience and shouted at them and laughed at private jokes. But there was quite certainly enormous excitement."[24] While Epstein wanted to maintain the excitement in the room, he challenged them to rethink their look and performance style if they wanted to move to a larger national stage. According to Hewitt, Epstein wanted to make them look more professional but "was not interested in the band copying others. He encouraged his boys to do what they would do throughout their career—subvert the norm."[25]

Epstein took the Beatles to his Liverpool tailor, Walter Smith, for new suits. But Smith did not design the new suits alone; the Beatles offered feedback on his designs, particularly insisting on extremely tight fitting, slim looking, drainpipe slacks. When the band moved to London, Epstein hired Millings, the tailor to the stars with a reputation for offering a cut that "was just a little bit more outrageous."[26] Millings had made suits for performers Cliff Richard, Bill Haley and the Comets, Roy Orbison, and others and was known for sharp touches, sleek designs, and tailoring suits that kept their look while the star performed. Epstein biographer Ray Coleman notes that for the first set of Beatles' suits, "Millings created a style envied by other stars for its simplicity and uniqueness and which Epstein applauded: a four-button, high buttoning jacket in dark grey, with black velvet collar and no outside pleats." Again, the band offered their input, asking for a form fitting style, and according to Coleman, Millings gave them "shoulders as narrow as each Beatle could carry. The skintight trousers were so tight the Beatle could hardly sit down in them."[27] Just as the music and the film both drew on a range of influences, their fashion was an appropriation of a previous style, but a creative shift into something new. And, as Hewitt importantly notes, "given the attention the band paid to the making and shaping of their suits, one does not detect a group being forced to act against its will."[28] And the Beatles clearly desired a style that looked slim, youthful, and erotic.

Epstein and the Beatles also wanted something modern. Millings designed suits that were modern and chic, clearly embracing the historical turn in the 1960s to giving men's fashion as much inventive attention as women's. He drew his inspiration from the designs of modernist groundbreaking designers such as Pierre Cardin, who led the way in revolutionizing menswear. With his unisex collection in 1958, Cardin began designing menswear, breaking a tradition in which *couture* houses did not design for men. In 1959, he offered a ready-to-wear line, again breaking new ground for a designer, which led to his being expelled from the *Chambre syndicale de la haute couture*, the governing body of the French fashion industry. In 1960, Cardin continued to remake men's fashion, moving it away from the conformist look of the 1950s with his collarless cylinder line jacket. Menswear columnist J. J. Lee claims that this jacket "tells the story of the vertical without distraction and heralded Cardin as a truly modern designer, pushing clothes towards pure geometric blocks of colour and extreme minimalism."[29]

Consulting with McCartney, Millings drew on Cardin's collarless jacket, adapting it for the Beatles in what became an iconic look for the group. Millings designed the jacket in several different shades, with distinct changes from the Cardin design, including braided edge pockets and a reduction of the number of buttons on the front from five to three, and his son Gordon observed that the group was "elated" and "just knocked out" with the new suit.[30] By the time of their appearance on *The Ed Sullivan Show* in 1964, Millings and the Beatles had moved back to lapels and collars. According to Lee, "the suits that the Beatles wore for their American debut created strong diagonals with lapels, contrast collars, and narrow ties, which helped visually separate the shirt collars. The suits served the same purpose as the Sullivan stage set composed of giant arrows and radiating lines. They provided dynamism and sexual energy. The set drew the eye to the Beatles, and the Beatles' suits drew the eye to their faces. The Beatles had arrived. With lapels. The girls went wild."[31] Hence, under Epstein, the Beatles were constantly changing their look, as well as music, suggesting a group that was leading in pop fashion, erotically charged, and not trapped by a single look. Millings and his son went on to make about 500 suits for the Beatles in the 1960s, and as a tribute to his importance, Millings had a cameo in *A Hard Day's Night* as a beleaguered tailor.

The form fitting, sleek suits worn by the Beatles in the film continue the look established during their American debut, and thus the film reproduces this success. While the suits offered a sensual dynamism for their performance on the *Ed Sullivan Show*, the film expanded this sensual dynamism into an off-stage world. The dark, solid colored, tightly fitted suits become like skin, always maintaining a lean, boyish shape, never slowing them down as they dash around escaping their fans and run, jump, and stand still during the musical interludes, such as "Can't Buy Me Love." The Beatles looked cool, seductive, and untroubled, in contrast to

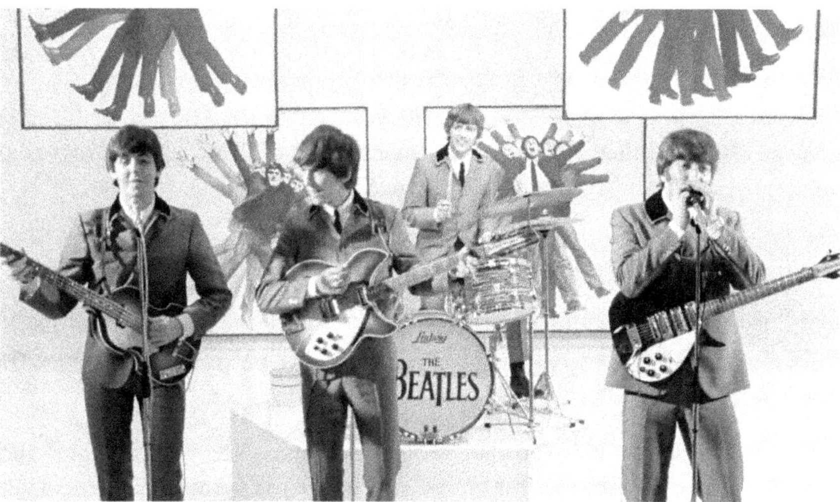

Fig. 1.2 The Beatles' suits offered skintight chic and "never wrinkled perfection," even during escapes from fans.

their earlier Liverpudlian look. The never-wrinkled perfection of the look, moreover, became a visual equivalent for the prerecorded musical perfection—every note polished and every line of the suit in place. The suits thus become a crucial part for constructing the Beatles' erotic presence in the film, in their flawless studio sound, and in television performance.

While the Beatles wear copies of the same design that defines them as a group throughout the film, fashion also allows individual expression and a way of identifying each Beatle to the newly initiated fan. In particular, John sometimes wears a Greek fisherman's cap and is often seen with his coat unbuttoned and tie loosened, suggesting his more rebellious, sarcastic demeanor. George changes up his look more often in the film from shirt and tie to turtlenecks and becomes the stylish Beatle who confidently challenges the corporate trendsetter. Playing on of his name, Ringo sports an assortment of jewelry, wearing rings on both hands and a watch and ID bracelet on separate wrists. Paul seems to brandish his comb more than the others and sometimes wears a vest. Like the more effeminate haircuts and seductive suits, these examples of individual self-fashioning—suggesting that like women, men can be narcissistic about their looks—seem to offer more evidence for Stark's assertion that the Beatles helped to change "the way men think about the way they look" at the time.

Even when John's tie is loosened, the Beatles always look neat and fresh-faced, seemingly parodying the criticism that they have been cleaned up. While the film emphasizes their spotless, pressed suits and clean hair and faces, it also signals that this is a different kind of clean than the previous generation. Throughout the film, the Beatles repeatedly note that Paul's grandfather looks like "a clean old man," setting him apart from their youthful, modern, cool image. Their image may be clean, but the hair, suits, and other aspects of their more androgynous look suggest that a revolution is on the move.

Sanitized Revolution through *A Hard Day's Night*?

A Hard Day's Night captures the Beatles in a moment of creative transition in their music, their performance in film and television, and their look. All these aspects suggested youthful modernism, but also a successful brand that the market could embrace. And if Epstein cleaned them up, so did Martin, Shenson, and others who helped to develop their image and sound. The band accepted this advice and the change that came with it, ready for success beyond Liverpool and Hamburg. In his study of their approach to creativity and competition, Greg Clydesdale labels the Beatles' artistic curiosity and openness to change a process of "continuous improvement."[32] And within change, there are often aspects of standardization and innovation.

While offering new innovative touches to their music, producer Martin "cleaned up" their sound, taking off the rough edges and making them more marketable within the pop music industry. In addition, the prerecorded studio sound that Martin produced for the album and film became the structure that was reproduced for their live performances. Every performance for each song was tightly scripted, structured and performed in the same way in every venue with no variation or temporal expansion. Therefore, at the time of *A Hard Day's Night*, the Beatles offered pop songs that were geared toward commercial success through innovation and recognizable repetition.

A Hard Day's Night is also about branding the Beatles image as a safe investment for commercial ventures. In this branding, they needed to hide from their rougher past. The film thus erases the history of drinking, use of drugs, and overt sexual carousing, moving the film and the band away from the image of the juvenile delinquent and the troubled adolescent films of the 1950s. Most telling, neither the film nor its publicity mentioned Lennon's marriage to Cynthia Powell, constructing a myth that all four Beatles were unattached and romantically available to their female fans. Here, the film participates in cleaning up the group for the masses and the entertainment industry, particularly for its young female consumers. While the film's presentation of the Beatles may unleash the fan's uninhibited passion, corporations hoped that this passion would translate into buying future albums and merchandise, as it did.

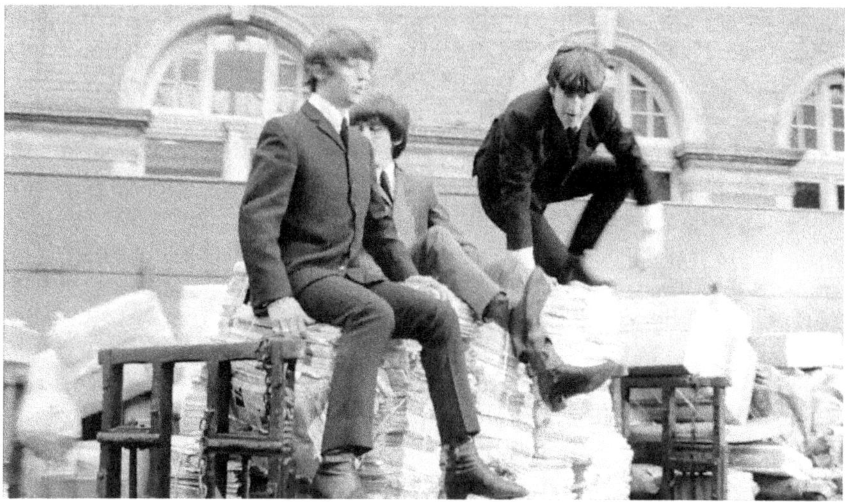

Fig. 1.3 The Beatles using fashion to signal youthful revolution and creative modernism.

Finally, the Beatles' fashionable dress in the film certainly offered a more respectable image than their previous on stage dress in Liverpool and Hamburg. However, like the innovations in their music and the new film styles used by Lester, fashion allowed them a further aura of creative self-expression. As Frank argues in *The Conquest of Cool*, many advertisers and their clients at the time excitedly embraced these modern styles as they desired to move away from the conformist, conservative 1950s through modern designs and attitudes. The Beatles may have been used to sell soap and love charms, but they also suggested "coolness" and revolution in the image that many advertisers wanted to embrace in their products and their own lives.

So, one seduction is between United Artists and other commercial interests and the fans. The romance is about consumption: buy our records and Beatles merchandise. However, while the film offers a cleaned up image of the Beatles for the market, what emerges as one looks at the trajectory over the 1960s is a movement towards groundbreaking innovations in music and visual image. The film questions established structures both through the group's androgynous image and through the uninhibited expression of youthful desire, challenging the suppression and conventions of the previous generation. The Beatles seduce the audience, particularly an adolescent audience, into an open, spontaneous, honest, intense, excited, playful, rebellious space of unleashed desire, which prefigures the countercultural embrace of many of these ideas later in the decade. With the id unleashed, as signified by the screaming, the film articulates an unapologetic openness about desire and a utopian space away from adult authority and structure. By screaming, they reject older structures of properness and shed their inhibitions, which is a step towards the sexual revolution of the 60s. The Beatles music, the film, and fashion become a space for articulating revolution, and the transition eventually takes the fan from "She loves you, yeah, yeah, yeah" to "You say you want a revolution." Within two years, the Beatles moved through Millings's 1964 designs to Carnaby Street and the psychedelic fashion that marks *Sgt. Pepper.* Of course, capitalism is not absent, but by then, capitalism wanted to be part of a revolution.

RONALD GREGG is Senior Lecturer and Programming Director in the Film Studies Program at Yale University. He has curated film and video programming for the Chicago Gay and Lesbian Film Festival, the South African Gay and Lesbian Film Festival, Chicago's Gerber-Hart Gay and Lesbian Library, and the University of Chicago Lesbian and Gay Studies Project.

Notes

1. Stephen Glynn, *A Hard Day's Night* (New York: I. B. Tauris, 2005), 30.
2. Arthur Knight, "Beatles, Anyone?" *Saturday Review*, September 19, 1964, 30.
3. Glynn, *A Hard Day's Night*, 3.
4. Neil Sinyard, *Richard Lester* (Manchester, UK: Manchester University Press, 2010), 39.
5. Glynn, *A Hard Day's Night*, 50.
6. Ian Inglis, *The Beatles in Hamburg* (London: Reaktion Books, 2012), 101.
7. Michael R. Frontani, *The Beatles: Image and the Media* (Jackson: University Press of Mississippi, 2007), 10–11.
8. Thomas Frank, *The Conquest of Cool: Business Culture, Counterculture, and the Rise of Hip Consumerism* (Chicago: University of Chicago Press, 1997), 26– 27.
9. Gilles Lipovetsky, "The Empire of Fashion: Introduction," in *Fashion Theory*, ed. Malcolm Barnard (New York: Routledge, 2007), 25.
10. Paolo Hewitt, *Fab Gear: The Beatles and Fashion* (New York: Prestell, 2011), 59.
11. Steven D. Stark, *Meet the Beatles: A Cultural History of the Band That Shook, Youth, Gender, and the World* (New York: Harper Collins, 2009), 3.
12. Sinyard, *Richard Lester*, 35.
13. George Martin and William Pearson, *Summer of Love: The Making of Sgt. Pepper* (London: Macmillan, 1994), 31–32.
14. Marc Myers, "He Had You Hooked on the Beatles," *Wall Street Journal*, September 10, 2012, accessed November 14, 2013, http://online.wsj.com/news/articles/SB10000872396390444327204577617182988336066
15. Marc Myers, "He Had You Hooked on the Beatles."
16. Tim Riley, *Tell Me Why: The Beatles: Album By Album, Song By Song, The Sixties and After* (Boston: Da Capo, 2002), 98.

17. Glynn, *A Hard Day's Night*, 15.
18. Barry Miles, *Paul McCartney: Many Years from Now* (New York: Henry Holt, 1997), 158.
19. Andrew Caine, *Interpreting Rock Movies: The Pop Film and Its Critics in Britain* (Manchester, UK: Manchester University Press, 2004), 165.
20. Riley, *Tell Me Why*, 98.
21. Hewitt, *Fab Gear*, 26.
22. Hewitt, *Fab Gear*, 26.
23. "Beatles Interview: Playhouse Theater, London, 10/16/63," *Beatles Interviews*, accessed November 28, 2013, http://beatlesinterviews.blogspot.com/2009_02_01_archive.html.
24. Hunter Davies, *The Beatles* (New York: Norton, 1996), 124.
25. Hewitt, *Fab Gear*, 47.
26. Douglas Martin, "Dougie Millings, 88, the Tailor for the Beatles," *New York Times*, October 8, 2001, accessed November 17, 2013, http://www.nytimes.com/2001/10/08/world/dougie-millings-88-the-tailor-for-the-beatles.html.
27. Quoted in Hewitt, *Fab Gear*, 54–55.
28. Hewitt, *Fab Gear*, 47.
29. J. J. Lee, *The Measure of a Man: The Story of a Father, a Son, and a Suit* (Toronto: McClelland and Stewart, 2011), 43.
30. Martin, "Dougie Millings."
31. Lee, *The Measure of the Man*, 43–44.
32. Greg Clydesdale, "Creativity and Competition: The Beatles," *Creativity Research Journal* 18 no. 2 (2006): 132.

2 The Art of Undressing: Automation and Exposure at the Margins of Cinema

Amy Herzog

I WOULD HARDLY BE the first scholar to point to Andy Warhol's fascination with the overlapping fields of fashion, celebrity, and pornography, three spheres in which art and commerce collapse into one another and offer up the human body as the ultimate commodity, simultaneously precious and utterly replaceable. Each industry operates via a machinelike modality, automated and impersonal, yet trafficking in the most intimate and private of desires: we wrap our bodies in the fabric and fantasies of stardom, desirousness, fulfillment—a commingled longing to possess, to inhabit, and to be the idealized image that is always suspended just beyond our grasp. Each industry, too, deals in surfaces, in self-presentation as a mode of being, a mode of working. Surfaces not as masks shielding an inner truth, but as an end in themselves, an endless series. These themes pervade Warhol's work as a whole, but are articulated in an extraordinarily fascinating way in his films of the 1960s.

Warhol's early cinema was created in the midst of an outpouring of experimental and independent filmmaking in New York City. Film distribution and exhibition were undergoing broad transformations during this period, as witnessed by the formation of experimental film collectives (such as the Filmmaker's Cooperative and the Millennium Film Workshop), by the distribution of foreign and independent films by financially-strapped major studios, by the rise of independent art-house distributors (such as New Yorker Films), and by the explosion of Times Square "grindhouse" theaters devoted to exploitation cinema. The films produced during this period were wildly divergent in their approaches, ranging from high-art abstraction to expanded cinematic "happenings" to the most base sexploitation; beyond their position outside the Hollywood film industry, many of these works appear to share little in common. Yet I would argue that certain tendencies within Warhol's cinematic style resonate with independent pornographic films being produced and distributed in New York during this period. In particular, the fixation on acts of dressing and undressing in each set of films illuminates a larger cultural and economic shift at work in New York at this time.[1]

My objective in this chapter is to read Warhol's portrait films, such as *Poor Little Rich Girl* and the "Screen Tests," alongside the typical pornographic peep show loops produced in the mid-1960s, which most often featured individual women stripping and posing for the camera. To coopt a phrase from Jonas Mekas, the Warhol film and the 42nd Street "beaver loop" are both shining examples of the "impure, naughty, 'uncinematic' cinema being made . . . in New York" in the 60s, both positioned squarely outside the established film industry and both straddling a line of ambiguity between spectacular performance and unembellished documentation.[2]

What follows is not an attempt to "rehabilitate" porn loops or to redefine them as "art." Nor am I seeking to contextualize Warhol's films in relation to contemporaneous porn. Instead, I would like to look at the modalities that both sets of films employ, modalities that inform one another and suggest provocative ways of rethinking questions of spectatorship, labor, and politics in cinema. Their affinity has everything to do with the politics and economics of that historical moment—the mid-1960s—conditions Warhol and the porn peddlers implicitly understood and exploited without inhibition. Three thematic frameworks will guide this inquiry: exposure, automation, and exchange. Critical here is the unusual system of rehabilitation that the early peep show loop and the early Warhol film share, what I would like to call the ethos of the "leftover." The strategies of recycling, cooptation, and recontextualization at work here challenge us to rethink many of the tenets of film studies, such as the distinction between spectator and text as the primacy of the theatrical model of exhibition, forcing us to confront one of the most foundational challenges that cinema poses: what does it mean, and what are the consequences, when we view another human body on the screen?

Exposure

Martin Hodas, the peep show king of 42nd Street, began his career servicing vending machines in the New York metropolitan area. In 1966, he encountered a Panoram jukebox that had been retrofitted to show burlesque films. The Panoram was a film jukebox from the 1940s that played "Soundies," three-minute musical shorts by jazz artists and novelty bands. When the Soundies corporation folded in 1947, the abandoned machines were recycled for more prurient purposes. The large format screens were boarded over, and binocular viewers were installed. These newly outfitted machines were sometimes placed in entertainment arcades that featured a range of devices, such as pinball machine and "games of skill."[3]

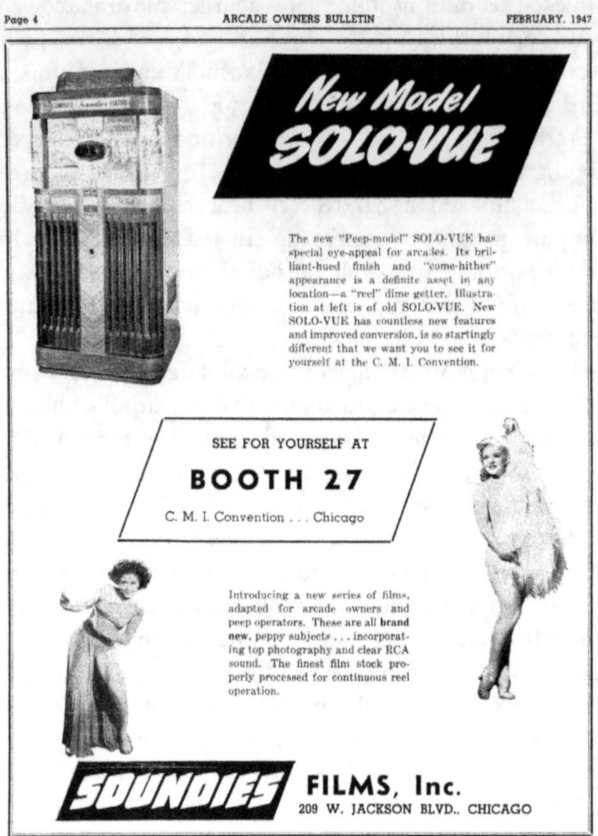

Fig 2.1 Soundies Films, Inc., advertisement, *Arcade Owners Bulletin* 2 no. 1 (February 1947): 4. This image depicts a Panoram machine that has been converted for peeping purposes. Image from the collection of the author.

Martin Hodas did not invent the peep booth as such, but he was instrumental in launching the pornographic arcade as a visible urban institution. He purchased a large number of discarded Panorams and convinced adult bookshop owners in Times Square to allow him to install and service groups of machines. He took advantage of changes in censorship law and loopholes in zoning regulations to establish a thriving franchise, and it is rumored that Hodas's operations accounted for 85 percent of the quarters deposited at the Chemical Bank branch at 42nd Street and 8th Avenue during the peak of his business.[4] As adult emporiums began to flourish throughout Times Square, the Panorams were replaced by privatized booths with curtains or doors.

The economy of the peep show is explicitly grounded in the commodification of a sexual experience. The apparatus of the peep booth both relies on and toys with notions of fetishism and control. Desire for sexual gratification (an affective experience) is objectified in the persona of the body on the screen. Yet, these visual fetishes are presented in a semiparadoxical way. On the one hand, the titles and stills posted on the fronts of the booths promise a unique, individualized encounter. On the other, the rows of identical machines point to the substitutability of this experience. And the rationing of only a short fraction of the film per coin fragments the event into regimented measures equivalent to a predetermined monetary value.

At the same time, at least in the series of films I am considering here, the performers have a relative degree of autonomy, evidenced by the affective surplus they are able to generate. Each performance is unique, occupying the space of the screen with varying degrees of control, but in all, there is an explicit, extended, and at times unsettling visual interaction with the camera.

Perhaps the most politically significant aspect of the peep arcades of the 1960s was the public venue they provided for activities not necessarily envisioned by the entrepreneurs who created them: cruising, hustling, and drug dealing. Indeed, in the early years of the arcades, when the majority of the film loops featured solo female performers or heterosexual couples, the film booths became accessible locales for gay male public sex. Particularly in the years before Stonewall, the peep arcades served as open sites for contacts and exchanges that, potentially, had very little to do with the content on screen.

The peep arcade thus represents a multifaceted site for recycling (of technology, of film, and of people) and co-opting (of diegetic and public space). A wide range of social and material "leftovers" are reactivated here and launched into new networks of exchange.

What ultimately, then, is being exposed within the peep arcade? The woman's body, to be sure, is exposed, as are her performative capabilities and her surroundings. Yet that exposure, as a commodity, remains hidden within the machine, accessed only via a purchase. Within the architecture of the arcade, the body of the spectator is, in fact, far more directly put on display than that of the performers, in some instances as a potential erotic offering for other patrons, much like the bodies on the screen. Exposed, too, is the complex traffic of urban public sexuality in all its diverse, polymorphous, and limited ways.

Fashion and Undressing

It might be helpful to consider what the act of undressing tells us about the function of fashion and film in general before delving further into the specificities of the peep arcades and Warhol's approach to film. Certainly the cinema has been fascinated by acts of undressing from the outset, building on traditions of erotic "revealing" that evolved from photography and other, earlier visual technologies. Mutoscope motion picture machines were often stocked with scenes of women undressing in their bedrooms or while preparing the laundry and with barely clothed dancers performing "exotic" routines. Early silent films, too, featured women disrobing before their baths and in more explicit burlesque routines, such as the 1901 Edison Manufacturing film in which a female trapeze artist strips whilst performing an aerial routine, much to the delight of her enthusiastic, male audience.[5]

Yet the relationship between cinema and acts of undressing cannot be reduced to the mere exposure of human flesh. Films about undressing engage in a curious depiction of labor—although rarely that of the labor of producing clothes, a subject that gets some rather oblique and heavily mythologized attention in cinema. Films about fashion might show the working girl struggling to climb the ladder in the glamorous-but-exploitative world of the fashion house, or we might see a backstage narrative about a young designer strategizing her way onto the runway, (although we'd almost never see a believable image of the clothes being cut and sewn en masse in a factory). Dressing, and undressing, however, is a different kind of work. For obvious reasons, the depiction of the body putting on or taking off clothing presents problems for filmmakers, particularly during the heavily restricted studio era. There's a further disincentive, however, in that the act of undressing breaks the spell cast by the unified image of body-and-dress.

An undeniable power is generated when the camera cuts to Joan Crawford in an Adrian gown. We know intellectually that these are costumes, and we may even know who designed them, but their emotional impact depends on a union of fabric and flesh, an embodied vision that would likely dissipate the moment we see that flesh exposed in the very mundane task of hoisting up its stockings, or struggling with a zipper. Is it the girl who makes the clothes, or do the clothes make the girl? Perhaps we don't want to know.[6]

But the film industry, and the industry of fandom, has always exploited our fascination with exposing the performers we adore. Fan magazines such as *Film Fun* and *Screen Fun* have existed since the silent era, offering salacious images of female celebrities provocatively undressed. *Celebrity Skin* was published from 1979 until 2015, providing helpful guides to which films feature which performers unclothed, with stills. A broad array of contemporary media outlets (such as TMZ, Celebrity Jihad, icanseeyourpants.com, celebritieswithoutmakeup.net, and celebritypussyblog.com) feature paparazzi shots of female celebrities caught unawares, not in makeup, or disembarking from vehicles with or without their underpants.

Wayne Koestenbaum has pointed to two primary subjects dominating Warhol's oeuvre: stars and disasters.[7] Is there any disaster more poignant than

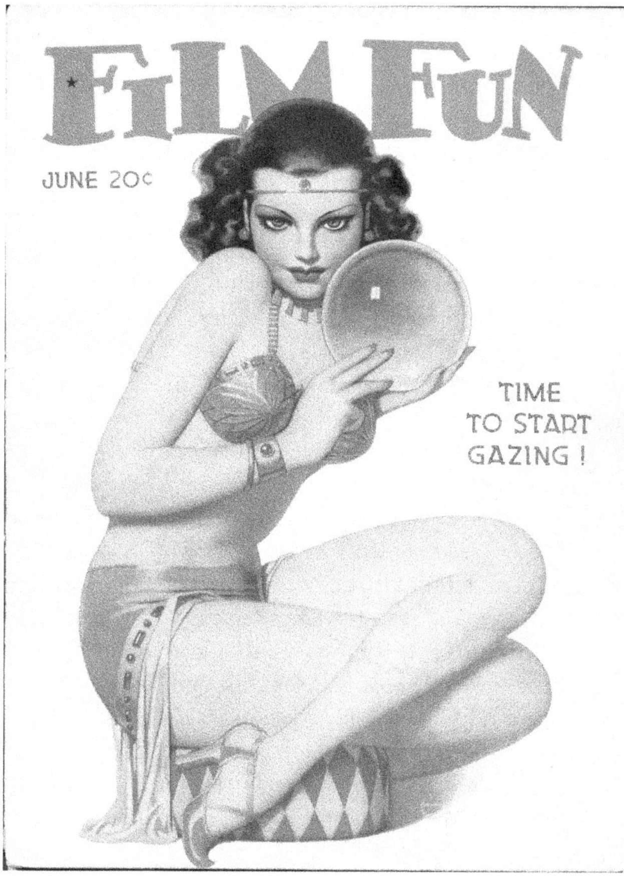

Fig 2.2 Enoch Bolles, *Film Fun* cover art (June 1938). Image courtesy of Jack Raglin, Indiana University.

that of the fallen star? And any more poignant fall than that of the female star, captured in a raw state, or forced to remove her clothes before the camera, to cash in on her most intimate assets?

Warhol was attuned to the magic of the fallen star, making her the subject of several of his films: *More Milk, Yvette* (1965), starring Mario Montez as Lana Turner, recounts the murder of Turner's lover by her daughter Cheryl, played by Richard Schmidt. Hedy Lamarr (played once again by Montez) is the subject of *Hedy* (1967), she the stunning beauty and military communications inventor exposed in the most fashionable of crimes: shoplifting. And his fascination with star performers culled without judgment from all stripes and strata of society granted him special appeal to those working at the margins of "legitimate" social circles.

As Kathy Acker reminisced: "I was working at FUN CITY, a combination magazine and peep-show emporium and a (fake) sex-show theatre. My boss' nephew, who worked in this family concern as the video booth cleaner, was friends with Joe Dallesandro. . . . In fact, one of the lines in our sex-shows was that we were waiting to be discovered by Andy Warhol. We weren't entirely joking, but we were hoping."[8]

Warhol was of course deeply invested in the fashion industry. He was particularly keen on exposing the shared paths of circulation that money, art, celebrity, and commodities trace—something we see manifest in his paintings, books, and films. And fashion figures prominently in his films, albeit in a far more improvisational and "downtown" context. For Ronald Gregg, style in underground cinema serves as a means of self-creation in which outsider stars fashion themselves via leftover, secondhand couture.[9] Performers are ceaselessly dressing and undressing in Warhol's films: Freddy Herko in *Haircut #1* (1963); Mario in *More Milk, Yvette*; and Edie in *Poor Little Rich Girl* (not to mention more explicit works like *Couch* and *Blue Movie*). But it is in the more understated portrait films that the dynamics of exposure are most evident.

The figure of the star, the star's body and face, serves as a nexus for this traffic in commerce, desire, and disaster. Stars are exposed, rendered as icons and plasticine images. But present here, too, is an affective excess. Warhol's attention to gesture is made possible by the relentless, unblinking gaze of his camera, trained on the faces and bodies of his superstars. He exposes the cruel, torturous relationship between the viewer and the viewed, between the performer and the camera. Exposed, as well, are moments of resistance: Taylor Mead's refusal to keep his ass still in *Taylor Mead's Ass* (1964), dancing and shoving objects up it; Edie's exquisite vulnerability and anger in lobbing an ashtray at Chuck Wein during *Beauty #2* as he tortures her from off-screen; and, of course, the sublimeness that is Mario Montez stealing every scene and twisting the words of his humiliators into triumphant performances. We see these stars ceaselessly exposing themselves, a gesture in direct opposition to the paparazzi photo that implies some kind of "truth" that might be arrived at beneath one's clothes. What is exposed is not the flesh or the self, but the perpetual necessity of performing that self, performing for—and against–all those other performers. "Being sexed," Warhol philosophized, "is hard work."[10] We strip ourselves and dress ourselves up again in an endless repetitive loop.

Poor Little Rich Girl

Poor Little Rich Girl was first shot in early April 1965. It was the second of Warhol's film's featuring Edie Sedgwick, the enigmatic and deeply troubled heiress he had recently met. Conceived as part of a larger film saga, *Poor Little Rich Girl* was meant to capture a day in Sedgwick's life in real time, as it unfolded.

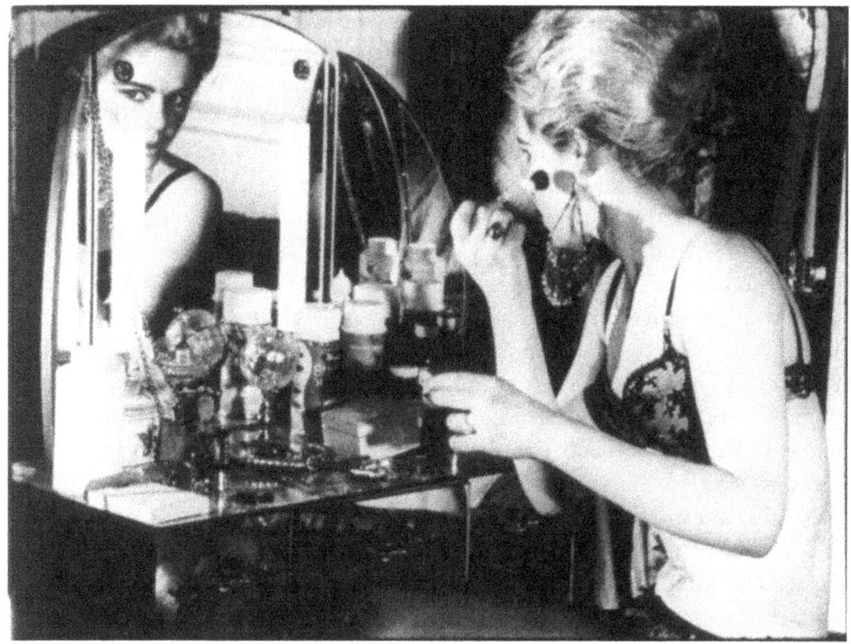

Fig 2.3 Andy Warhol, *Poor Little Rich Girl*, 1965. 16mm film, black and white, sound, 66 minutes. © 2016 The Andy Warhol Museum, Pittsburgh, PA, a museum of the Carnegie Institute.

The title is borrowed from one of Warhol's other favorite muses, a 1936 vehicle for Shirley Temple.

There was a problem with the lens during this shoot, and thus, the entirety of the two reels were out of focus. Warhol's team obtained new equipment and shot the entire film again two weeks later; this is apparently the only time Warhol reshot a film due to a technological accident. Based on subsequent reviews of the film, it appears that Warhol first screened both reels of the in-focus, second version of the film on April 26. He then repremiered the film in June on a bill with *Vinyl*, but now combining the first of the out-of-focus reels with the second of the in-focus reels. The inclusion of the technological mistake is intentional and serves as cryptic sort of unveiling.

In the first reel, Edie appears cloaked in a protective haze. Aside from her phone conversation ordering coffee and juice, she remains relatively quiet, with an Everly Brothers record providing the main soundtrack, but all of this changes in the next reel. Edie is now in crisp view, laughing and chatting with Chuck Wein, who prods and questions her from off-screen. Dressed only in a black bra, panties, and stockings, Edie tries on different outfits (including a leopard coat she declares "the most beautiful in the world") and applies layer after layer of makeup. To quote Callie Angell, "The contrast between the romantic elusiveness of the first reel and the realistic immediacy of the second creates a minimal narrative of visual suspense and resolution, in which Edie's extraordinarily mercurial, vulnerable presence is literally brought into focus through a subtle, yet strangely moving drama of loss and recovery."[11]

Throughout the film, Edie slips between performing a prepared character discussing her squandered inheritance (the spoken credits at the opening of the film introduce her as "Mazda Isalon") and intimate revelations of her naked self. I think we might find here what Wayne Koestenbaum cites as a tendency in Warhol's work for the fusing of "the deliberate gesture and the unwilled spasm."[12] And is this not precisely what pornography attempts to bring us, the deliberate gesture and the unwilled spasm? A performance that is artificial yet documents and elicits a natural affective response? What is so haunting about each of these film portraits, for me, is the palpable, almost unbearable labor that goes into the performer's gestural and spastic self-presentation.

Yet one question looms here, particularly given the kinds of exposures these films elicit: what degree of agency might we assign to any of the selves involved with either of these film factories? Can one truly speak of self-representation in a world of automation, potential exploitation, and serial replication?

Automation

> JOSEPH GELMIS: It's been suggested that your stars are all compulsive exhibitionists and that your films are therapy. What do you think?
>
> ANDY WARHOL: Have you seen any *beavers*? They're where girls take off their clothes completely. And they're always alone on a bed. Every girl is always on a bed. And then they sort of fuck the camera.
>
> GELMIS: They wriggle around and exhibit themselves?
>
> WARHOL: Yeah. You can see them in theaters in New York. The girls are completely nude and you can see everything. They're really great.
>
> GELMIS: Have you actually made a beaver yet?
>
> WARHOL: Not really. We go in for artier films for popular consumption, but we're getting there. Like, sometimes people say we've influenced so many other filmmakers. But the only people we've really influenced is that beaver crowd. The beavers are so great. They don't even have to make prints. They have so many girls showing up to act in them. It's cheaper just to make originals than to have the prints made. It's always on a bed. It's really terrific.[13]

Seriality rules the peep loop aesthetic. Each filmic artifact is at once unique and replaceable. The body is literally a commodity, a vehicle for exchange that traffics the porous boundary between public and private, between product and person, and between perception and bodily reflex. In this context, image production serves not only as means of self-creation but also as a point of entry into what Michael Hardt and Antonio Negri have identified as an affective economy. "Being seen" is a form of productive labor, and the product being sold is our own affective response.

Serial imagery and machine aesthetics are, of course, key to Warhol's philosophy. Many of his silkscreen portraits originated as strips taken in the coin-operated booths located near the Factory, his studio in Times Square. It is no accident, I would argue, that the photobooths so closely resemble the motion picture peep machines nearby, and it was not uncommon for photobooth patrons to disrobe inside.

The art dealer Holly Solomon recalls her own photobooth session with Warhol:

> We went to Broadway and 47th Street, where they had this photobooth. Andy met me there, and we had a bunch of quarters. He was very particular about which booth. We tried a whole bunch of them. . . . Actually, if you're in a photobooth for a long time it gets pretty boring; being photographed anyway is pretty boring. After you do one pose, how many poses can you do? I got so bored that I started to really act in them. . . . Fifty dollars is a lot in a photobooth![14]

Solomon later told Wayne Koestenbaum that she was "dismayed" when she first saw the silkscreen he created from her photobooth strips, as "she thought it made her look like a 'cocksucker.'"[15]

What Warhol has tapped into here is a new capitalist model: the "Factory society," an interminable busman's holiday where life and work become indistinguishable. Hardt and Negri locate an epochal shift in the structure of capitalist production in the early 1970s, from a modern economy based on industrial manufacturing to a tertiary, postmodern economy dealing in "knowledge, information, communication, and affect."[16] Within this new service-based economy, the products of affective labor may be immaterial (a sense of personal satisfaction, of belonging to a community, of arousal, of being cared for, and so on) but they are most frequently and most successfully achieved when they are produced or felt via the body. Feminists have long pointed to the ways in which traditionally female spheres of labor (domestic work, childcare, nursing, sex work) operate at the margins of the industrial economy and through various forms of corporeal work. This body labor relies on human interaction (whether direct or indirect, in the case of the entertainment industry) but produces something that is nevertheless ephemeral: "social networks, forms of community, biopower."[17]

This kind of work is not new, of course, but the manner in which it has become instrumentalized within the broader economy is. And it is acutely manifest in the spheres of fashion, celebrity, and pornography. In the 60s and 70s, we see a dramatic acceleration in the ways in which images circulate and in the meanings that they generate, especially in relation to the notion of a "fashioned self." What was once nominally private is increasingly drawn into the public sphere in no small part because of the way in which an affective economy places a value on something immaterial, like sexual arousal, and uses technological networks (advertising, film, television) to produce and profit from it.[18]

"Advertising," Walter Benjamin observed, "seeks to veil the commodity character of things. In the allegorical the deceptive transfiguration of the world of the commodity resists its distortion. The commodity attempts to look itself in the face. It celebrates its becoming human in the whore."[19] I would like to suggest that the foregrounding of portraiture in the two sets of films I am examining here represents precisely this attempt to look one's self in the face. And I suspect we might best locate this effort in the seemingly automated ways in which both Warhol and the peep loop producers operated.

Elizabeth Wissinger, in her work on affective labor and the modeling industry, quotes a makeup artist describing the ideal fashion model, one who can enter into the "flow" of a shoot without needing direction: "it's almost like watching an actress where there's no direction required; they're just flowing with it, they get it, and they've paid attention, and the photographer can take pictures for over an hour and not have to say one word because everything is just wonderful."[20] Indeed, what strikes me as most resonant between Warhol's film portraits and the peep loops is the painful absence of a directorial presence, a lack that becomes increasingly apparent during the course of the films. I find that watching the pornographic peep show loops is remarkably similar to watching one of Warhol's *Screen Tests*, where the subjects were asked to sit still in front of the camera for the duration of a 3-minute reel. Over the course of the ten-to-twelve minute peep loops, the performance tends to disintegrate. The women run out of material fairly quickly, sometimes bursting into nervous laughter, making eye contact with the unseen camera person for guidance, or beginning to play with props in a manner that I found burlesqued the very notion of "sexiness" (biting a hula hoop, or, in a series of six reels featuring a potted plant in the background, the inspired moment where a performer turns and begins licking the plant). Even in the more mundane loops, what we see performed might best be described not as sex, but as the performers' imperfect idea of what sexiness on the screen ought to look like. I am reminded here of Judith Butler's observation that "heterosexuality is always in the process of imitating and approximating its own phantasmatic idealization of itself—*and failing*."[21]

The void created by the ambiguous gaze of the camera implicates the viewer as well. There is no cutaway shot, no narrative suture, and no fictional character to stand in for us. The machinations of the apparatus are painfully felt, and we, like the performers, begin to squirm. Duration becomes unbearable, deliciously

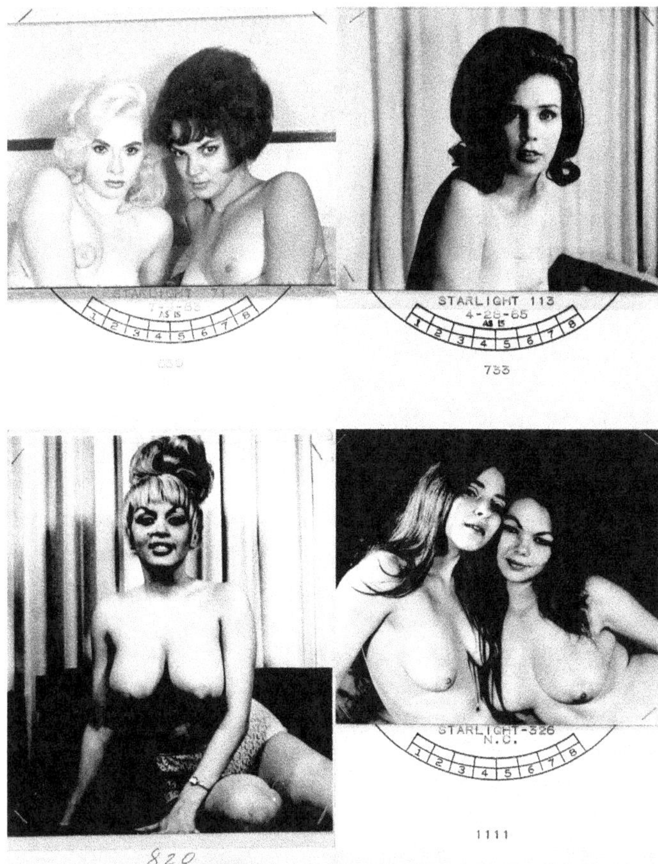

Fig. 2.4 Marquee card used to advertise the models featured in peep loops (1963–1968), courtesy of Albert Steg. Starlight Films and Photographs nos. 113, 820, and 326 are part of the Richard B. Kornbacher Collection.

masochistic, and we, too, are caught up in a system of conflict, exchange, desire, and suffering, in concert with those others on screen.

Exchange

In his work on Warhol and machines, Jonathan Flatley has argued that the significance of the machine model is not that it allows the artist or the viewer to isolate themselves but that it forces us to recognize the messy and imperfect ways in which the many machines and systems that comprise our world intersect. "Warhol's interest in faces, in celebrity, in technologies of reproduction, in collecting can all . . . be productively thought about in terms of system interface, the (mis)translation between systems."[22] Faces and naked bodies are replicated, but imperfectly, via technological transformations that bring into focus a wide range of similarities, and variances. "The imitation of the machine does not increase our alienation; instead it rescues us from our isolation by reminding us to notice our likenesses."[23]

There is a collapsing of being, being alike, and liking in Warhol's work that is decidedly queer and that engages with what Homay King identifies as a queer temporality.[24] I would point here to the emphasis on deferral, the absence of a teleological purpose, and the production of displaced responses that implicate, rather than placate, the viewer. And I would like to suggest, somewhat paradoxically, that there is something inherently queer about certain types of pornographic peep loops, including many that are ostensibly heterosexual in focus.

The loops that I am drawn to are nonnarrative, noncopulative, and resplendent with colors and textures that adorn the body of the film. There is an exquisite vulnerability to many of the subjects, serendipitous occurrences, inspired performances, and absurdist humor in which we encounter sameness, difference, imitation, and failure.

If affect is a vehicle for exchange in our late-capitalist economy, it is also highly unstable and unpredictable, a force or flow that can generate unintended reactions and that can be redirected or subverted toward unsanctioned purposes. I am thinking about the co-opting of discarded technologies by the pornographers and the poignant performances of the stars of the loops, and most especially of the appropriation of the peep show arcade as a site for hustling, dealing, and cruising.

Warhol's philosophy stresses the need to democratize exchange: "Everybody does something for everybody else—your shoemaker does your shoes for you, and you do entertainment for him—it's always an exchange, and if it weren't for the stigma we give certain jobs, the exchange would always be equal."[25] Yet the exchange is not equal, and perhaps there are moments when this can be productive. Douglas Crimp has described the ethos of the Warhol world as "misfitting together."[26] "If people never misunderstand you," Warhol wrote, "and if they do everything the way you tell them to, they're just transmitters of your ideas, and you get bored with that. But when you work with people who misunderstand you, instead of getting *transmissions* you get *transmutations*, and that's much more interesting in the long run."[27]

A component of the misfit relationship is the remainder, the leftover, which contains a latent potential to set its machine on a different course. Warhol wrote of this phenomenon:

> I always like to work on leftovers, doing the leftover things. Things that were discarded, that everybody else knew were no good. . . . When I see an old Esther Williams movie and a hundred girls are jumping off their swings,

> I think of what the auditions must have been like and about all the takes where maybe one girl didn't have the nerve to jump when she was supposed to, and I think about her left over on the swing. So that scene was a leftover on the editing-room floor—an out-take—and the girl was probably a leftover at that point—she was probably fired, so the whole scene is much funnier than the real scene where everything went right, and the girl who didn't jump is the star of the out-take.[28]

The ethos of the leftover creates a space for an alternative economy of exchange, one that is often fickle, parasitic, and unruly. Misunderstanding, miscommunication, and failure become a means creating of transmutations, stutters in the system. It is important not to over-romanticize the capacities of practices that are still deeply embedded within systems of exploitation: the pornography industry is ruthlessly sexist, and there is an unsettling degree of cruelty in many of Warhol's works. Nevertheless, there is something happening in these films that is endlessly fascinating to me, that makes me uncomfortable, and that makes me rethink what it means to look at a face, or a naked body, what it means to be naked, and what it means to be a spectator. I feel confronted by these images, and by the exchanges with multiple others that they have engendered. They suggest a politics of looking that is mutual, if uneven, that is corporeal and serial, and in which similarity and difference can coexist. And they suggest the fantasy of a space in which the leftover girl on the swing can become, if just for a moment, a star.

AMY HERZOG is Coordinator of the Film Studies Program at the CUNY Graduate Center and Associate Professor of Media Studies at Queens College, CUNY. She is author of *Dreams of Difference, Songs of the Same: The Musical Moment in Film* and editor with Carol Vernallis and John Richardson of *The Oxford Handbook of Sound and Image in Digital Media*.

Notes

1. My thinking about Warhol's filmmaking throughout this project is deeply indebted to the insights and advice provided by Callie Angell. I am further grateful to Claire Henry at the Andy Warhol Film Project at the Whitney Museum of American Art, who generously shared resources and her knowledge of the production logistics for Warhol's *Poor Little Rich Girl*.
2. Jonas Mekas, as quoted in Marc Siegel, "Documentary That Dare/Not Speak Its Name: Jack Smith's *Flaming Creatures*," in *Between the Sheets, In the Streets: Queer, Lesbian, Gay Documentary*, eds. Chris Holmlund and Cynthia Fuchs (Minneapolis: University of Minnesota Press, 1997), 91.
3. An earlier version of this section appeared in "In the Flesh: Space and Embodiment in the Pornographic Peep Show Arcade," *The Velvet Light Trap* 62 (Fall 2008): 29–43. Both projects are part of a larger manuscript that is in process.

4. Anthony Bianco, *Ghosts of 42nd Street: A History of America's Most Infamous Block* (New York: William Morrow, 2004), 162–64.

5. *Trapeze Disrobing Act* (Silver Lake, NJ: Edison Manufacturing, 1901), film, 2:40 min., accessible via the Library of Congress, http://www.loc.gov/item/96514756/. Bieke Gils discusses this film and the fascinating career of its star, Charmion, in "Flying, Flirting, and Flexing: Charmion's Trapeze Act, Sexuality, and Physical Culture at the Turn of the Twenties Century," *Journal of Sports History* 41 no. 2 (Summer 2014): 251–68.

6. For an extended treatise on the relationship between costume and constructions of gender, see Stella Bruzzi, *Undressing Cinema: Clothing and Identity in the Movies* (London: Routledge, 1997).

7. Wayne Koestenbaum, *Andy Warhol* (New York: Viking, 2001), 62–63.

8. Kathy Acker, "Blue Valentine," in *Andy Warhol: Film Factory*, ed. Michael O'Pray (London: BFI, 1989), 65.

9. Ronald Gregg, "Fine Vintage," in *Birds of Paradise: Costume as Cinematic Spectacle*, ed. Marketa Uhlirova (London: Koenig Books, 2014), 293–304.

10. Andy Warhol, *The Philosophy of Andy Warhol (From A to B and Back Again)* (San Diego: Harcourt Brace Jovanovich, 1977), 98.

11. Callie Angell, *Something Secret: Portraiture in Warhol's Films*, Exhibition Catalog (Sydney: Museum of Contemporary Art, 1994), 14. Edie's brother Bobby had died in a motorcycle accident shortly before the filming, and she discusses her anxiety about meeting with several of his friends during the shoot.

12. Koestenbaum, *Andy Warhol*, 24.

13. Joseph Gelmis, *The Film Director as Superstar* (New York: Doubleday, 1970).

14. Holly Solomon, as quoted in "Early Celebrity Photographs," *Andy Warhol Photographs*, New York: International Center for Photography, exhibition January 11 to March 18, 2001, http://museum.icp.org/museum/exhibitions/warhol/early_celebrity.html.

15. Koestenbaum, *Andy Warhol*, 99.

16. Michael Hardt, "Affective Labor," *boundary 2* 26, no. 2 (1999): 91.

17. Hardt, "Affective Labor," 96.

18. See Elizabeth Wissinger, "Always on Display: Affective Production in the Modeling Industry," in *The Affective Turn: Theorizing the Social*, ed. Patricia Ticineto Clough and Jean Halley (Durham, NC: Duke University Press, 2007), 233–35.

19. Walter Benjamin, "Central Park," trans. Lloyd Spencer and Mark Harrington, *New German Critique* 34 (Winter 1985): 42.

20. Wissinger, "Always on Display," 242.

21. Judith Butler, "Imitation and Gender Insubordination," in *The Lesbian and Gay Studies Reader*, eds. Henry Abelove, Michèle Aina Barale, and David M. Halperin (New York: Routledge, 2003), 313.

22. Jonathan Flatley, "Art Machine," in *Sol LeWitt: Incomplete Open Cubes*, ed. Nicholas Baume, Wadsworth Athaneum Museum of Art (Cambridge, MA: MIT Press, 2001), 93.

23. Flatley, "Art Machine," 101.

24. Homay King, "Girl Interrupted: The Queer Time of Warhol's Cinema," *Discourse* 28.1 (Winter 2006): 98–120.

25. Warhol, *Philosophy*, 100.

26. Douglas Crimp, *"Our Kind of Movie": The Films of Andy Warhol* (Cambridge, MA: MIT Press, 2012), 96–109.

27. Warhol, *Philosophy*, 99.

28. Warhol, *Philosophy*, 93.

3 Pasolini's *Teorema*: the Eroticism of the Visitor's Discarded Clothes

Stella Bruzzi

TEOREMA (*THEOREM*), MADE in 1968, is an odd, almost surreal movie; it is also arguably Pier Paolo Pasolini's masterpiece and offers an exemplary portrait of the "swinging sixties." The casting of English heartthrob Terence Stamp as the anonymous "visitor" was enough to secure the film a kind of cult status, and its blasphemy (that the seductive visitor was an allegorical representation of Christ) led to a certain notoriety. Having appeared the previous year as the caddish Sergeant Troy in John Schlesinger's adaptation of Thomas Hardy's *Far From the Madding Crowd*, Stamp started stepping out with that film's female lead Julie Christie, sparking a popular fantasy that they were the "Terry and Julie" of The Kinks' 1967 single "Waterloo Sunset" (a reading that Ray Davies, who penned the song, denies). Pasolini's fixation with Terence Stamp is evident throughout *Teorema*, from the tight crotch shots to the lingering, dreamy close-ups of his delicate yet surly facial features.

Yet, the film's allusions to other 1960s concerns—sexual liberation, class, and Italy's concentration of wealth in the industrialized north, especially around Milan—also demonstrate the many sides of Pier Paolo Pasolini himself: the Marxist, the director of documentaries (such as the feature-length *Comizi d'amore* [*Love Meetings*] in 1965, in which the director appears on camera interviewing Italians about their attitudes toward sex and sexuality), and the poet. Though it is a concise and relatively short film, *Teorema*'s title points to its schematic complexity and, in passing, to Pasolini's intellectuality and his intellectualization of "art" cinema in the 1960s. Beyond being understood as a critique of European bourgeois society and values, and despite its superficially detached tone, the film is also frequently interpreted as an allegorized expression of Pasolini's (furtive) homosexuality. For, although the visitor awakens the sexuality of all the characters—male and female—the liberation of the men (the father and the son) remains especially intense. Pasolini's humor is often neglected, and I have always found *Teorema* to be not only a profound but also, in parts, a funny film.

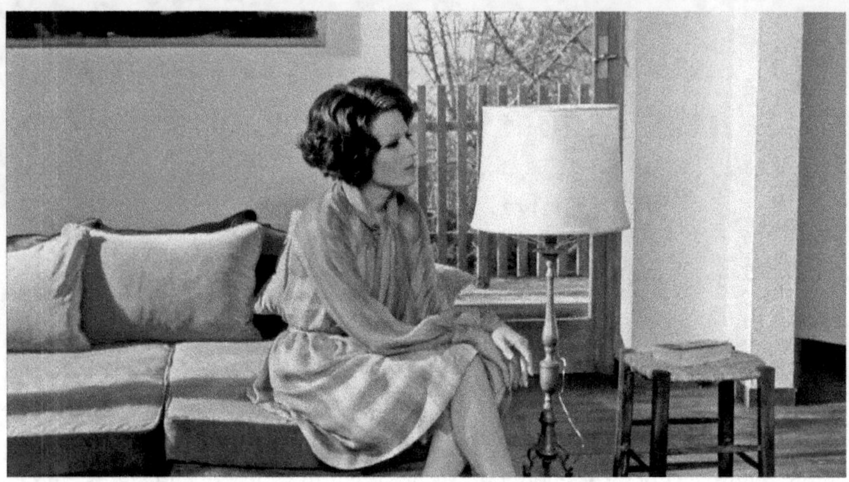

Fig. 3.1 Silvana Mangano.

Teorema is famous for many things, but its costumes are not usually among them, despite the fact that it exhibits many of the traits of the "clothes movie" and is acutely design conscious (the family's Milanese mansion now looks like a modernist museum). Costuming is a notable visual feature of the film. In what proved to be his one foray into cinema, 1960s Italian couturier Roberto Capucci provided the clothes for Silvana Mangano as the mother Lucia, while Marcella de Marchi, Roberto Rossellini's former wife, confidante, and collaborator, designed the remainder of the costumes for Stamp and others.[1]

Teorema centers on the arrival of an unnamed "visitor" to a wealthy house in Milan's affluent San Siro suburb. Upon his arrival, the visitor swiftly proceeds to have sex with all five members of the household in turn: Emilia, the maid (Laura Betti), Pietro, the son (Andrés José Cruz Soblette), Lucia, the mother (Mangano), Paolo, the father (Massimo Girotti), and Odetta, the daughter (Anna Wiazemsky). The effect of these sexual encounters on the family members is traumatic: Emilia, for example, returns home, refuses to eat, and is found levitating by her neighbors; Odetta becomes catatonic; and Lucia, hitherto an impeccable bourgeois housewife, goes cruising. The controversy surrounding *Teorema* revolved around the evident similarities between the visitor and Christ: that the name of the postman who brings news of his arrival and departure is Angelo (i.e., the Angel Gabriel), that the effect of the sexual encounters themselves are extraordinary and catastrophic; and that inserted into most of the seduction scenes are sporadic images of the bleak slopes of Mount Etna, which recall, for most critics, the biblical wilderness into which prophets and others went for spiritual contemplation.

In a film so lacking in the conventional narrative traits of character development, dialogue, logical exposition, and cogent plot development, additional signifiers such as costume are granted elevated importance, and within this elliptical framework, clothes feature prominently, used at various times to carry and create, not merely reflect, meaning. For instance, being a study of sexual and spiritual awakening, undressing features prominently in *Teorema*: the visitor and Pietro, compelled to share a bedroom when other visitors descend, undress awkwardly in front of each other; Lucia undresses while waiting for the visitor to return from running with the dog; and most notably, right at the end, the father Paolo divests himself of all his clothes (his conventionality, his heterosexuality, perhaps even his "mortal coil") on the concourse of Milan station before running naked and screaming into the wilderness in the film's concluding image.

Lacking certain conventionalized modes of exposition, piecing together the film's meaning is much like—as its titular allusion to mathematical formulae implies—piecing together a puzzle: moments and gestures in isolation appear opaque and even irrelevant, but they start to make sense once viewed in tandem with each other. The undressing scenes noted above are three such incidents. Pitero's and Lucia's scenes function relatively straightforwardly as preludes to sex with the visitor, and although the third does not lead to a literal sexual encounter, if the visitor is likened to Christ, then the naked and screaming Paolo's flight into the wilderness, when taken in conjunction with the cumulative connotations of undressing, could be read as an empathetic flight towards both spiritual and sexual enlightenment.[2]

There are several such exemplary clothes moments in which the specific conjunction between desire, sexuality, and Terence Stamp's quintessentially cool 60s look is made central, and I discuss a crucial scene in more detail below. Coolness is indeed key to *Teorema* because, despite the prominence accorded sex and desire in its plot, the sexual act remains repressed, mimicked by the repressive implications of many of the costumes. Stamp dons the 1960s "capsule wardrobe" for the casually dressed young man: slacks, shirts, and pullovers in subtle and unremarkable shades. His unremarkable appearance, however, is ironic considering the remarkable effect he has on the household, but also complements his character: that he is promiscuous and bisexual but also emotionally detached. As if reconfirming this, the film dwells on the build up to and the traumatic effects of desire, rather than on the sexual encounters themselves. Within the film's mannered and precise but ultimately cold style, the oddly tactile yet unsensuous costumes start not to reflect the characters, but rather to create barriers for them.

The quintessential costume moment in *Teorema* is an extended prelude to the visitor's seduction of Lucia, who comes across a set of clothes that he has left on one of the sofas in the Po Valley summer house while out running with the family dog. The sequence opens with a static wide shot of the exterior of a luxurious, contemporary house whose modernity is at odds with the unkempt, woody landscape in which it sits. A somber church bell tolls and continues to do so for over a minute. The visitor's presence in the house is signalled by a close-up of his copy of Arthur Rimbaud's complete works left on the floor.

Earlier in the film, in his first full scene after the party to welcome his arrival, the visitor had sat in the garden of the Milan villa reading first a law textbook and then this same edition of Rimbaud's complete works. The casual but repeated interest in Rimbaud, the restless, peripatetic lover of fellow poet Paul Verlain, brings the visitor's own promiscuous bisexuality to the fore. In the summer house, Lucia picks up the volume and places it purposefully on a footstool before looking across the room towards a sofa on which lie the visitor's casually discarded clothes.

The parallels between the dynamics of this scene and the earlier encounter with Rimbaud are significant, for on both occasions, the visitor's inferred interest in homosexuality is witnessed by a woman (in the first instance Emilia, in the second Lucia) who then finds herself irresistibly and maybe masochistically drawn to him. The sequence in the garden culminates in the visitor's sexual encounter with Emilia, just as the later Po Valley scene will conclude with the visitor's seduction of Lucia, a seduction that marks the midpoint of Terence Stamp's cycle of sexual conquests. In that later scene, as one quickly realizes, the clothes on the sofa are not laid out with entirely dishevelled abandon, and Lucia feels compelled to go over to them, just as Emilia had felt compelled in the garden to rush over and brush away the cigarette ash that had fallen from the visitor's cigarette onto his thigh as he had sat reading Rimbaud.

Here, Lucia is similarly drawn to the visitor's clothes but, unlike Emilia, walks toward them in a measured, one might even think haunted, way. Rimbaud is again proposed as a rival for the visitor's affections, and as if signalling this threat, Lucia's control recedes as she reaches the sofa. As she moves toward the clothes, a rougher handheld camera style takes over from the slow, steady low-angle pan that had followed her across the room. The agitation implied by the rougher visual style conveys—within a film so pointedly reluctant to use dialogue for this purpose—the urgency and encroaching passion of Lucia's thoughts as she surveys the shirt, trousers, jumper, and underpants strewn before her.

The first item of clothing is a pristine white shirt which, lit from the left, acquires the quality of coldly sensuous alabaster (an apt substitute for the visitor) as its folds, collar, and buttonholes are picked out and accentuated by the directional light, their sculptural whiteness luminously pale against the muddy green of the sofa behind. The second is a salmony pink pair of trousers, the third a flecked pink and white pullover with a white vest nestling in its folds and the last a pair of decidedly grubby briefs.

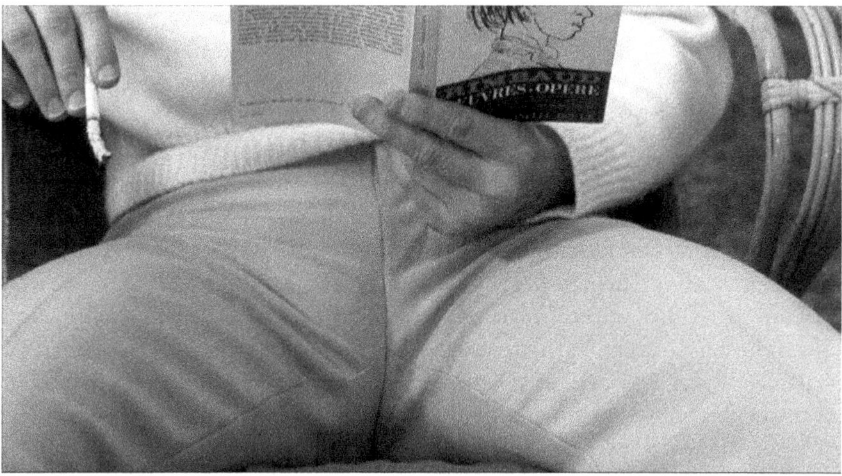

Fig 3.2 The Stranger reading Rimbaud.

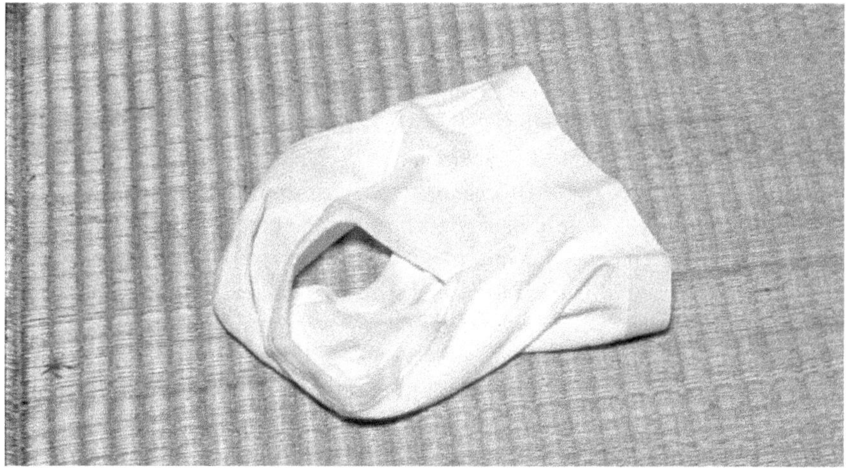

Fig. 3.3 The Stranger's underpants.

Particular emphasis is placed on the trousers Terence Stamp has only recently vacated, which as garments feature prominently in several of *Teorema*'s seductions. The opening shot of the garden scene, when we first see the visitor reading Rimbaud (and the first time we see him in a close-up), is a low-angle view of his crotch as he sits back in a low chair.[3] Stamp is fond of recalling how Pasolini's minimal direction included the command (conveyed in English through Pasolini's close friend Laura Betti, who played Emilia) to keep his legs open and get an erection.[4] Although the actor failed to oblige, the eroticism generated by the juxtaposition between the disconcertingly bland light wool beige slacks and the sexual promise they cocoon is an adequately tumescent substitute.

The irony is that all this promise of arousal is never matched by the perfunctory and cold sexual gestures that ensue once the women have expressed their interest in the visitor. The garden sequence, for example, concludes with a close-up of Stamp's buttocks sheathed in the comically unerotic banality of his bland, fitted trousers as he shifts mechanically around on top of Emilia, a familiar motion heralding an act of perfunctory lovemaking. The slight sheen of the trouser fabric, their taut 1960s cut that reveals the lines of some underwear lurking beneath, their neat little pocket, and the freshly ironed crease inching down the back of Stamp's thigh all serve to kill the eroticism of the moment, the final deadly flourish being the postdubbed sound of mixed fibers brushing up against each other. This earlier indication of the complex erotic importance of Terence Stamp's trousers is the veiled force that informs the later scene.

What sets the visitor's clothes apart in the Po Valley sequence is that they do not adorn a body: they have become objects rather than adornments, spectacular in their own right, but also sculptural and inert. Roland Barthes articulated the eeriness of clothes detached from the body thus: "It is not possible to conceive a garment without the body . . . . The empty garment, without head or limbs (a schizophrenic fantasy), is death, not the body's neutral absence, but the body decapitated, mutilated."[5] Barthes's nihilistic notion of unattached clothes as death is just one theorization of the detachment between clothes and the body. There is also the idea, grounded in Freud, of unattached clothes as fetishistic sexual substitutes for the veiled genitalia or sexual object. Both of these arguments find their way into the moment when Lucia contemplates the visitor's abandoned garments, which come to function as eroticized substitutes for the absent body but also as signals that such a dislocation between body and clothes will prove traumatic.

Throughout *Teorema*, Stamp never regards his seduced victims warmly; instead he looks through or away from them even as he gets close to them, and the actor has, in interview, referred to his mannered performance style emanating from his intention to remain "not in the moment," but divorced from it.[6] This detachment is also signalled through the distancing of costume and body. In the most often cited scene in Paul Schrader's *American Gigolo* (a film in which, like *Teorema,* the prioritization of the male protagonist's costume signals both his desirability and his ability to remain emotionally detached from those whom he attracts), Richard Gere, the eponymous gigolo, chooses his clothes for a date by laying a selection of Giorgio Armani ensembles on his bed. The gesture of looking at the clothes to scrutinize them indicates that he is about to assume a role. These are costumes, not extensions of the self. Likewise in *Teorema,* the visitor's clothes, so frequently set apart from his body, are not part of him. The clothes wear the man.

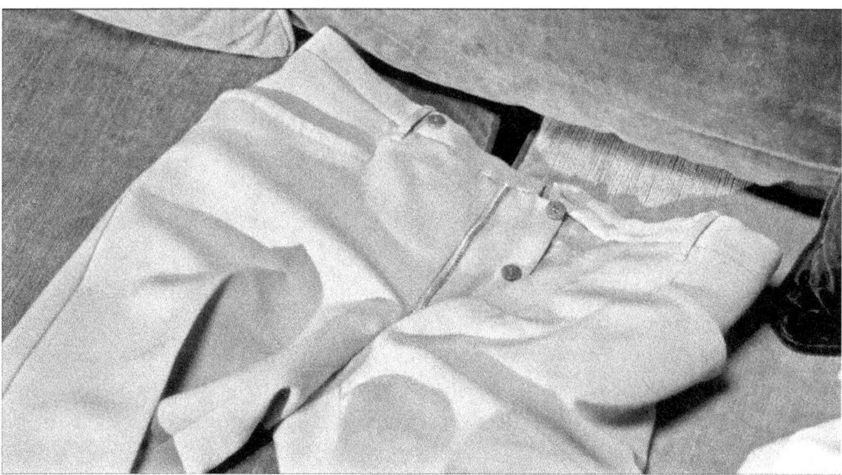

Fig. 3.4 The Stranger's trousers.

This disassociation is brought sharply into focus by what we see of the visitor before he returns to the summerhouse. In one of *Teorema*'s rare energetic and spontaneous asides, we understand that he has abandoned his clothes to frolic in the woods with a dog, dressed only in sneakers and a pair of grubby grey shorts. This juxtaposition is heavily ironic. First, this dog is not only the one partner with whom the visitor does not have sex but also the one partner with whom he appears to have fun. Second, his carefree running reminds us that the prim but provocative clothes lying on the sofa should not be mistaken for him; they are only impoverished, empty, and even fraudulent fetish objects.

Lucia's contemplation of her guest's clothes is thereby infused with lack: lack of passion; lack of corporeality; lack of fulfilling consummation. The object of her desire is not merely "not in the moment"; he is away enjoying himself, his body unshackled from his external layers of respectability, his clothes. This absence is most keenly felt when Lucia alights on his trousers. Beige-salmon in colour, they offer a classic example of the late-1960s styling with their flat-fronted fit, their visible stitching around the hems and their small front pockets. Lucia finds them unzipped at the fly with one side folded back to reveal a distinctly more sensuous silk blue lining inside, a metonymic representation perhaps of the visitor's repressed passion, the vivacity he is capable of expressing when with the dog.

The trousers have been (as always) neatly pressed, with a crisp pleat down the front of the leg, and one would not automatically mistake these slacks for the garment of a sexual predator. The trousers' shade, though unusual, blends in with its surroundings, in keeping as it is with the soft browns and pinks that permeate the scene, from Lucia's striped dress to the décor. The pink is also an androgynous mix of femininity and homosexuality in conflict with the aggression of the opened fly, and its fleshy tone recalls what is absent here but was present the first time we saw the visitor's crotch close-up: his penis. The pornographic juxtaposition of the heavy, fleshy penis emerging from a three-piece suit in Robert Mapplethorpe's photograph *Man in Polyester Suit* (1979) is also absent here, but the intercutting of Lucia's observation of the clothes with the visitor's cavorting in the woods alludes to it.

That his pinkish slacks are the site of trauma comes to the fore specifically as Lucia picks them up. The bell that has been tolling mournfully until this moment finally ceases, and on Silvana Mangano's face we see that desire has given way to panic. In this instant, *Teorema*'s tense elusiveness, its intellectualization of desire, its detachment, and its persistent repression of feeling become focused in one moment that conveys to us more or less definitively that the members of this household are not attracted to the visitor per se, but to what their longing for him unleashes in themselves.

The provocatively opened trousers serve paradoxically to figuratively evoke again the visitor's body, but his actual absence makes it possible for the essentially passive Lucia to access her own hitherto repressed carnality, the expression of which is the moment when she discards *her* clothes and sits naked on the terrace of the house waiting for the visitor to return from his run with the dog. The erotic potential of clothes to function as substitutes for the body is evident throughout *Teorema*: eroticism is there even if the erotic object is elsewhere, jogging through the rustic woods. The film's final, triumphant perversity is that, while it remains Pier Paolo Pasolini's most explicitly homosexual film, it also remains resolutely inexplicit in terms of how it speaks about sex and coldly, intellectually dispassionate. Its costumes are similarly ambivalent: precise and inherently unsensuous, yet overloaded with erotic promise.

Pasolini died on November 2, 1975, in Ostia, Rome's seaside resort, having been run over several times by his own car. Although a teenage rent boy, Giuseppe Pelosi, confessed to his murder soon after, he later retracted his confession. Pasolini may have been murdered for his homosexuality or, as Pelosi later intimated, for his political views. Just as the Altamont Free Concert on December 6, 1969, signalled the end of the hippie-inspired sixties, so the contrast between the extreme brutality of Pasolini's murder on the beach at Ostia contrasts markedly with the elegant 1960s detachment of *Teorema*, a film close to Pasolini on a personal level (courtesy of its homosexual inferences), and also one of relatively few films set in contemporary Italy.

Teorema is quintessentially of its time, a poetic 1960s parable, but it is also elliptically timeless. Throughout much of his career, Pasolini did not appear to pay too much attention to costumes. They were just clothes. But the late 1960s garments on display in *Teorema* introduce a different sartorial sensibility altogether, one very much rooted in sixties.

STELLA BRUZZI is Professor of Film and Dean of Arts and Humanities at University College London. Her publications include *Undressing Cinema: Clothing and Identity in the Movie* and *Bringing Up Daddy: Fatherhood and Masculinity in Post-war Hollywood.* She is coeditor of *Fashion Cultures* and *Fashion Cultures Revisited.*

Notes

An earlier version of this chapter appeared in *Film Moments*, eds. Tom Brown and James Walters (London: BFI, 2010).

1. Capucci was an ardent admirer of Mangano, referring to her as a woman "of such refinement, beauty and elegance. . . . She wasn't an ordinary woman, an ordinary actress" ("Di una raffinatezza, di una bellezza, di un'eleganza . . . Non faceva parte delle donne normali, delle attrici del cinema"), http://www.modaemodi.org/rivista.

2. Just prior to undressing, Paolo had made eye contact with a younger man at Milan station whom he seemed to be going to follow into the gents' lavatories. Instead, he undresses himself and runs off, arguably preparing himself for the visitor, in whom are combined the twin attractions of religion and homosexuality.

3. This moment is the one used on the British Film Institute's DVD edition of the film (2013) as the backdrop for the root menu, so it appears on a continuous loop until you press "play."

4. In the interview on the BFI's DVD edition, Stamp recalls how Betti came up to him just before shooting and said "He just wants you to keep your legs open. Keep your legs open. . . . He wants you to get erection in this take. Can you get erection? He wants you to have erection. . . . So I dreaded Laura Betti coming towards me."

5. Roland Barthes, "Erté, or A la lettre," in *The Responsibility of Forms: Essays on Music, Art and Representation*, trans. Richard Howard (Oxford: Blackwell, 1984), 107.

6. See the interview on the BFI's DVD.

4 Rite of Passage: The Hat That Wouldn't Disappear in the 1960s

Drake Stutesman

In the 1960s, after thousands of years as everyday wear, the hat began to disappear in the industrialized world. Almost overnight, hats that had defined people's status and desires were swept out of style. Gone or going were the top hat, fedora, bonnet, bowler, boater, cap, custom hat, coif, and cartwheel.[1] The hat continued to be used in religion and government and other occupations,[2] but even as the hat was diminishing as a regular part of dress, there are indications that it remained a strong cultural presence with an ineradicable symbolic value. This was evident in the constant public discussions about the hat's disappearance,[3] its retention in aphorisms[4] (such as "a feather in your cap"), and, arguably, in its use as a signifier of *gravitas*. Diane Crane, in her analysis of the meaning of clothes, cites hats as "closed texts," fixed and constant because "universally understood." The hat's broad use as both synecdoche and metonym suggests that the conceptual "hat" was an enduring, even crucial, part of society.[5]

Two American films from the 60s, one released in 1963, *A New Kind of Love*, directed by Melville Shavelson, and one released in 1970, *Puzzle of a Downfall Child*, directed by Jerry Schatzberg, both about the fashion industry, use the hat as a symbol and can be read as using this symbol to send key information to the audience.

It was in the 1960s that for the first time since late antiquity, women and men went bareheaded as a rule, not as an exception. This was a cataclysmic shift, as to be hatless had long been met with suspicion.[6] But by the mid-60s, hatlessness was normal. When fashion advanced from the 50s wasp-waisted, pale Dior model posing at a stiff angle in an alluring hat to the 60s Sassoon-coiffed girl in exaggerated black eye makeup doing the frug in Mary Quant's A-line mini dress, the hat did not adapt well. By the 1960s, the hat that completed a "look" was no longer a de rigueur part of an outfit, but rather an afterthought or a uniform, such as the hood-like shape made by André Courrèges, Halston, or Pierre Cardin. Though the bold or witty woman's hat continued into the 70s with millinery by Yves Saint Laurent, Mr. John, Adolfo, and a few others, it had been phasing out for some time.[7]

Reasons for this loss vary. One is hair: products such as hairspray, invented in 1940s America and popularized in the 1950s, began to undermine the hat's monopoly. Hairspray froze hair into a crowning glory and allowed a style to announce a person's élan as a hat had done.[8] But in 1963, hairspray was usurped—by hair itself. Vidal Sassoon created the "five point" cut that allowed hair to move easily but perfectly return to its contour, undoing the dependence on perms, sprays, and hats. Within the year, 75 percent of Sassoon's clients chose the five point.[9] A second key reason for the hat's demise is that hatlessness came to signify a kind of democratization because the bare head did not identify status as the hat had always done.[10] This was evidenced well in the controversy over John F. Kennedy's inauguration. It was much discussed (and contested) whether he did or did not wear a hat for the 1961 presidential swearing in. Kennedy, a thin man who relied on his luxuriant hair to make himself seem more virile, had, from the 50s, courted the hatless look, a look so out of place that the press constantly noted it as either novel or inappropriate. There was buzz about whether or not he would arrive hatless for the ceremony but, for Kennedy, this was never in question and he wore the traditional top hat. He removed it during his acceptance speech not, as myth determines, because he had cast it aside as an undemocratic marker, but because every incoming president removed his top hat during his speech as a sign of respect. That the hat controversy is so fabled and that some still claim that JFK did not wear a hat (despite photographs of the event) reveal how vigorously the hat, whether materially present or not, plays on the social imagination.[11] After this watershed moment, the hat took on a new incarnation—that of "missing." And, in that incarnation, as an inherent and still potent paradigm, it has continued to exert influence.

Did cinema reflect this change? Arguably, it did, and in ways both subtle and complex. In *A New Kind of Love* (1963) and *Puzzle of a Downfall Child* (1970), the films' hats, seemingly irrelevant to the two stories, acted as a stabilizing semiotic. In the wildly spiking times of the 60s, which were moving so fast by the end that extreme change was the constant,[12] the "hat" epitomized Marshall McLuhan's "medium," referenced constancy and standards while carrying new, unacceptable, or difficult information for an audience who still easily recognized the hat's "closed text" status.

Each movie had mixed reviews. *A New Kind of Love* was dismissed as "thin" and is still considered a fluff film.[13] It was, however, nominated for an Oscar for both best costume and best score, and Joanne Woodward and Thelma Ritter were nominated for, respectively, a Golden Globe for best actress and a Golden Laurel for best supporting actress. *Puzzle of a Downfall Child*, a serious art film, was a financial failure, panned by many American critics but loved by European ones, who nominated Faye Dunaway for a Golden Globe. Its screenplay, written by Carole Eastman, won an Oscar. It gained cult appreciation after a 2011 restoration and gala screenings, including a night at the Cannes Film Festival.[14] Though one film is a comedy and one a tragedy, both demonstrate the role fashion played in expressing the 60s. Both appeared on the cusp of social reforms, and present the fashion industry as a mirror of the era's zeitgeist. Both recreate fashion through costume design. Both connect haute couture with asexualization and depict the former as stifling. Both discard couture as extraneous yet retain couture hats as symbols. Both are women's films with stars at their career peaks portraying accomplished professionals. In both, the leads pursue sexual satisfaction that becomes a metaphor for the era, but with very different outcomes.[15] These different endings reflect the sixties' extremes, with the films made, respectively, at the decade's beginning and end. Finally, both films come out of the dominant culture of white, heterosexual perspectives, the very culture that was being attacked and from within which a counterculture was emerging.

A New Kind of Love, written and directed by Melville Shavelson, with costumes by Edith Head, is a light sex comedy, starring Joanne Woodward, Paul Newman, Maurice Chevalier, Eva Gabor, George Tobias, and Thelma Ritter. The film is about the fashion trade, set in the New York garment industry and the Parisian couture houses.[16] Though it may seem like merely fluff, the film, from Paramount Pictures, was made with all of the studio's expertise.[17] Moreover, the fashion contributors were famed: photographer George Hoyningen-Huene, who redefined the fashion image in the 1930s, devised the title sequences of humorous credits (which declare, after a long list of contributors, "if we forgot anyone, sue us") that reveal that the film contains "Paris originals designed [and] executed" by the couturiers "Lanvin-Castillo, Pierre Cardin, and Christian Dior," as well as clothes "pirated" from them. The credits include the "amused cooperation" of high-end American department stores such as Bonwit Teller and Bergdorf Goodman and the respected discount department store Ohrbach's, known for quality couture replicas. They even boast the "somewhat horrified participation" of eminent accessory labels,[18] including hats by the milliner Mr. John, who was still a fashion luminary after three decades.

The year 1963 was a turbulent one, in many ways deeply marking the onset of the era's full frontal attack on current governing systems. The year ended in the assassination of President Kennedy and the uneasy beginning of the Lyndon Johnson administration. The year held turning points for women that would also have far reaching consequences. Betty Friedan's best-selling exposé of inequities experienced by many women, *The Feminine Mystique*, was published, raising Second Wave feminism, which ultimately fueled massive demonstrations in the 70s. The Equal Pay Act of 1963 was passed in the United States, making it illegal to pay one gender less for the same work and at least publicly highlighting the practice as unlawful, even if the law was not widely followed.[19] Fashion's silhouette was recut radically by young designers such as Quant and Barbara Hulanicki.

Quant in particular was considered by many to be, as Ernestine Carter put it, the "symbol for the sixties."[20]

A New Kind of Love seems to be a frivolous film that was released during this electric period almost by chance. But it is not. Using a subplot of design theft, the film looks at relationships between couture, ready-to-wear, and costume design and intriguingly reduces these relationships to one thing: sex and youth versus couture and age. The film is a tribute to fashion as a national industry that honors both high-end and low-end, but it covertly lauds the modern over the outdated and dares to set this up as a contest between American sensual crassness and European jaded good taste.

The jazzy title sequence reveals Woodward walking late at night past expensive store windows on New York's Fifty-Seventh Street and Fifth Avenue, secretly photographing their displays. Later, in daylight, we see a stampede of customers rushing into a department store (not named but situated in the Garment District, the city's manufacturing/*atelier* center) for bargains. Finally, in the offices above the public floors, we see Woodward, buyer and industry spy, and her two bosses, Ritter as head of design and George Tobias as the chief executive, discussing and making their signature merchandise: cheap knockoffs of luxury lines. Thus, the film's first few minutes reveal the American brand-to-counterfeit formula (theft by photograph, then construction, then purchase), the executive telling his team that he wants to rival Ohrbach's by producing fake French couture. They travel to Paris, the setting for the film's main story, where they plan to "buy, buy, buy" custom work and steal ideas from the grand couture houses. Woodward must memorize what she sees on the catwalk, as a camera is risky, and in this sense, she works as an early-twentieth-century copyist had worked (drawing from memory), and though seemingly small, this detail subtly establishes a major theme: American futurism. America has been introduced as producing low art of a good grade that is in touch with contemporary methods and contemporary people, and Europe is introduced as creating high art of a good grade but from a place that remains in the past. Through this pairing, a subtext surfaces that promotes the United States as the new fashion strength,[21] and the use of the hat as a rite of passage conveys this. Just as in the JFK story, this reveals that the hat, though on the wane, retains intense metonymic signification.

Romance is the story's juice, of course, and the film is built on the device of a woman's sexuality emerging once she, in the guise of a femme fatale, seduces a man.[22] The man (Paul Newman), in this case is an educated (he references Baudelaire, Herrick, and Montaigne) and womanizing New York columnist whose philandering with the boss's wife has forced him to transfer to the paper's Paris office. Woodward is introduced, as was the era's cliché of a professional woman, as somewhat tomboyish and hardheaded, focused on her job and little else. Her professionalism is associated with clothes of a masculine cut and details with

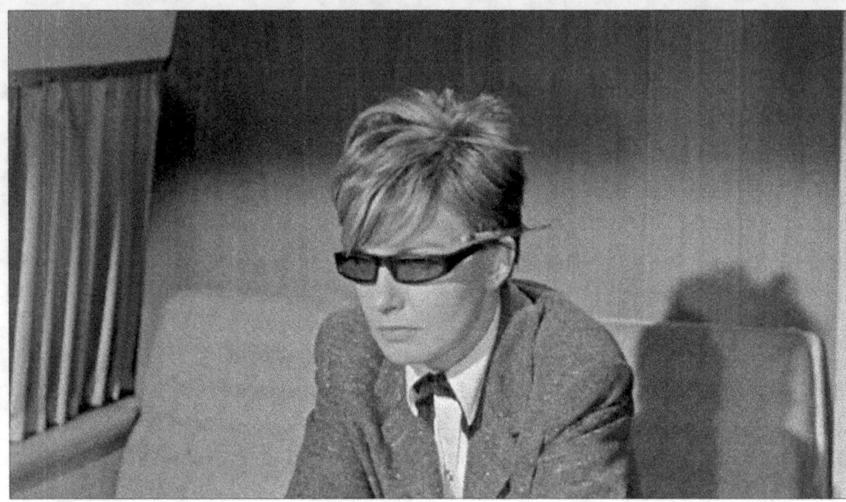

Fig. 4.1 Sam in blue dark glasses, jacket, and tie.

male tonality. Dressed in a pencil skirt, man's jacket, shirt with small tie, white trench coat, white flat driving cap, and wraparound blue sunglasses, she has a clipped mannish haircut and is called Sam (short for Samantha).[23]

However, despite the stereotype, several aspects of the narrative reveal the 1963 film as progressive. Sam has renounced relationships and sex because of a bad love affair but she does not fear humiliation when she talks matter-of-factly about this with her older colleagues Leena (Ritter) and Joe (Tobias). She describes herself as "half a maiden," indicating sexual experience, but is determined to try again once she meets Newman whom she attracts by pretending to be a high-class French "call girl," Mimi, who slinks around in uber-chic (though unrevealing) outfits, wears a long platinum wig, and smokes cigarettes through a ten-inch cigarette holder. The sexism that defines Woodward's character (as really looking for marriage) does not imply, as it would have a few years earlier, that she will leave (or lose) her job if she is a wife. Her problem in 1963 is not a choice between virginity and matrimony; it is how to find sex that she likes. The film fools endlessly with sexual innuendo and with the reality of erotic desire. This is done not as a crude joke but rather the film poses sex as vital and playful, and sought after by women and men of any age. Woodward, on reading Shavelson's film treatment, said it was "the dirtiest thing I ever read and I love it."[24]

As is typical of the "false femme fatale" genre, the leads become a couple once they have stripped themselves of all pretense, a condition that *A New Kind of Love* links with youth, sex, and America. In the last scene, when the couple are lovers, Sam's clothes have been codified into a basic lingerie chemise—the modern, simple, carnally explicit garment—in which she, at last, is herself, a young, sexually eager, skillful career woman. She has cast off pretend womanness (as created by the couture disguise and defined by its old feel) and pretend maleness (in her tomboy appearance) and has arrived at her unaffectacious being.

According to Edith Head's biographer, David Cherichetti, Shavelson wrote the treatment as an homage to Head.[25] Shavelson's respect for Head likens her to a couturier. Though her costumes mimicked French workmanship, her work was American, and though her "couture" costumes imitated couture, her film work was already well-known and prized.[26]Publicly, Head was tantamount to a fashion designer, with a career studded with trend setting[27] and fashion advice, even as late as 1967.[28]

So what are we really seeing? The film layers the authentic (authentic couture designs and authentic costume design) and the imitative (costume design's imitation of couture and the fashion industry's imitation of couture). Furthermore, American garments are represented by Ohrbach's, the store already legendary by 1963 for its distinguished remakes of haute couture.[29] Jacqueline Kennedy, according to Marylin Bender, from 1960 onwards, successfully introduced the couture look to the masses as no one before her had done. Kennedy bought French couture but also bought "Balenciagas and Givenchys in Paris, at Chez Ninon, a New York custom copyist of French clothes, and at Ohrbach's, the bargain store that excels in mass-produced translations."[30] Criticized for favoring European dress, Kennedy chose an American, Oleg Cassini, to create many of the clothes that became part of the celebrated "Jackie Look." Cassini, who considered these designs to be "haute couture at its highest and purest level," was a well-recognized costume designer with his own fashion line.[31] According to him, the Jackie Look brought "world wide recognition, for the first time, to an American designer."[32] Though it is open to question whether Cassini's work was the first to put US fashion on the international map, the Jackie Look had impact and a lasting influence. Kennedy's endorsement of Cassini and her endorsement of mock couture clouds the distinction between "high" and "low" and reveals that *A New Kind of Love*'s nexus of fake–real and Cassini's nexus of design in costume and in couture was reflective of early 1960s consumerism.

A New Kind of Love's tensions are acted out in the good girl versus bad girl sex drama, as well as in the "up market" versus "down market" of fashion industries and the no-nonsense drama of working girl versus the modish whore. But the film is tilted fully towards a broader identity: the contemporary 60s generation and American style. The film has a love of women dressed in sexual (versus chic) clothes and a love for American "lowbrow." *A New Kind of Love* goes further—it shows lowbrow as superior to "highbrow," because, like JFK's hatlessness, the film presents lowbrow as a part of a vibrant American persona embodying the current, charged world. Teri Agins, in *The End of Fashion*, views the 1960s as a breaking point in France when the "first hair line cracks in the couture world began to appear" due to rising costs and lowered subsidies.[33] Valerie Steele's history of Paris fashion characterizes that problem as a "profound identity crisis" as France, having not cultivated its newcomers but relied instead on couture prestige, lagged behind the latest British and American artists and designers who now were leading the way, such as the Beatles, Quant, Elvis Presley, and Rudi Gernreich.[34] The new generation not only drove the style, but defined it. Quant (and Courrèges) produced the miniskirt in 1964, a moment, underscored by Agins, that marked a "change in women's values," when the consumer suddenly flaunted her youthfulness and rejected the adult aura that the customer always had expected from fashion (an objective that Quant hated).[35]

Karl Lagerfeld, head of Chanel, agreed that "sexiness and youth didn't come in until the sixties," the era of "youthquake."[36] This rise of this "quake" contributed to the political agitation that would explode by the middle of the decade, but early in the decade, this energy still expressed itself, by and large and in the main, in newness. Fashion embodied it. Historian Caroline Milbank situates the early 60s look not just in "youth" but also in "freshness, charm, simplicity and ease,"[37] and *A New Kind of Love* perfectly suited that focus. 1962–1963, when the film was created and released, were years on the cusp. At this time, fashion began to leave the styles of the late 1950s more completely and move toward definitive 60s gear as it appeared by 1964 with the work of Gernreich, Quant, Courrèges, and Ossie Clark.

In 1962, Head was out in front of the curve, already creating elements of what would become distinctive to the 60s mode, and in a notably American way. *A New Kind of Love* anticipated the unconcealed sexuality of mid-60s clothes. Its costumes reach, under the covering of "light comedy" easiness, into a modern look that was about to burst onto the London scene. Though the film's rejection of, as the film portrays it, European couture's dull heaviness is similar to the designs found in the elegant, dynamic, American sensuality of a late 1950s designer like McCardell, Head goes further. She showcases early 1960s "freshness" but radicalizes it with adult eroticism. The film's US "fashion" (as found in Head's costumes) is not in Fifth Avenue glamour, Seventh Avenue practicality, or Ohrbach's cultured rendition, but rather in a fashion space of its own, a subversive and *au courant* American underground.

This appears in an inset story rendered in a split screen. During a French couture fashion show, the screen is divided suddenly into two entrances to two different rooms, shown side by side. One is the brightly lit couture house and the other a murky, reddish-hued burlesque strip club with flashy lights. On the left, haughty French models in clothes austerely couture and asexual (ballooning capes that hide the body, high collars, and hats that obscure the face) coldly walk through a demure but splendid interior filled with wealthy clients. On the

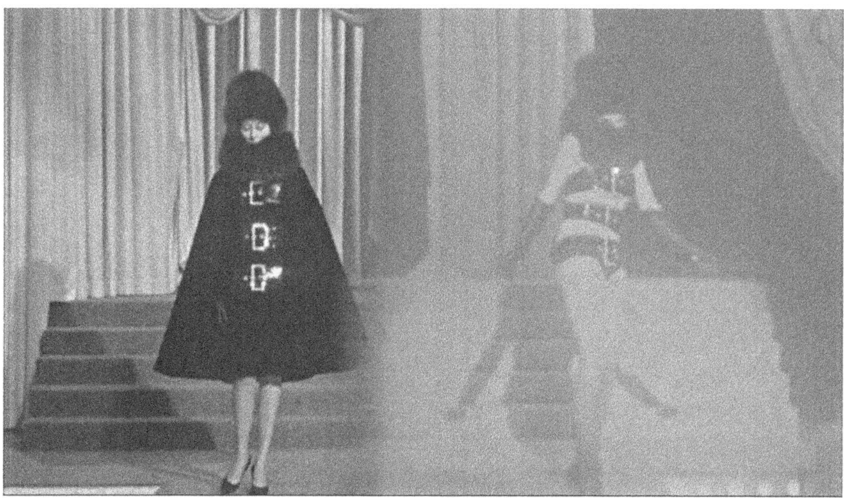

Fig. 4.2 Strip-couture in Edith Head's three-belt costume, *A New Kind of Love*, designed in 1962.

screen's right, in the rosy strip club, young women stand in a doorway wearing outfits matching or almost matching those of the couture models. The girls then fling open the clothes to reveal their lithe bodies in flimsy, bedizened, over-the-top versions of the high-end outfits.[38] There is no nudity or actual stripping (though the inference of stripping is clear). The girls are not the weighty, womanly strippers of the time.[39] They have svelte, teenage shapes, and though they bump to exciting music in a few burlesque moves, they smile and dance down their runways with an air of amused enticement. The club scene does not have the prurience or power contest of stripping, per se; rather, the audience and the young women seem to be on par with them, delighting in the fun and the insider world of "strip" wear versus couture wear.

This is the world of "now" and the future. The clothes anticipate, arguably, styles that emerge in the mid- to late-60s or even twenty years later (or more),[40] as shown in figures 4.2 and 4.3.

In one episode (figure 4.2), a model wears a black fur hat and a wool cape over a three-banded, buckled, shapeless, knee-length black dress while a striptease girl wears a black fur hat, fur collar muff, elbow length black gloves, a black patent leather buckled belt as a brassiere, a black patent leather buckled belt at the waist, and a patent leather buckled black belt as a bikini bottom at the hips. The latter's outfit mixed the stripper, the model, and the athlete such as Madonna's (and Jean Paul Gaultier's) merging of these three in the 80s and 90s, which, prior to Madonna's pioneering, had been kept as separate "types." Gaultier's costume

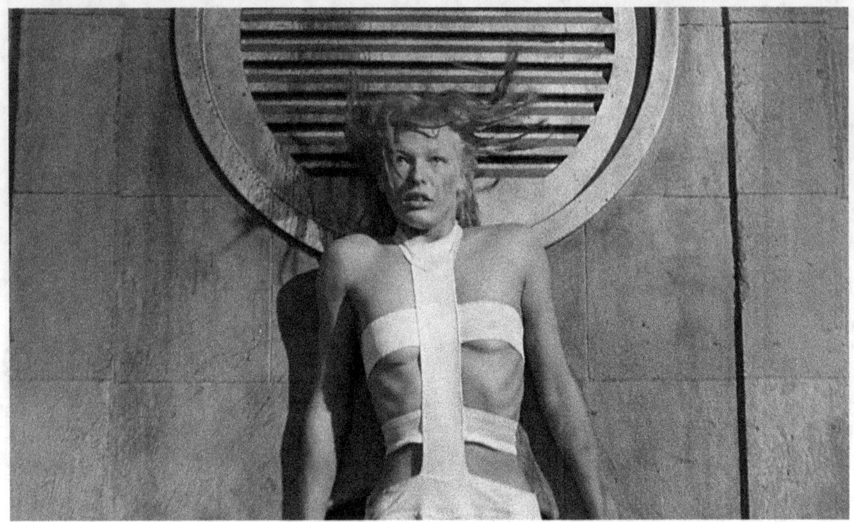

Fig. 4.3 John Paul Gaultier's 1997 costume, *The Fifth Element.*

for the 1997 film *The Fifth Element* (figure 4.3) is almost identical to Head's, and in 2012, Krizia brought out a dress with Head's same elements. The mix of dance and catwalk anticipates Ossie Clark's mid-1960's shows. His models cavorted down the runways, which was how he felt his clothes came to life and (ultimately) became erotic. Manolo Blahnik, Clark's 1970s shoe designer, so eloquently described his designs as doing "what fashion should do—produce desire."[41]

The link between clothes, youth, seduction, and movement that exemplifies the mid-60s fashion-produced "desire" is bound together already in the 1962 *A New Kind of Love* scene. The European house seems dead, while the strip club (which is American in feel because, as Rachael Shteir defines it, in her history of striptease, stripping is a "distinctly American diversion"), is alive with fashion's potential because these designs are current, if not innovatively offbeat, and the scene's atmosphere full of dynamism that will take it forward. [42]

The sequence is done with droll irony, but in using striptease, Shavelson chose something already in the culture at large by 1963.[43] Burlesque, long viewed as sordid, had been merging with dramatic theater and Hollywood since the 40s.[44] A telling shift in the sexual climate came in 1960 when semipornmeister Russ Meyer began a film genre (and a financial hit) with his *The Immoral Mr. Teas*, a narrative using burlesque stereotypes with full nakedness meant to titillate. Shteil argues that Meyer "used undressing as a metaphor for ripping the veil off the 1950s hypocrisy."[45] "Undress" in *A New Kind of Love* is doing something similar: exposing the weakening of France's hold on couture and offering an alternative.

The *A New Kind of Love* strip club girls are in undress, but in much the same spirit as the mini skirt undressed women by 1964. It was not lewd, but rather showcased an active body toned more by rock and roll or sex than by starvation, and one, according to Quant, that was looking for sex.[46] Shteil argues that by the sixties, the decade's new dances (free form, solo, and uninhibited), though they seemed to have evolved from strip, had nothing in common with original tease and its shapely bodies and slow peeling of clothing. She argues that the 1960s go-go dancers who danced with unhesitatingly erotic energy on the stages, in club cages, behind singers, and on the dance floor "asserted irreverence, a disdain for formality, and more movement than striptease could contain."[47] In 1962, go-go dancing had hardly begun, becoming commonplace only in the middle of the decade. Thus, *A New Kind of Love* anticipates its blend of lustfulness and spirit and takes the striptease sequence out of striptease itself, places it on a catwalk-burlesque runway, and adorns it in what will be the new "60s" look. In juxtaposing a classic couture model against a go-go girl with striptease moves, the film promoted American taste as debatably declassé but undeniably striking, sybaritic, inventive, and enviable.

In the film, the two design fields (European couture and American knockoff) are pitted directly against each other through costume design and its American originator (Head). Head unifies the two but, out of that amalgam, creates a fashion impact that is distinctly American, made from the new American mode (strip undress) and moving toward the forthcoming European mode (mini-clothes undress). In 1962, Head's freewheeling, arousing "undress" garments that blurred adult stripping, go-go youth, agile bodies, and direct female sexuality only were hinted at in fashion. Curvaceous stars such as Marilyn Monroe, Elizabeth Taylor, and Sophia Loren were foremost beauties, and their styles, and styles in general, even those that were sexualized, lingered in the 50s cosmopolitan look. Lingerie was about foundation, with stiff brassieres and long girdles. The mini, with all its meaning, would not launch for another year or more. *A New Kind of Love*'s costume design was presenting the public with the next generation's explosive taste, not only overtly presenting it as wild, but also covertly offering it as having gravitas, as able to authoritatively take over.

It is the symbolic hat metonymically standing in for authority that the film uses to bridge the styles. It is the couture hat (with all its undertones of old European haute art), but one made by a renowned American milliner (with all its overtones of new American haute art), that is the conduit. Sam's concern about her womanliness is a theme not uncommon in romantic comedy. If she is a workaholic, a woman could be stereotyped as too masculine, and Sam's hats reflect this. Initially, she wears a man's cap (and is more than once mistaken for a man),[48] and when she dances with Chevalier at a party, she wears his trademark straw boater (while surrounded by women in colorful, gigantic, over-the-top feminine hats).[49]

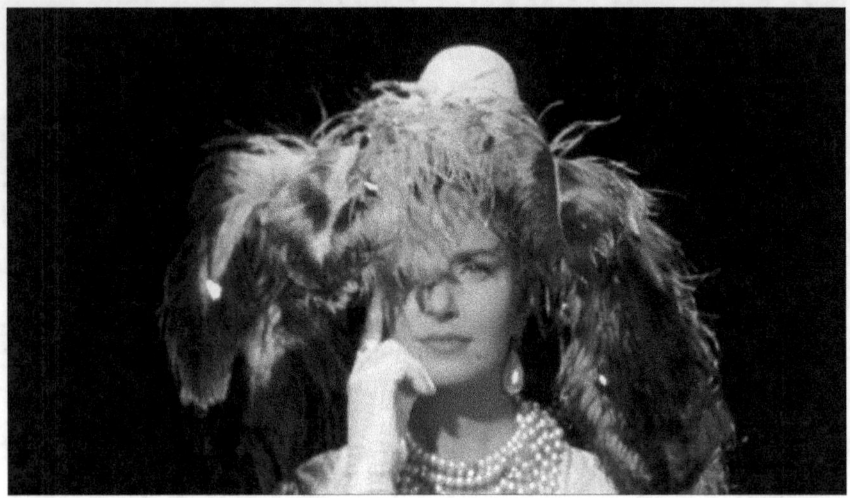

Fig. 4.4 Sam's unworkable dream makeover in a Mr. John couture hat.

Hats also define her attempts at femininity. There is a larger-than-life fantasy sequence in which Woodward's dream of femme mystique is displayed through a series of outrageous hats made by Mr. John. In the scene, Sam decides she needs feminizing through artificial arts and, though in Paris, the film cements its American favoritism when Sam chooses the American Elizabeth Arden for her makeover. The sequence begins with facials, workouts, excessive makeup, and sculpted lavender and pink wigs. After she is "ready," she wears four madcap hats as if in a photo shoot. The first is a sumptuous platter with falling grey and black ostrich plumes, followed by a bright blue satin turban, an orange, contoured headdress with three feather-constructed, curved prongs like bird wings, and finally a gigantic red fez with a huge skirt of red, wide-ringed mesh that encompasses her fully, falling over her shoulders. Their idiosyncratic, couture beauty shows a reverence for hats. Yet, the hats are contradictory (as the 1963 film is at the beginning of the end of hats as de rigueur attire) and are all finally rejected as impossible for a woman like Sam. She looks stunning in them but finds fault with each: she blows at the soft, dangling feathers (and they seem limp), she doesn't know what to do with the turban (which seems like a costume), and she can't get the cigarette holder through the fez's mesh (and it seems nutty).

Despite its expertise and refinement, and despite the respect towards the couture names in the opening credits, high fashion is shown in *A New Kind of Love* as out of reach and out of touch. The hats are too much work! They do not offer her the world that Sam/Samantha is really looking for, which is ultimately the place the strip girls inhabit—larky, unpretentious, libidinous, adventurous,

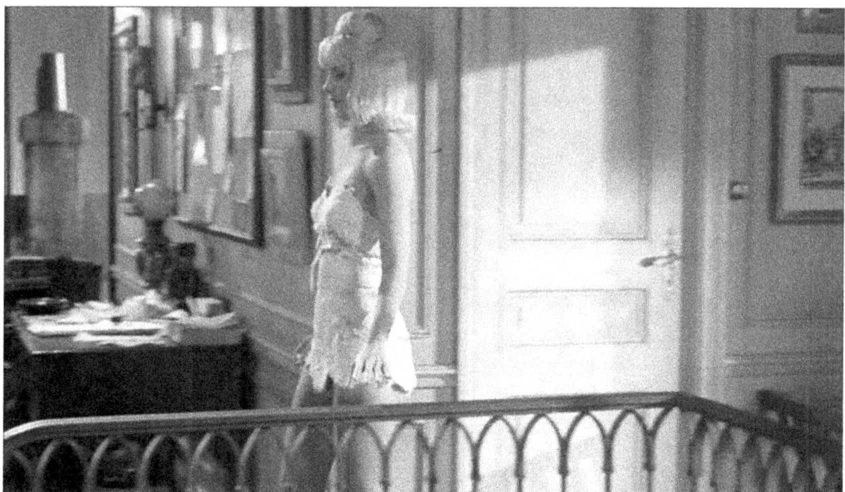

Fig. 4.5 Sam dressed in her chemise and "Mimi" wig.

and cutting edge. Their movement is free and not encumbered by the dictates of haute couture. But the strip girl's own constricting outfit (the three-belted one) during the dance also counters couture. It "outs" the sadomasochism found in 1950s frozen Dior model's tightly bound silhouette, because the strip girls openly enjoy their clothes' bondage eroticism and its heightened sexuality.

But these alternate-to-couture clothes (skimpy, scintillating, silly, sexy, edgy, and hip) are also unique as new fashion in their mix of the risqué and the not classically tasteful. As such, they are unlike previous unhindered styles, from Poiret to McCardell, whose creations, even if scandalous, were not without decorum. This overriding of the "refined" (as what one looked for in the dominant fashion) was the mark of the 60s. When Sam is finally herself at the film's end, hatless (and wigless) and about to go to bed with her chosen lover, she wears something most like that which is worn by the girls in the club: her short lingerie chemise.

This is not just "a new kind of love," but a "new kind of" everything. In 1963, *A New Kind of Love* shows a woman's hat as still representative of the cool, but it is depicted as unattainable (the hats are send ups). It's obvious that the hats aren't wearable and, for all their craft, their sophistication is worn out. As such, the film uses the fantasy hats as a distinct sign of change in fashion and, more so, of change in self-perception. The hats are between the two worlds of the 1950s and the 1960s—they are "old hat." Their place in fashion is over (Woodward discards them), but their importance as signifiers of status, much as the removal of JFK's hat signified status (as much as the real hat on his head once had done), remains. In *A New Kind of Love*, the rejecting of the hat serves much the same purpose: it is a rite of passage

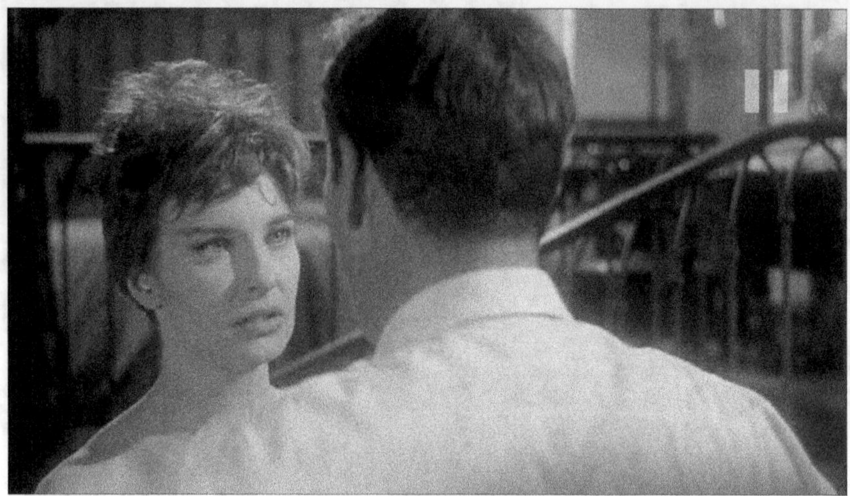

Fig. 4.6 Sam as herself, hatless and wigless, in her chemise.

taking Sam/Samantha from frustrated "half a maiden" to one who is sexually satisfied and from a woman who is "too male" or "too female" in her assumed dress to a self-accepting woman in "undress," reflecting the "fresh" start of the 1960s.

Seven years later, in 1970, the couture hat in cinema *still* acts metonymically, but now it is used to pose the "new" as negative. The authority invested in the hat is used in *Puzzle of a Downfall Child* to show that authority in general has dissolved, a reflection of the disturbance in the late 60s culture at large. In 1968, Tod Gitlan, then a leader in the activist Students for a Democratic Society, felt that the "nation went into shock."[50] Robert Kennedy, who was killed that year, spoke of that shock as a consequence of the "shattering" of the "mask of official illusion with which we have concealed our true circumstances, even from ourselves."[51] In *Puzzle of a Downfall Child*, the world displays no handover between generations. There is no sexual completion. There is no "fresh start." Contemporary historian William O'Neill, in his 1971 history of the era, saw the nation as in a "frenzy."[52] The assassinations and burning cities of 1968, the use of martial law, the ongoing Vietnam War, the civil rights conflicts, the separatist movements and the outflowing of their new diatribes, the rise of violent opposition, and the antiwar demonstrations were only some of the crushing uncertainties that dominated the culture. In 1969, the grisly, manifesto-driven Manson murders, one of the twentieth century's most famous crimes, so heightened the public's fear of how far people would go that Joan Didion, in her collection of essays on the culture of the 1960s and 1970s, *The White Album*, marked them as the decisive end of the 60s because "the paranoia had been fulfilled."[53]

Puzzle of a Downfall Child is an art house film set behind-the-scenes in the world of modeling.[54] It was directed by fashion photographer Jerry Schatzberg in1969 and released in 1970 and starred Faye Dunaway (at the height of her fame with *Bonnie and Clyde* [1968] and *The Thomas Crown Affair* [1969]) and Barry Primus, with costume design by Jo Ynocencio and Terry Leong. Like *A New Kind of Love*, this was a film with illustrious collaborators, written by incisive screenwriter Carole Eastman,[55] who was known for Jack Nicolson's breakthrough film *Five Easy Pieces* (1970), one of the most influential movies of the 1970s, and for the arcane, subtle western *The Shooting* (1966), also with Nicholson. Schatzberg went on to make the successful *The Panic in Needle Park* (1971) on drug addiction, which shook audiences with its realism, and *Scarecrow* (1973), a tight, eccentric road movie, both with Al Pacino. Structured as a fragmented story, through a disjointed, flashback narrative, *Puzzle of a Downfall Child* is about a supermodel, Lou Andreas-Sand (Dunaway), now a recluse at her East Coast beach home after a severe nervous breakdown, who tells her life story to photographer friend and lover, Aaron Reinhardt (Primus). The film follows Andreas-Sand's recollections of many jobs and many affairs and of her adolescent sex abuse, culminating in hallucinatory scenes of her stay in a mental hospital years later, where she had psychotic episodes.

Despite its diverse critical responses,[56] *Puzzle of a Downfall Child* was in tune with what has been referred to as the "tectonic shift" in American cinema in the early 70s.[57] The period from 1970 to 1975, known as New Hollywood, produced introspective, ambiguous films with themes often centered on people displaced within their own worlds. The male-driven films such as *Five Easy Pieces*, *The Godfather* (1972), and *The Godfather II* (1974) enjoyesuccess at the box office and portrayed men who tried to leave their origins but could not. Their dilemmas had no straight answers, and they were conflicted, not easy to like, and not reconciled to the roles into which they had been forced.[58]

But films about women in the same situation were less acceptable. *Puzzle of a Downfall Child* is one of the few that could be said to fit the 1970s male genre but still have a focus on women's lives: Andreas-Sand tries to leave her past but cannot; the film offers no straight answers to her problems; and like the men, she is conflicted, not easy to like, and not reconciled to the role into which she has been forced. What she suffers is similar to what Eastman ascribed to her Nicholson character in *Five Easy Pieces*: he "has lots of artistic temperament, but his ability and discipline are not equal to it. . . . His harsh treatment of others has to be seen in relationship to his own pain."[59]

In the film, Andreas-Sand is defined as much by her sexual life, which is portrayed as catastrophic, as by her professional life, which becomes catastrophic. Though she is the cliché of the shaky, semi-mean, toying model, Eastman nevertheless writes her as an intelligent woman but one so splintered that she cannot build a solid life. As an adult, she has numerous liaisons, but they offer little enjoyment and she moves on quickly. Any grounding through her work or her sexuality eludes her. Andreas-Sand is given a reason for her breakdown—childhood sexual abuse. This link (between trauma and pedophilia) was unusually direct for 1970, as this exploitation was a taboo subject and not part of the public dialogue. The film's serious approach to sex abuse sets it apart for the 1970s, but it also sets a theme (so different from *A New Kind of Love*'s sense of arrival) of disruption. In 1969, part of the "frenzy" of the late-60s zeitgeist was that society was, as O'Neill describes it, "coming part."[60]

In *Puzzle of a Downfall Child*, Eastman and Schatzberg look starkly at the nature of psychological disintegration and place it in the fashion scene that spoke to the chaotic world at large. The confidence of the early 60s, in barely five years, began to shift, much as Andreas-Sand does in *Puzzle of a Downfall Child*. Fashion moved from "youth" and "freshness" to, as Milbank argues, "mock innocent" and cynically "hip" becoming, by 1969, "experimental, even weird."[61] By the 70s, fashion, as an identity, was declining. It was a time, as Steele explained, when "fashion was not in fashion" and viewed as elite and about money.[62] Fashion styles had become so eclectic and undefined by then that they were disparaged as lowbrow.

Puzzle of a Downfall Child can be taken as characterizing a germinal cusp between the 1960s and the 1970s, just as *A New Kind of Love* was for the transition from the 1950s to the 1960s. The film was about *fin de décennie* uneasiness as much as it was about the Andreas-Sand persona. It was a time when everything was a "showdown, shootout, and face-off."[63] How could the fashion world mirror this? Schatzberg worked as a career fashion photographer for many years and knew the difficulties of the industry. John Fairchild, acerbic editor and publisher of *Women's Wear Daily* from 1960 to 1996, railed against the industry's brutality in 1989. He saw it as a world that "seeth[ed] with double deals and political ploys" and felt that the exposure of its duplicities was nearly impossible. "The real issue is that in the fashion business, it's almost against the law to tell the truth, and anyone who steps behind the silk curtain to show how raw the business is can expect a rough time."[64]

Andreas-Sand's character was based on Anne Saint Marie, a model with whom Schatzberg had worked and whom he loved from a "distance," according to Michael Gross's exposé *Model: The Ugly Business of Beautiful Women*.[65] In the opinion of photographer Roger Prigent, the job stress was so great that Saint Marie "lived in a fantasy world, completely dedicated to her work,"[66] which was something felt by others. "All the girls started to drink because of the pressure."[67] Much like Andreas-Sand, Saint Marie, "broke and broken," had a breakdown and was hospitalized.[68] Schatzberg could make fashion, a secretive, cutthroat world, into a metascape for the cusp between the 60s and 70s. Unlike *A New Kind of*

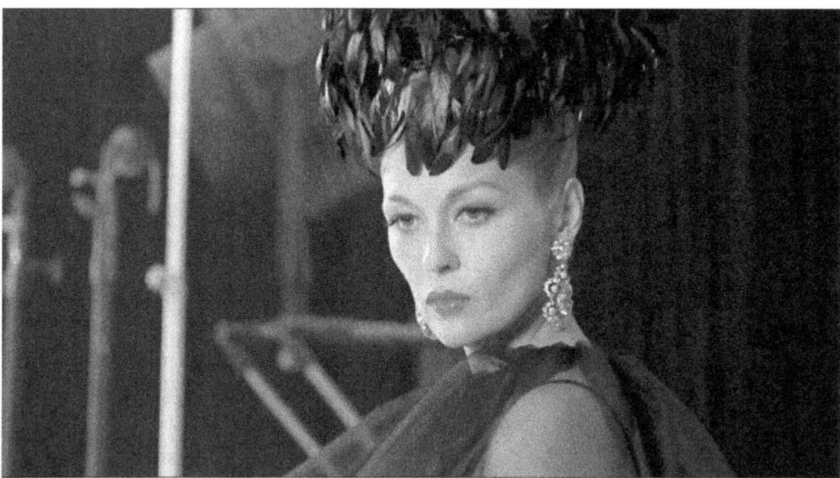

Fig. 4.7 Andreas-Sand in the perfect vogue hat in the beginning of the fashion shoot.

Love, which showed growth from the 1960s transition and had a respect for venerable European couture and a love of the American system's "nuts and bolts" ingenuity, *Puzzle of a Downfall Child*'s fashion industry was seen as insubstantial and vicious.

The hat, though no longer central in culture, was still strong enough in the era's collective unconscious to be used in the film as a symbol. In the opening flashback, virtually the film's beginning, Andreas-Sand wears a spectacular couture hat on her first fashion job. She is initially an incandescently beautiful model, but by the end of the shoot, the hat *and* Andreas-Sand have transformed and become almost grotesque. The scene and its focal hat are paradigmatic both of Andreas-Sand's breakdown and of the late 60s, merging the two into one.

Andreas-Sand tells Reinhardt the story of the day that she started in the industry, portraying herself as a vulnerable young woman who is willing to learn but who becomes unglued in the harsh modeling world that she has just entered. When she arrives at the shoot, the photographer insults her. As she comes on set, she is seen in close-up with a neckline of black toile, long diamond earrings, and a tall, dark hat perched on her head with her hair pulled tightly back in a bun. The hat is made of flowing short black feathers set on single stems so that they tremble and fall into a loose beehive shape.

The still above, a close-up of Andreas-Sand in the hat, became internationally famous and, as beautiful as Dunaway is, it is the hat that strikes the strongest note, doing what hats are meant to do—make an impression. The hat, awesome in its fragility, art, coherence, and balance brings the whole image together and makes the look dazzling.[69] But once the shoot begins, as the hard photographic

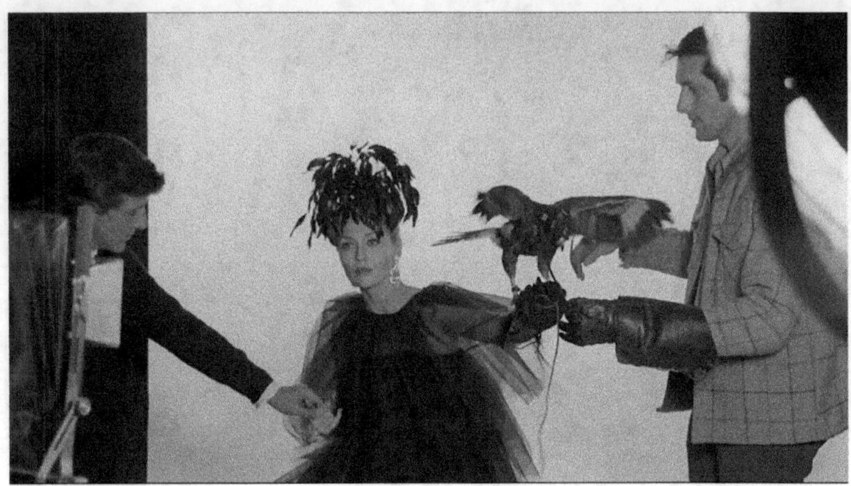

Fig. 4.8 A distressed Andreas-Sand with hawk, skeletal hat, and "bag" dress at the end of the fashion shoot.

white light shines through it (not on it), the voluptuous hat becomes skeletal and askew. A long shot reveals the striking black toile to be part of a misshapen dress that bulges in a desexualizing manner, which the photographer names "an insipid bag," condemning the ensemble by calling Andreas-Sand's head "pointed." Finally, she is given an agitated, flapping, live hawk to hold on her arm, which frightens her and her face becomes distressed and frozen. The final photo makes the cover of *Vogue*, but only Andreas-Sand's arm and the bird are in the picture. Andreas-Sand has been excised completely.

Thus, the film's first (and only important) hat also acts as a rite of passage and subtly represents Andreas-Sand, who in turn represents the anxieties of the new 1970s era.[70] The hat signifies collapsed authority. It is exactly the opposite of what it has been throughout its long, long history. In the past, the hat made the wearer a part of society. In *Puzzle of a Downfall Child*, the broken hat stands for a final social breakdown, the revelation that the person was not part of society because society itself was "coming apart" and its constituents fraying. By 1970, US politics was so raw that, as Gitlan summed it up, it exploded daily in "a succession of exclamation points."[71] The young disavowed the older generation as treacherous: "Never trust anyone over thirty" was a late 1960s cliché. In both conservative and radical positions, "extremity was the commonplace style," as was destabilization.[72] The Vietnam War's realities, such as the Tet Offensive, the My Lai massacre, and the secret bombings in Cambodia, undermined public support[73] and eventually exposed the war as "the longest, most brutal, and most destructive guerrilla war in modern history."[74]

The sexual revolution, it turned out, was riven with age-old sexism. Even the past was upturned. Feminist and gay activism was reclaiming and, thus, rewriting history, as was the civil rights movement, forcing new ways of seeing the "traditional" past. A looming recession, ominously known as "the malaise," was predicted in the near future.

As Sam/Samanthas's couture dream hats did, Andreas-Sand's couture feather hat stands for a transition from one kind of woman/citizen (naïve) to another (experienced). The black hat, which transforms through the shoot from glamour to ugliness, epitomizes Andreas-Sand's life: it seems intact (we see glamour's illusion), but it is falling apart (we see beneath glamour's illusion). Unlike those in *A New Kind of Love*, the hat in *Puzzle of a Downfall Child*'s loses all vitality. It is not even "old hat." It is empty, characterless, only a blunt metaphor. The hat signifies false security (represented by glamour, which, as Steele notes, was out of style in the early seventies, a time of antifashion). The fashion shoot (as a microcosm of society) so demoralizes Andreas-Sand that she and the hat (her would-be sense of self) are a wreck by its end. Her hat, as its shape wilts, acts as a sign of dehumanization, deterioration, and gimmickry, which is reinforced by the abusive fashion shoot. Unlike Sam in *A New Kind of Love*, Andreas-Sand does not find stability by usurping a previous generation. Rather, she is not given that option (of a stable past) and only descends further and further into confusion.

Though the hat appears only briefly in the narratives of these two films and seems buried in mise-en-scène, both *A New Kind of Love* and *Puzzle of a Downfall Child* show that the hat's reflection of a culture's sense of its soundness, structure, permanence, and transition is arguably too important to disappear. Culture, along with its stand-in, the fashion world, is intact in *A New Kind of Love*'s 1962–1963. Modernity is bound with time past and time future. While radicalizing the present, culture/fashion is presented as nevertheless integral to what has preceded it. Society is new but part of a whole, as symbolized in the coitus (to come) of the two lovers. Fulfillment is fulfilling, and it leaps from the past and moves culture onward. *Puzzle of a Downfall Child* does not have this kind of cohesion in time. The sophisticate's hat, which comes apart, mirrors the state not only of the Andreas-Sand character but also of the culture of 1969–1970. The connection between past, present, and future is disrupted. Sexual union does not unify; it is incomplete (unsatisfying affairs) and destructive (sexual abuse). The critiques by O'Neill, Didion, Gitlan, and many others that the culture was in a "frenzy" and that people's "paranoia" was "fulfilled" suggest that, by the end of the 60s, a state of amorphous fear had replaced the anticipated success that marked the beginning of the 60s as seen in *A New Kind of Love*. *Puzzle of a Downfall Child* has no resolution, and the fracturing of the ever-reliable hat displays that unequivocally.

DRAKE STUTESMAN teaches theoretical approaches to film costume design at New York University, where she coorganizes the annual conference on film costume. She is the author of *Snake* and the editor of *Framework:The Journal of Cinema and Media.*

Notes

1. The businesses of hatters (men's hats) and milliners (women's hats) suffered constant decline in the 1960s. By the middle of the decade, in trade journals such as *Millinery Research,* these statistics dominated the news. In New York, considered the "heart of the industry" and in the highly productive New England region, the industry began to slip. "What has happened to the industry since 1963? . . . All indications are that millinery shipments did not exceed $140.0 million for 1965, down some 30% from the base years of 1957–9" (*Millinery Research,* April 12, 1967, p. 7). In 1965, it was reported that millinery employment "continues to slide down," with approximately 12,000 workers in Massachusetts, New Jersey, and New York, only "half the number employed in the industry in 1947!" ("Hat Industry Shrinks in 1965," *Millinery Research,* March 15, 1967, 1, pp. 4–7). In New York City, men's hat production dwindled further in 1966 ("Hatters Lose 600 Workers in October," in *Millinery Research,* January 18, 1967, p. 13), and numbers decline continued to be reported through the decade.

2. Hats remained dominant in religion (e.g., turban, mitre, yarmulke, habit), official capacities (e.g., in the municipal, national, and sport realms) and governance (e.g., crown), and in social customs in areas as diverse as beauty, adulthood, and sexuality.

3. See discussion of President Kennedy's hat below.

4. The word "hat" exemplifies an array of behaviors, emotions, and situations: "hat in hand" (humility), "wear two hats" (allegiance or duplicity), "keep it under your hat" (discretion), and a "feather in your hat" (status or award)," to name but a few.

5. Diane Crane, *Fashion and Its Social Agendas: Class, Gender, and Identity in Clothing* (Chicago: University of Chicago Press, 2000).

6. Neil Steinberg, *Hatless Jack: The President, the Fedora, and the History of an American Style* (New York: Plume Books, 2004), ix–xvii, 216–17. Before the 1960s, internationally, the hatless head had an aura of vulnerability, even immorality: hatless women could be considered underdressed, hatless men considered weak.

7. The couture hat somewhat revived in the 2000s led by the elite British millinery of milliners such as Philip Treacy and Stephen Jones.

8. Milliner Mr. John declared hair spray and its creation of "orthopedic hairstyles" as the end of millinery (in interview with Drake Stutesman, 1990).

9. Vidal Sasson, *Hair Heroes,* ed. Michael Cordon (New York: Bumble and Bumble, 2002), 235.

10. Steinberg, *Hatless Jack,* 212–16. Steinberg argues that, after World War II, men rejected uniform hats and that, after the Korean War, young soldiers distanced themselves from the older generation and their hats. Cars with low ceilings, heaters, and/or convertible tops made hats unnecessary or too difficult to manage.

11. The influence of Kennedy's choice is still a burning question. For example, "Did Kennedy Kill the Hat?" appeared on the November 1991 cover of *Esquire Trade Talk.* On January 21, 2013, during Barak Obama's inauguration, *New York Times* columnist David Brooks commented inaccurately that Kennedy did not wear a top hat at his inauguration.

12. Tod Gitlan, *The Sixties: Years of Hope, Days of Rage* (New York: Bantam, 1987; repr. 1993), 274. Gitlan, leader of the Students for a Democratic Society (SDS), wrote in his memoir, "In the collective memory of what "The Sixties" looked and sounded like . . . the landscape was cluttered with landmarks and watersheds. The politics of the late Sixties [were viewed as] a succession of exclamation points. . . . One can see the late Sixties as a long unraveling. . . . Whatever the image, the contending forces labored under a cloud of impending doom, or salvation, or both. . . . How is it possible to hazard a strictly political account of even the single apocalyptic year 1968 without casting at least a sidelong look at the surrounding culture of politics? On every side, extremity was the commonplace style."

13. Bosley Crowther, *The New York Times*, October 31, 1963.

14. *Puzzle of a Downfall Child* was screened at the 2011 festival and introduced by the festival director, Thierry Fremaux. A Shatzberg image of Dunaway as *Puzzle's* model (though not from the film) was the festival's poster. *Indie Wire* critic Simon Abrams hailed *Puzzle* as a "must see" film and a "knock-out psychodrama." http://blogs.indiewire.com/thompsononhollywood/cannes_update_trabalahar_cansa_hard_labor_polisse_puzzle_of_a_downfall_chil [accessed on July 3, 2014]

15. The films also do not pose sexual pursuit as displacing their careers. Their jobs are shown as unquestionably part of their lives and not as a substitute for sex.

16. The film has many undercurrents about unions. Clara Lemlich, a Ukrainian immigrant who married Joe Shavelson in 1913 in New York, was one of the twentieth century's great union organizers. Lemlich's work in the unionization of the shirtwaist workers evolved into the International Ladies' Garment Workers Union (ILGWU), the garment industry's most powerful union for the next sixty years. Melville Shavelson was possibly related to her.

17. Paramount's crew were cinematographer Daniel L. Fapp (*West Side Story*), editor Frank Bracht (*Hud*), art director Arthur Lonergan (*Beyond the Valley of the Dolls*), Hal Pereira (*Vertigo*), set decorators James Payne (*The Sting*) and Sam Comer (*Rear Window, Sunset Boulevard*) and George Masters (*Vertigo*) and Nellie Manly (*The Ten Commandments*) for hair. Shavelson directed films such as *Houseboat* (1958) and *Cast A Giant Shadow* (1966), wrote comedy for Bob Hope, and was president of The Writer's Guild of America, West.

18. These were, as listed verbatim in the credits, "perfumes by Lanvin, furs by Maximilian of Embra mink, jewelry wardrobe by Richelieu, gloves by Kislav, handbags by Park Lane."

19. Many events in 1963 America created breaking-point confrontations, such as the murder of civil rights leader Medgar Evers, the enrollment of James Meredith as the first black student in all-white University of Mississippi, the deaths by bomb of four children in a Birmingham African American church, the drug Thalidomide being widely prescribed for pregnant women and then sourced as the cause of mutilating birth defects (corroding public trust in the medical world and the FDA), and the U.S. presence in Vietnam (heightened by the U.S.-backed assassination of South Vietnamese President Ngo Dinh Diem).

20. Ernestine Carter, *The Changing World of Fashion: 1900 to the Present* (New York: G. P. Putnam's Sons, 1977), 97.

21. This has been an American design theme since the early part of the twentieth century. Costume designers such as Clare West and Gilbert Adrian were vocal about the inventiveness of American costume and couture and were internationally influential.

22. Other films include *Madame Satan* (1931), *Two-faced Woman* (1941), and *Love in the Afternoon* (1957). There are many more.

23. Despite the implication of Woodward as masculine (she is mistaken for a man), her boyish haircut was seen on, for instance, Doris Day, Paramount's most popular star (male or female) from 1961 to 1965.

24. David Chierichetti, *Edith Head: The Life and Times of Hollywood's Celebrated Costume Designer* (New York: Harper Collins, 2003), 159–60.

25. Chierichetti, *Edith Head*, 159.

26. The film has further complexities of design. In their rush to complete (they had six weeks), they used a dress that Paramount's previous Head of Costume, Travis Banton, had made for Marlene Dietrich and, in a fantasy wedding scene, Woodward wears this bouffant satin gown and runs across a football field chased by Newman. This, in itself, is an amazing image (of a Dietrich-worn, Banton-made 1930s gown turned into a 1963 wedding dress retailored by Head and worn by Woodward on a sports field) and very reflective of *A New Kind of Love*'s schematic, which moves back and forth between "real" couture of the design houses, "fake" couture of costume design, and the "real couture" in the innovations of costume design.

27. These included Elizabeth Taylor's flowered bustier dress in *A Place in the Sun* (1951) and Dorothy Lamour's sarong in *The Hurricane* (1937), both created fashion crazes.

28. Edith Head and Joe Hyman, *How to Dress for Success* (New York: Abrahams, 1967; repr. 2010). This was a style handbook. Head also wrote Edith Head and Jane Kesner Ardmore, *The Dress Doctor* (Boston: Little and Brown, 1959), and Edith Head and Paddy Calistro, *Edith Head's Hollywood* (New York: Dutton, 1983; republished Santa Monica, CA: Angel City, 2009). Style advice from experts was common, and both fashion designers (such as Claire McCardell and Elizabeth Hawes) and costume designers (such as Howard Greer and Irene Sharaff) alike published guides and/or stories of their lives in design.

29. Tom Mahoney and Leonard Stone, *The Great Merchants: America's Foremost Retail Institutions and the People Who Made Them Great* (New York: Harper and Row, 1949, repr. and updated 1974), 327–35. Ohrbach's opened in New York in 1923 on Fourteenth Street and quickly was known as the "Rolls Royce of low-margin retailing," with a streamlined approach to discount selling using low mark-ups, steady prices, and quality clothes supplied from quality outlets, often bought in large lots. They targeted various kinds of customers, from the wealthy client to the bargain hunter. The wealthier women bought Ohrbach's "lower-priced, line-for-line- copies of creations by French, Italian and Spanish designers" such as "Dior, Givenchy, St. Laurent, Chanel, Valentino, Balenciaga, Fabiani, Simonetta and Capucci." The owner, Nathan Ohrbach, so promoted French imports after the late 1940s that France awarded him the Chevalier of the Legion of Honor.

30. Marylin Bender, *The Beautiful People* (New York: Coward-McCann, 1967), 50.

31. Oleg Cassini, *In My Own Fashion: An Autobiography* (New York: Pocket Books, 1987), 328.

32. Cassini, *In My Own Fashion*, 328.

33. Teri Agins, *The End of Fashion: How Marketing Changed the Clothing Business Forever* (New York: Quill, 2000), 27.

34. Valerie Steele, *Paris Fashion* (New York: Berg, 1998, repr. 1999), 277.

35. Agins, *The End of Fashion*, 27.

36. Agins, *The End of Fashion*, 27. Lagerfeld also added that women previously expected fashion to make them look adult.

37. Caroline Reynolds Milbank, *New York Fashion: The Evolution of American Style* (New York: Harry Abrams, 1996, repr. 1986), 200.

38. Head and Calistro, *Edith Head's Hollywood*, 189–90. Bob Mackie drew all the costume sketches for this sequence but his work would appear under Head's name, as was common costume departments practice. A "third sketch" assistant, Mackie remained at Paramount a few months. He went on to work for Cher and Carol Burnett in his partnership with Ray Aghayan.

39. Rachael Shteir, *Striptease: The Untold History of the Girlie Show* (New York: Oxford University Press, 2004), 279.

40. Krizia's Fall 2012 season shows a model wearing three separate black bands (at breasts, waist, and hips) with skin showing between each. The band on the hip connects to a flowing white skirt.

41. Blahnik, who, as his career began, designed shoes for Clarke's 1972 runway show, and described Clarke's work effusively: "He created an incredible magic with the body and achieved what fashion should do—produce desire."

42. Shteir describes stripping as a "distinctly American diversion (*Striptease*, 1).

43. Newman's voice-over is a humorous send up of each model's clothes.

44. Sara Maitland, *Vesta Tilley* (London: Virago, 1986), 35–36. Maitland argues that burlesque, a specifically American form, did not emerge from theater but rather evolved, before the Civil War, as brothel entertainment for men breaking from long isolated jobs such as cattle drives. Originally known as "specialist shows," what would become burlesque developed in the 1860s for an all-male audience, with shows designed to be sexual. As these men were also whorehouse clients, the association with brothels always remained close.

45. Shteir, *Striptease*, 306–07.

46. John D'Emilio and Estelle Freedman, *Intimate Matters: A History of Sexuality in America* (New York: Harper and Row, 1988), 306. Quant is quoted from *Newsweek*, November 23, 1967: "Am I the only woman who wanted to go to bed with a man in the afternoon? . . . Lots of girls don't want to wait. Mini-clothes are symbolic of them."

47. Shteir, *Striptease*, 317.

48. Newman initially thinks she is man, and later a female prostitute thinks the same. Newman twice refers to her as the woman whom he "picked up in the men's room," since he spoke to her while she was waiting in the line for the wrong toilet. This extends to her transformation into Mimi when, as he recounts the memory, he describes her as "never being directed to the men's room again."

49. These hats were designed by Mr. John.

50. Gitlan, *The Sixties*, 286.

51. Gitlan, *The Sixties*, 286, quoting Harris Wofford, *Of Kennedys and Kings: Making Sense of the Sixties* (New York: Farrar, Straus, and Giroux, 1980), 117. This is from a speech Kennedy made in direct response to the January 1968 Tet Offensive in Vietnam.

52. William O'Neill, *Coming Apart: An Informal History of America in the 1960s* (New York: Time Books, 1971), 396.

53. Joan Didion, *The White Album* (New York: Farrar, Straus, and Giroux, 1979; repr. 2009), at 47: The 60s "ended abruptly on August 9, 1969," the night of the first Manson killings.

54. *Puzzle of a Downfall Child* costume design sketches exist in the Mr. John archives at the Los Angeles County Museum (LACMA). It is known that John worked on at least ten to twenty films, and this suggests involvement with this production. Costume designer Ynocencio, who worked on most of Schatzberg's films, did not recall his involvement (interview with Stutesman, 2004), but further research may alter this.

55. Eastman wrote this script under the pseudonym Adrian Joyce.

56. Though some critics praised the film as experimental, others dismissed *Puzzle of a Downfall Child* as an imitation of European cinema with gamey, jagged stylistics. The setting of a model's world was demeaned as irrelevant.

57. *Hollywood Reborn: Movie Stars of the 1970s*, ed. James Morrison (New Brunswick: Rutgers University Press, 2010), 2.

58. Nicholson's character in *Five Easy Pieces* is a classically trained musician from a wealthy, cultured family who tries to lose himself as a laborer in the American oil fields but cannot escape his past. In *The Godfather*, Al Pacino plays the youngest son of a New York Mafia don who is forced to take over the business against his wishes when his older brothers

cannot. Both men are embittered be their experience. Though *The Godfather* was produced by Paramount Pictures, a major studio, it was guided by executive Robert Evans, legendary for developing iconoclastic material. *The Godfather II* plot follows a "New Hollywood" character formula, developing the first film's dilemma substantially. Furthermore, director Francis Ford Coppola declared that the films were representative of 1970s America: "I feel that the Mafia is an incredible metaphor for this country" (Peter Bondaella, *Hollywood Italians: Dagos, Palookas, Romeos, Wise Guys, and Sopranos* [New York: Continuum, 2004], 240).

59. Lizzie Francke, *Script Girls: Women Screenwriters in Hollywood* (London: British Film Institute, 1994), 94 (quoting an interview in *The Los Angeles Times* on May 2, 1971.

60. In using the subtitle *An Informal History of America in the 1960s* for his book *Coming Apart*, O'Neill portrays this zeitgeist as distinct to the 1960s.

61. Milbank, *New York Fashion*, 200.

62. Valerie Steele, *Fifty Years of Fashion: New Look to Now* (New Haven, CT: Yale University Press, 1997), 79.

63. Gitlan, *The Sixties*, 275.

64. John Fairchild, *Chic Savages* (New York: Simon and Schuster, 1989), 18.

65. Michael Gross, *Model: The Ugly Business of Beautiful Women* (New York: Icon-It Books/Harper Collins, 2011; repr. of 1995), 228.

66. Gross, *Model*, 228.

67. Gross, *Model*, 228.

68. Gross, *Model*, 228.

69. This picture became prominent again after 2011. For example, the image hangs in jeweler Waris Ahluwalia's House of Waris and he has been photographed with it.

70. The film has two other kinds of hats, both plain but with several iterations that differ only in color: one is a fedora (in black, red, and light blue), and the other is a pillbox (one black and one white, with diaphanous but solid straight veils to the chin).

71. Gitan, *The Sixties*, 274.

72. Gitan, *The* Sixties, 274.

73. *The New York Times*, May 9, 1969: William Beecher exposed the bombing of Cambodia secretly ordered by Presidents Johnson and Nixon. *Associated Press*, November 12, 1969: Seymour Hersh exposed the My Lai massacre, which in turn exposed the US military's "body count" policy.

74. William R. Polk, *Violent Politics: A History of Insurgency, Terrorism, & Guerrilla War from the American Revolution to Iraq* (New York: HarperCollins, 2007), 180.

PART II

Cities, Nations, and Fashion

5 Fashion Apart: Godard and Fageol in 1960s Paris

Astrid Söderbergh Widding

In the cinema of the 1960s, the French "New Wave" made Paris a new center of international interest by renewing global film culture through its innovative and fashionable portrayals of the city. This chapter seeks to explore the particular relations between the New Wave in Parisian cinema, fashion, and urban space in the 1960s. During this decade, these three aspects of modernity—new cinema, new fashion, and new urban life—appear as closely interrelated. Moreover, in the intersection of the three, a new way of conceptualizing urban space seems to appear by means of cinema and fashion together.

The French New Wave started with a journal, *Cahiers du cinéma*, in which a number of future directors first appeared as critics and a vision of cinema as something radically new was formulated with inspiration drawn from the Italian neorealists. The idea was to leave the studios and the heavy equipment behind and, instead, to use the new technical possibilities, such as lighter Éclair Caméflex cameras, to go out into the streets and capture real life, everyday life in its reality. By the turn of the decade, films by Claude Chabrol, Jean-Luc Godard, Jacques Rivette, Éric Rohmer, François Truffaut, and Agnès Varda had all premiered, which together formed the New Wave and changed the direction for the future development of French cinema.

In his two books on cinema, Gilles Deleuze seeks to define certain characteristics of the French New Wave.[1] He also emphasizes its connections to Italian neorealism; in fact, the New Wave seems to follow closely in its footsteps in construing pure optical and sound situations where the viewer's act of looking and observing has replaced action on the screen.[2] This new cinema, characterized by its disconnection from the earlier dominant sensory-motor schemas, was also developing what Pascal Augé once termed *espace quelconque*: "any-space-whatever." These spaces are never universal, but rather are quite unique. However, while they are unique, they can never be clearly determined, rather carrying a number of potentials, because they have lost their homogeneity, their clear connections both internally and externally, and have thus turned into instable, heterogeneous spaces. I will argue in the following that the new urban space of the French New Wave shares a number of these characteristics with Augé's *espace.*

With the French New Wave, at least three things were at stake. Firstly, the *cinéma d'auteur* was reinvented. The French magazine *Cahiers du cinéma* had discovered Hollywood authorship in the films of John Ford, Howard Hawks, and Alfred Hitchcock, but now the time had come to develop a new kind of auteur cinema on its own conditions, *à la Parisienne*—in Parisian style. Secondly, the New Wave also introduced a new relationship between fiction and reality. According to Jean-Luc Godard in an interview by *Cahiers du cinéma*, this particular relationship was defined partly by regret, by nostalgia for a cinema that no longer existed.[3] Thirdly, if the 1950s had been a highly stylized decade in cinema in general, both in France and internationally, the 1960s seemed to bring about no less than a revolution. The French filmmakers went out of the studios and into the streets of Paris. But at the same time, these streets became highly ambiguous. On one hand, they seem to be haunted by nostalgia, carrying along a fictional quality as if they were also reminiscent of a cinematic past. But this cinematic past also seemed to have entered everyday reality. On the other hand, the streets remain ordinary Parisian streets with very real cafés, shop windows, and ads of different kinds.

This departure from stylized studio productions also brought about a change in fashion in favor of more casual streetwear on the screen instead of the earlier designed costumes. At the same time, already in the 1950s, fashion designers had started to glance at the new street fashion, which had originated from the working class but had spread to middle and upper classes. Here, the fashionable was rather an antifashion, a return to the real, leaving both the film studio and the fashion studio for the streets in order to connect with ordinary people.

Thus, it is quite typical that, in Godard's first film *A bout de souffle* (*Breathless*) from 1960, no particular costume designer was credited. Here, Jean Seberg and Jean-Pierre Belmondo were both supposed to wear whatever they always wore. But this was bound to change, and the fashion industry quickly adapted to the new circumstances.

In two later films, *Vivre sa vie / My Life to Live from* 1962 and *Bande à part / Band of Outsiders* from 1964, Godard worked with costume designer Christiane Fageol, who later, as head of a costume and wardrobe department, designed the costumes for more than twenty films, both in Europe and the United States. As Catherine Deneuve acted in no fewer than sixteen of these films, Fageol could be characterized as one of her personal costume designers (actually, in one of the films, *Je vous aime* from 1980 by Claude Berri, she created only Deneuve's dresses). Otherwise, however, Fageol has remained relatively anonymous as a dress designer for cinema. In the case of the two Godard films, she has rarely been mentioned, obviously due to auteur cinema's tendency to credit only the director.

These two films in which Godard collaborated with Fageol are, however, both quite similar and both typical of Godard films from the period: they are shot in black and white; Anna Karina stars; different dimensions of urban space are explored; and they share a strong relationship to film history as well as a general cultural history. But they also remain dissimilar in certain ways, as they represent different directions in Godard's filmmaking. *My Life to Live* is a film in twelve chapters, all of which describe the main character, Nana, and her gradual degradation through prostitution. In *Band of Outsiders*, the lead woman, Odile, is one of three main characters, along with Franz and Arthur, and she lives with her aunt Madame Victoria. Odile aids the men to gain access to her aunt's hidden money.

As do most of the films during the French New Wave, these two films share a number of significant and innovative features. Both were cheap productions in which the street had become the scene, with handheld cameras and natural light. The ideal of direct sound turned out to be difficult and, due to its poor quality, had to be completed by postsynchronization. Both films were, to a large extent, based on improvisation. There were a number of jump cuts, as well as direct address to the camera. Also, a number of quotations and references to film history were added. These films, however, represent a New Wave not only because of their particular cinematic features but also because of their general qualities in expressing a new urban mode of life. As Jean-Louis Leutrat has noted, *My Life to Live* rather takes part in a predominantly documentary mode, whereas *Band of Outsiders* inscribes itself in a predominantly fictional mode, with both series indexed to the present. A third category, according to Leutrat, would be films that mix these modes (which to a certain extent both *My Life to Live* and *Band of Outsiders* also actually do), prefiguring a new problem central to Godard: how to make political films politically. The opening image from *Band of Outsiders* is quite revealing. If this film is generally supposed to belong to the fictional mode, it opens in a rather documentary style, focusing on a kind of dead, industrial space somewhere on the margins of the city. Thus, to quote Leutrat, "in this period, three series are displaced and modified in parallel fashion around an interlacing of common themes: love, betrayal, torture, prostitution, cinema, industrial society, among others."[4] The two films thus also serve as excellent examples of these three modes for exploring the relations between Parisian fashion and styles of filmmaking in New Wave films, as well as for examining urban space becoming fashionable anew during the 1960s, all under the auspices of the modern.

It is obvious that, thanks to the French New Wave, Paris had indeed become a new center of interest. The New Wave directors excelled in filming the city from odd angles, as well as both exploring and displacing the frontier between center and periphery, between urban and suburban space.

In *My Life to Live*, Parisian monuments like the Arc de Triomphe at the Place de l'Étoile on the Champs-Élysées are shown from unexpected angles. This was a commonplace in portraying the new Paris, so as to appear different from the well-known postcard clichés. These urban landmarks are thus revealed from new perspectives so that new facets may appear. The Arc de Triomphe all of a sudden does not appear as that triumphal, but rather as a monument among others, or even as equal in status, according to the film, with any building at all: a random building in the suburbs or an anonymous one in central Paris. Likewise, there is a photograph of the Champs Elysées on the wall behind Nana in a café where she is trying to write a letter to apply for a job. From this angle, it appears as any street whatever—in the Deleuzian sense of any space whatever—far from the general touristic views.

Urban and suburban spaces here appear as interconnected. The general idea is that they have to be connected, meaning that the general relationship between urban and suburban space is not innocent. The threatening character of anonymous buildings somewhere in between center and periphery is revealed through the tragic ending of *My Life to Live*, where the anonymous street allows for equally anonymous crimes.

"Are we inside or outside Paris here?" asks one of the characters in *Band of Outsiders* at the sight of the house in Joinville, where Odile lives, as they are there for the first time. This question, however, remains unresolved throughout the film, in spite of its being quite crucial; Joinville seems to hover in between and, thus, to be consigned forever to the divide between urban and suburban.

On a similar note, in both *My Life to Live* and *Band of Outsiders*, *les boulevards extérieurs* ("the exterior boulevards") are explicitly mentioned. This is another dead space, neither urban nor suburban, endless boulevards with almost no life. It is here that Mademoiselle Nana Untel—("Miss Girl So-and-So") in *My Life to Live* stumbles upon her first client as a future prostitute. And in *Band of Outsiders*, it is here that Odile and Arthur spend their first (also to become their last) evening together, under the sign of hopelessness. The exterior boulevards obviously carry no hope, no potential of development—only iron fences, empty spaces, and a constant threat of crime. Once again, they appear as Deleuzian *espaces quelconques*, spaces in between.

Nana's two appearances in different hotel windows in such "in between" spaces in *My Life to Live* reveal both the continuity and the change between these two scenes, the first of them being at an early stage in her "career" and the second towards the end of the film and of her life. In the first case, there is little to see through the window, and Nana does not seem to close the curtains against anything but possible peeping toms, even though the street appears deserted.

In the second case, she is in the hotel room with the anonymous young man who really cares for her, and she talks about leaving her pimp. As she closes the window in this scene, she rather seems to close her own last chance for an opening toward another life. Outer space, really neither urban nor suburban, appears here as both a possibility and a potential trap. Nana's dresses, so similar in these two central scenes, also suggest that she has remained essentially the same and true to herself in spite of whatever may have happened to her and whatever outer changes she may have undergone.

There is an oscillation in these films between conflicting *idées-images*, as French philosopher Jacques Ellul has called them in an essay on the contradictions of urban life—contradictory "image-ideas" particularly between "liberty" and "destiny" in which man appears as trapped *as l'homme quelconque*, as any-man-whatever. One might say, "I can live *my* life, without anyone interfering," and on the one hand, urban space thus liberates from taboos or obligations and allows for freedom, thanks to the anonymity of the crowd. On the other hand, this utopian view at closer look only reveals a seemingly abundant system, where in fact everything at closer look appears as calculated and precise, without any gratuity. According to Ellul, these contradictions are not dialectic and, thus, cannot produce anything new. Rather, they are charged with threats for which mankind knows of no remedy.[5] Hence, there is in both films a striking dark note that underlies the seemingly everyday quality of fashion and fiction.

From the point of view of fashion, however, there is a clear difference between Nana in *My Life to Live* and Odile in *Band of Outsiders*. On the story level, as we saw, Nana really remains herself. However, on the plot level, she also undergoes a clear development from a timid assistant in a record shop to a full-fledged prostitute, and this change is, as could be expected, clearly revealed by means of her clothing. In the beginning of the film, Nana starts out with quite a strict coat, turning her back towards the spectator, and then appears in her shop assistant outfit. When she picks up her first client, she has the same clothes on, but with a different black coat with an added degree of luxury. Later, she appears in another black, fur-trimmed coat, more elegant than the first. Under this coat, it later turns out that she also wears a ruffled blouse, which also appears as more vain than her previous working dress.

Odile in *Band of Outsiders*, on the other hand, changes only a little. She is dressed in almost the same way throughout the whole film. She has the same checked skirt, and only changes her sweater from grey to black. Unlike her classmate at the café, who is performing a full-scale makeover, Odile prefers a natural look and adds only a few details to her basic dress: a coat, a cap, and different hair dressings. She changes from knee-highs to stockings with an obviously unintended lack of continuity effect; whereas the stocking add a slightly erotic dimension (both Arthur and Frantz note her white legs of which they catch a glimpse), the knee-highs make her look more childish. Frantz's hat, which he puts on her head in the famous dance scene, also emphasizes a cross-gender quality in her style—which has already appeared in the opening of the film, in a rapid crosscutting between Frantz, Arthur, and Odile in close-up, a montage sequence which blurs their specific traits and emphasizes what they have in common. Unlike

Nana's character, Odile remains for the most part quite static from the point of view of fashion.

The male characters in both of the films are rather like Odile in that they never change. Neither Paul nor Raoul in *My Life to Live* undergo any essential transformations at all. In their early scenes in the film, both of them are shown—just like Nana—with their backs to the camera, and they appear as quite anonymous, in standard overcoats. In *Band of Outsiders* on the other hand, Arthur or Frantz may not change, but they still have their distinct stylistic markers: Arthur with his cap and his checked pullover that makes him appear as the joker of the game, a narrative function that he also fulfils, and Frantz with his costume and the hat (which Odile also borrows at times), which clearly makes him the elegant one of the piece. They could all have been cut out of a pulp fiction novel, a genre quoted on several levels in the film, both by Frantz within the plot and by the narrator at the end. The narrator also announces a sequel in color and cinemascope, and in such a film from the 50s on youth rebellion, Odile would indeed have been equally at home.

The nostalgia for a cinema lost is also, as already noted, a feature for the New Wave in general, not least for these two films. For instance, in a scene from *My Life to Live*, Nana performs a dance around a pillar that strongly resembles Asta Nielsen's famous dance in *Afgrunden* (*The Abyss*; aka *Woman Always Pays*; Urban Gad, Denmark, 1910), a scene that caused a scandal in its time. And in *Band of Outsiders*, several scenes recall the famous *Fantômas* or *Les Vampires* series (Louis Feuillade, France, 1913–1914), where dark zones within both urban and suburban spaces are explored. For example, when the band park their Simca in a parking lot using wooden rolls made for telephone cables, the imagery is strongly reminiscent of the wooden barrels in *Fantômas*. Likewise, when the two guys in the film put on Odile's black stockings before the attempted robbery, they both seem to be turning into *Les Vampires*' black-clad characters. And nocturnal space, as evoked in a number of scenes, also echoes Feuillade's nightly universe. Silent cinema is thus fully alive in these films, in spite of Godard's regretting its disappearance.

But it would be wrong to believe that a film like *Band of Outsiders* only looks back to the past. On the contrary, it broke new ground both in fashion and in cinema. And if Fageol has indeed remained quite anonymous as a dressmaker for film, as stated initially, her dresses for *Band of Outsiders* have nevertheless contributed significantly to the fact that the film has become an important source of inspiration to filmmakers and fashion designers alike. The filmmaker Quentin Tarantino was inspired by its dance scene, which interrupts the "action," and remade his own version of it in *Pulp Fiction*, and even named his production company "Band Apart." French designer Agnès B, who has often testified to her own inspiration from Godard, also created a photo exhibition in Hong Kong called

Bande à part in obvious homage to his film: a peek at the individuals behind New York's downtown scene in the 1960s, 1970s, and 1980s and a number of photos with visual qualities and fashion reminiscent of the film. But not least, there is also a contemporary designer company named Band of Outsiders that clearly takes inspiration from the film both in their dress designs and in the visual presentation for the company: a suburban villa that could have been the house in Joinville and a constellation of three, a girl and two boys, posing for the camera.

"Faire bande à part" literally means to do something apart from the group, which makes it a good fashion label: it should distinguish itself clearly from the rest. But is it still modern? Or has it become classical today? The question may seem less relevant in retrospect; when Odile goes to her English course in the beginning of *Band of Outsiders*, the teacher quotes T. S. Eliot, who claims that classic equals modern. However, Arthur complains to Odile in a note that he scribbles down that she looks unfashionable, or even old-fashioned, with her coiffure (a hairstyle that seems to prefigure Princess Leia in *Star Wars*). She then immediately undoes her hair. In general, though, Odile's basic outfit throughout the film are rather on the classical side and, thus, according to Eliot, also modern. Classic or modern, fashionable or unfashionable, regardless of which, these films contributed to creating a new way both of fashioning and perceiving the world.

The French New Wave, as we have seen, picked up references to old films, both American and European, but it also added something completely new, not least through new ways of seeing and portraying urban space. Fashion in the New Wave films also picked up references to classical fashion with hats, striped costumes, or checked skirts, but here, too, a completely new note was added in the way of combining elegance and playfulness, the street-smart with a fashion unaffected by time. Finally, the characters also constantly oscillate between the timeless and the trendy.

To think and rethink the urban through film and fashion in the 1960s Paris, through Godard and Fageol, indeed offers an unexpected point of view, a new perspective. Through the Deleuzian pure optical and sound situations, through the idea of an any-space-whatever, and through the disconnection to any simple sensory-motor schemas, a new cinematic urban space is revealed in which fashion plays a key role. Finally, this new perspective on the urban and on film and fashion offered by Godard and Fageol also includes several contradictions: on one hand, a nostalgia for the past or the classical both in film and fashion, and on the other hand, a bursting renewal.

ASTRID SÖDERBERGH WIDDING is Professor in Film Studies and Vice Chancellor at Stockholm University. She is coeditor of *A History of Swedish Experimental Culture* (Indiana Univerity Press, 2010) and *Moving Images: From Edison to the Webcam.*

Notes

1. Gilles Deleuze, *Cinéma 1: L'image-mouvement* (Paris: Les Editions de minuit, 1983) and *Cinéma 2: L'image-temps* (Paris: Les Editions de minuit, 1985).

2. "Italian neorealist cinema" refers to the group of low-budget films made in Italy in the 1940s and 1950s with social problems, working-class settings, and poverty on the agenda, clearly breaking with the dominance of glossy, escapist films made in Italy before the Second World war.

3. "'L'art à partir de la vie,' Jean Luc Godard par Jean Luc Godard," *Cahiers du cinema Éditions de l'Étoila*, 1985, 9–67.

4. Jean-Louis Leutrat, "The Declension," in *Jean-Luc Godard: Son + Image* (New York: The Museum of Modern Art, 1992), 23–34.

5. Jacques Ellul, "Les contradictions de l'urbain," in *Penser la ville*, eds. Pierre Ansay and René Schoonbrodt (Brussels: AAM Editions, 1989), 315–21.

6 Fashion, Film, and Rome

Eugenia Paulicelli

Introduction

"Hollywood on the Tiber" was a phenomenon of the 1950s and 1960s, during Italy's reconstruction and economic boom, which was fuelled by the marriage of fashion and film. Together, the two industries helped to construct an attractive idea of Italy that turned a nation in ruins at the end of World War II into one of the world's most desirable tourist destinations.[1] Although this phenomenon has received a great deal of critical attention that has given special focus to cinema and Rome and offers a rather descriptive and partial account of films and *sartorie* in Rome, not enough analytical work has been devoted to the role fashion played in defining a narrative of urban experience and desire. In particular, critical studies have overlooked, first, how fashion took a central role in the process of the hybridization of Italian and American cultures, and second, how fashion developed connections with the film industry and the multilayered history of Rome. These are stories that have often been considered separate.

In this chapter, I would like to offer some reflections on how the complex phenomenon "Hollywood on the Tiber" paved the way for several important events that were to have profound resonances in the film, fashion, and tourism industries. It was in the early 1950s that the global launch of what later will be called "made in Italy" took place. The success that Italian fashion and design enjoyed projected a new image and perception of the Italian peninsula: Italy had become, almost overnight, a modern and appealing country. Italian fashion became sexy and glamorous, thanks to the media and cinema that materialized these new images in the imagination not only of those who could afford to visit Italy but also of those, the great majority, who were virtual visitors attracted by the country's beautiful products and designs that they saw on the screen and in magazines. Since low-cost and more affordable flights were not available, films became "air travel," transporting audiences to places they could not afford to visit and also serving as a showcase for styles and fashions that they might not otherwise see.[2] The fact that many of the Italian films made during this time were shot on location against the backdrop of breathtaking Italian art and architecture contributed enormously to the way both Italy as a whole and its individual cities

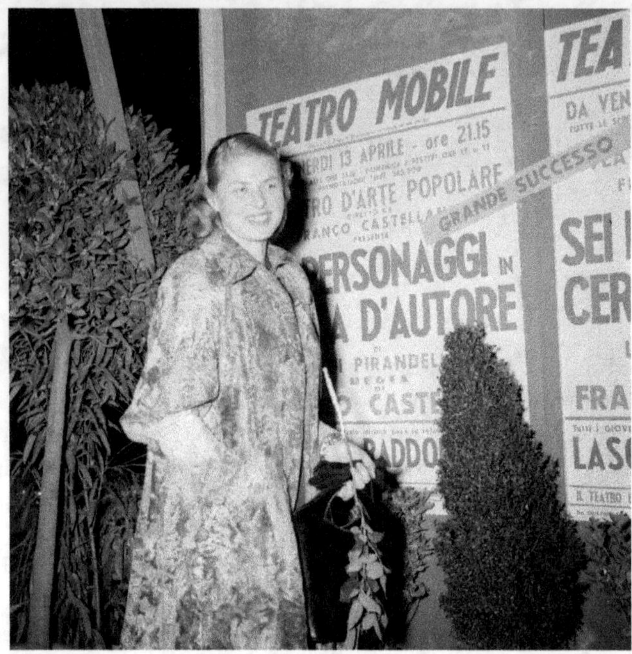

Fig. 6.1 Ingrid Bergman, Swedish actress, Rome, 14 April 1956. Photo by Giuselle Palmas. Image courtesy of Roberto Palmas and the Giuseppe Palmas Photographic Archive, Italy.

were experienced. It is these links between fashion, film, and the specific city of Rome and how certain films helped to construct a narrative of a glamorous Italian identity that I propose to investigate.

Through the eye it gives to fashion, to the work of fashion houses, to the highly skilled people working in them, and to the emergence of costume designers and creative laboratories for cinema, this chapter also aims at connecting the glamorous side of Italy's postwar narrative of success with the labor that fuelled and materialized the media success of Rome, fashion, and film. These narratives were constructed and sewn with fashion, film, and the locations that allowed the viewing publics to have the experience of Italy through its cities. My hope is that this analysis may contribute to a wider understanding of how fashion, film, and the city shape discourses of modernity and negotiations of individual and collective identities.

In connecting the important objects of experience, fashion, film, and the city of Rome, I take my lead from the work of film and media scholar Francesco Casetti on the "filmic experience." His reflections on experience and the theoretical framework he develops are useful for a better understanding of how the fashion experience too must have a central role in relation to film and the city and how they all share, although in different capacities, what we may call the "market of experience." Let us see how Casetti defines the meanings and function of the "filmic experience" and how it overlaps with what I would like to call the "fashion experience." In Casetti's words:

> . . . a discourse is always a representation, but also an action. On this note, one can say with certainty that the filmic experience is not really a filmic experience if it is not certified at the level of discourse as well; it is this certification that leads to the emergence of that social and individual consciousness without which the filmic experience would not effectively exist. In other words, the filmic experience, like any other experience, would not be such if it did not find an echo in the network of the discourses that surround it.[3]

Casetti goes on to say that, if cinema, "thanks to its apparatus, embodies the real, . . . fashion takes the process of embodiment almost literally." In fact, if cinema provides the means for a virtual or symbolic identification ("mental garments," as Casetti calls them), fashion "responds quicker and more aptly to the needs of expressing/performing oneself."

In his most recent book, *The Lumièr Galaxy* (2015), Casetti has further explained that experience is a "cognitive act, but one that is always rooted in, and affects, a body (it is 'embodied'), a culture (it is 'embedded'), and a situation (it is 'grounded')."[4] As these three levels work interchangeably, we can use them to connect fashion, film, and the city, but further clarification is needed to explore the meanings and implications of experience in our context. Both fashion and film have implications with the senses (Casetti's "embodied experience"). The typology, however, is and could be different: in wearing clothing, one has an immediate physical, bodily, and symbolic response to the object a person is wearing, but the action of wearing also elicits a response from people looking at him or her. A wearable object can also be possessed in one's own wardrobe, whereas one cannot wear a film or a city except at a fantasy level. "Wearing" for film and the city has to be symbolic, or both embedded and grounded, in Casetti's terms. Fashion, then, establishes itself as a bridge that activates and facilitates the process of embodiment in film and the city.

For generations of viewers, iconic films such as *Roman Holiday* and *La Dolce Vita* have spurred a process of desire that has led to a symbolic wearing of the city of Rome simply because the spectator acquires the experience of fashion, film, and the city. Fashion, style, and film are sewn on the body of the city at different levels of the imagination. In this way fashion, film, and the city create a sensuous and emotional experience in which there are inter-exchanges of different domains and affective layers: embodiment, embedding and grounding, in Casetti's classification. Cinema starts out as an optical experience and then becomes haptic, and fashion and clothing on the screen facilitate this passage. Fashion, for its part, starts out as a haptic experience and then becomes optical. The city, Rome in our case, becomes the location in which optical and haptic experiences and discourses take shape, rendering the living experience palpable, readable, and consumable in different historical and geographical contexts. For, while fashion functions as the specific device (both optical and haptic) that binds together the different levels of experience, each discourse that surrounds the living experience of fashion and film requires that it be contextualized and historicized.

Robert Gordon has discussed the intertextual relationship between *Roman Holiday* and *La Dolce Vita* as two iconic "snapshots from a proliferating web of connection and hybridisation between 1950s Hollywood and Italy," to which I would add that fashion and the parallel development of costume design for cinema in Rome greatly contributed to this process of Italian and American hybridization.[5]

It was thanks to the success and widespread diffusion of the "Hollywood on the Tiber" phenomenon that Rome came to be perceived as a "filmic and fashion experience" to be lived and consumed by the city's visitors. More precisely, because of its history, art, and architecture, Rome itself became an object of experience similar to the ones engendered by film and fashion. Rome came to embody a series of emotional experiences and fantasies that had a special force for visitors from outside or abroad and constructed for them a picture not only of the city but of the whole nation. As Angelo Restivo has noted, "Rome remains throughout [the economic boom] the center of image production within the nation, so that the Roman story stands in for the story of the nation itself."[6] In the same vein, the major producers of images (fashion and film) mediate and materialize the urban experience, shape personal and collective identities, and shape the myths of the city.

It is, then, quite important to examine closely the operations of fashion and the cinematic experience to see the different modalities in which this relationship manifests itself and to productively explore the experience of cinema, fashion, and the city of Rome. These three share more than ever the modes defining experience. An experience first implies the involvement of the senses and the sensual. This initial emotional involvement leads to a set of practices and consumption choices. In this way, both fashion and cinema find a correlation in the social discourses that create a narrative structure that cements and certifies the social practices. For instance, it is interesting to note that, in the last decade, studies in neuroscience have found the fields of fashion and consumption to be a fertile terrain of application and study, generating a branch called "neuromarket," a term often used in fashion marketing strategies and in the storytelling that aims at giving a brand a luxury identity (but also in the process of branding in the market in general).[7] Branding, though, is a concept that can be extended and connected to the cultural capital of a city or country. The bridging of the fashion–film–city experience is a productive framework that helps us to understand the operations of their discursive processes. Fashion and film enable us to think of experience not as an origin, but rather as the site of the questioning by which discourses and practices of embodiment unfold in their historicized contexts. Our firsthand experience of streets, shops, neighborhoods, and urban space in general signify specific contexts, thanks to the way we as viewers and consumers perceive and breathe reality, and they are always mediated through those contexts, including our baggage of culture and sensibility. In this way, the field of analyzing fashion and film can be very productive insofar as these foreground the nature and the process of knowing, apprehending, and desiring.

The examples I will draw on, which are all taken from the world of the art films of the 1950s and 1960s, pose questions that concern the temporality of fashion, which—according to Roland Barthes—has two durations: one strictly historical and the other "memorable."[8] It is the "memorable" that possesses the quality to affect and have a longer life beyond the strictly "historical" time to which it belongs. It is this interplay between the historical and the memorable, between the optic and the haptic, that nourishes the relationship between film and fashion and links them to the notion of experience. Cinema, like fashion, has the power to activate new sensibilities and identities, masquerades, fictions, and performances. But in viewing the world on screen (any permutation of it: frame, mirror, skin, window) the result is a "magnification" of reality. This process determines a "new" (other) version, a new skin, a new layer, perception, and experience of the world. In the process of mediating between observer and observed, "filmic vision depends on technology but also presents itself as an essential condition in order for something to be seen."[9] Fashion too would not and could not exist without mediation; it is a manifestation of the technologies of body and mind, of history and identity.

Nowadays, of course, the mediation of fashion takes place more and more on multiple screens of multiple sizes and forms (the cell phone, the computer, the window display) and has narrowed the boundaries among different media, rendering them more porous but also generating a sense of loss and nostalgia, for the 1960s, for example.[10] But, for younger generations, the 60s also exert a continuous attraction toward a decade characterized by the "youthquake" in fashion, sexual mores, pop art, and design.

Keeping the two experiences of fashion and film connected, we can see how productive this relationship can be as we explore Italian style and its tropes as they appear in Rome, one of the most cinematic Italian cities and one of the most "looked at" cities in Western culture.[11] As Gordon has noted, "Rome-on-film is, inevitably, layered into a panoply of images and sites, histories and representations."[12] It is to postwar Italy, and especially Rome, that I now turn.[13]

Rome as a Fashion City in the Postwar Era"

As a preliminary, we need to look at the process by which Rome was designated as Italy's fashion capital and the specific historical contingencies that have contributed to this identity.[14] In contrast to the case of Paris and the identification of France with Paris, studied by many scholars, Italy has always been a composite nation. The history of Italian fashion reflects the nation's plurality and diversity insofar as there has always been more than one fashion city on the Italian peninsula, which makes the task of establishing a history of Italian fashion far more complicated and multidimensional, and not only in terms of geography. Although recent scholarship has given us a deeper critical understanding of fashion and its "many direct points of contact with the study of a city," we have to critically adjust the paradigmatic structure for Italy in order to answer the question "Just how many Italian fashion cities are there?"[15] And in what way and to what extent do they contribute to the umbrella concept of the "Made in Italy"? Indeed, Rome was far from being the sole competitor in the race to be considered the capital of style. Competition with other fashion cities, most notably Florence, was rife. After World War II, before Rome and Milan had established themselves as centers of fashion, it was from Florence that Italian fashion was launched nationally and internationally. In addition, Turin could boast an important privilege: that of being nominated Italy's first fashion capital during the fascist regime. It was in Turin, in fact, that the biannual fashion shows were established around 1932. Despite (or perhaps because of) the fascist regime's hatred of France, it was no coincidence that Italy's fashion capital was located geographically and culturally close to Paris, the then undisputed fashion capital of the world. Florence became Italy's fashion capital in 1951 thanks to the "Sala Bianca" shows, in which Italian fashion had first been marketed to an audience of American buyers, triggering the trend for Italian fashion. After Florence, though, it was Rome (the "eternal city") that became the center for *alta moda*—high fashion.

After World War II, the city of Rome underwent a cultural rebirth, leaving behind the images of destruction that had appeared in the film *Roma città aperta* (*Rome open city*, Rossellini, 1945). In the aftermath of the war, the city reconstructed itself within ten years to become a cultural destination of choice. As an intrinsic aspect of this cultural reimagining, fashion had a great impact in constructing and reshaping the postwar city.

The *annus mirabilis*, the "magic year," of Roman fashion and style was 1949. It was on January 27 of that year that Tyrone Power, who was in the city to film *The Prince of Foxes*, married the young actress Linda Christian in the medieval basilica of Santa Francesca Romana. The couple celebrated their marriage, a Catholic rite, amid the most cinematic scenery: the Fontana Sisters had made Christian's dress and Caraceni did the suit for Power. The wedding was one of the most important media events of the time, and Italians experienced the beginning of celebrity culture, as did the world.[16] As a result, Italy and Italian style became appealing and, as Micol Fontana recalled in an interview: "That day sanctioned our success as a Roman based fashion house."

But it was also the day that Italian fashion became and showed itself to be inextricably linked to film, almost sewn to it through the bodies of the stars and their iconic status. The dress the Fontana Sisters made for the wedding became famous worldwide and was featured on the cover of *Life* magazine. In fact, the Fontana Sisters have claimed that this was the origin of the glamorous idea of the "made in Italy," as well as the beginning of their international fashion fame, which began when the Hollywood stars they had dressed advertised their creations in the media and popular press, as also happened for male fashion, making the fortunes of Roman tailors such as Brioni and Caraceni.

It was also in May 1949 that the Chamber of Commerce in Rome organized the First National Conference on Fashion, which was followed on November 5 by the formation of the Committee on Fashion charged with developing production and design and with maintaining relationships in the national and international markets.[17] The year 1949 was also an important one for Italian and American political and economic relations and those with France, another country that benefitted from the Marshall Plan. It has been argued that what happened in Italy between 1949 and 1951 was an attempt to transform Italian cinema from a state of artisanship into one of industry. Italian–French coproduction agreements were first signed in 1949 with the government legislation of July 26 and December 29 of that year, followed by the 1951 agreements Italy's ANICA (Associazione Nazionale Industrie Cinematografiche Audiovisive e Multimediali) and America's MPAA, the first stepping stones toward the America—Italy film exchange. The relationship between Italy and the United States was cemented thanks to the Marshall Plan, also known as the European Recovery Program (ERP), and a series of national government measures that "certified" and promoted cultural transformation.[18]

This was also the time in which the process of modernization brought about a radical change in the Italian economic and social landscape. A massive migration of Italians in search of a better life took place from the rural south to the industrial north, as well as to Rome. It was also at this time that the films of directors such as Antonioni, Fellini, Visconti, Pasolini, Pietrangeli, Monicelli, and others recorded a profound anthropological revolution. If the Marshall Plan succeeded in helping the economic recovery of the European countries defeated by war, it also guaranteed American cultural hegemony and economic expansion in Europe and especially Italy. New legislation on Italian cinema such as law 958, which was designed by Giulio Andreotti (then State Undersecretary in Charge of Entertainment) and passed on December 29, 1949, had the aim of protecting the Italian film industry. Nevertheless, this law was the official permit that allowed what Pescatore called the "invasion" on the part of the Hollywood studios of the newly reconstructed Cinecittà Studios.[19]

The year 1949 was also one in which radical changes took place in the organization of the world into two main blocks with the beginning of the Cold War and Italy's official participation in the NATO Alliance. As several film historians have argued, Hollywood landed on the Italian peninsula, and Rome in particular, along with the US army of liberation. This complex economic, political, social, and emotional conjuncture allowed the America to exercise what Gian Piero Brunetta has called a *sguardo telescopico*, which perhaps could almost be translated into the Foucaldian "panoptical gaze." The United States exercised overall control thanks to the presence of its diplomatic offices in Italian territory, especially in Rome.[20]

It is relevant to note that fashion followed a similar pattern of development and branding as a result of the American presence in Italy. Fashion too was transformed from artisanship to industry, and it is also for these reasons that some scholars maintain that Italian fashion started in the postwar years.[21] The international recognition of Italian fashion was facilitated and cemented by international relations between Italy and the United States, and through public relations and business relations that were mutually beneficial during the Cold War. Fashion shows at the Sala Bianca or in the fashion houses themselves were more than just spectacle and exhibitions of beautiful young women wearing wonderful clothes: they were a new genre of diplomatic performance. The bodies of models in the where, why and how of performance were not only presenting clothing; they were the embodiment of a new tangible, modern, and attractive nation that looked to the United States. Fashion shows performed a postwar Italian national identity that was dreamt of and much desired, and as a manufacturing industry and a powerful symbolic force, fashion acted both for the Europe of the Marshall Plan (Italy and France in particular) and for the United States as "economic and diplomatic rehabilitator."[22] At the same time, business and government officials made sure that European goods appealed to and reached the American market and thus fulfilled policy and public relations goals.[23]

But 1951 and Florence were far from being the zero year and place of Italian fashion. An Italian exposition opened in Macy's in New York City in the same year as Giovanni Battista Giorgini organized the fashion shows at the Villa Torregiani in Florence and invited buyers from the major US department stores Bergdorf Goodman, B. Altman, and Lord & Taylor, and the press. The Macy's fair, which took up the whole of the fifth floor, was the result of eighteenth months of preparation. But this was not the only Italian event at that time: the previous year, in 1950, the show "Italy at Work" had opened at the Brooklyn Museum and then travelled to the Art Institute in Chicago.[24]

These historical contingencies and media practices can clearly explain how and why one city or place acquires the iconic and status symbol of a fashion city more than another. David Harvey has identified fashion as one of the strongest vehicles through which cities acquire a mark of distinction that is, in turn, transformed into capital that attracts tourism and other business.[25] According to Harvey, it was in the postwar boom that Rome acquired the status of "monopoly rent," a term he borrows from economics: it was Rome that became the center of fashion and film and had the monopoly of this status over the other Italian capitals of fashion. The notion of monopoly rent is different from that of symbolic capital as developed by Bourdieau. Many Italian cities had symbolic capitals, as in the example of Florence and the Sala Bianca's fashion shows. But what Florence did not have was film production studios. The shift from Florence to Rome can be explained by the presence of Cinecittà, which in turn paved the way for the development of costume design as a profession parallel to that of fashion. It is also at this time that costume designers such as the legendary Piero Tosi came to be professionally recognized and his remarkable sense of style and beauty admired.

Since the end of World War II, Americans, including those involved in the film industry, spent more and more time in Italy—especially Rome—filming in the Cinecittà Studios. This was "Hollywood on the Tiber." Interestingly, some of the big American productions in these years revisited the past of Imperial Rome— starting with *Quo Vadis?* (Mervyn LeRoy, 1951), *Ben-Hur* (William Wyler, 1959) and later *Cleopatra* (Joseph Mankiewicz, 1963)—while in other films, Rome was a tourist destination for Americans, as in William Wyler's classic *Roman Holiday* (1953).[26] Fashion houses such as the Fontana Sisters (located in Piazza di Spagna) and Fernanda Gattinoni (near Via Veneto and strategically close to the American embassy and Rome's nightlife) were instrumental in establishing the relationship between glamour, cinema, and the city, designing and collaborating with Americans to make clothes for the stars in the films made in Italy.

This was a sign of a further step in the process of the hybridization of the relationship between Italy and United States: fashion shows, fashion parades, and models started to appear in films. This had already happened in the 1930s in, for example, Alessandro Blasetti's *Contessa di Parma*, a film about a dress and the fascist attempt to nationalize fashion, but fashion shows within film narratives became much more prominent in the postwar years. Luciano Emmer set his film *Le ragazze di Piazza di Spagna* (1951), starring Lucia Bosè, in the Fontana Atelier in Rome in Via Sebastianello. In 1950, Bosè had been transformed into a star by Sarmi's incredible costumes in Antonioni's first feature film, *Cronaca di un Amore*.[27] In 1951, the couturier Emilio Schuberth, playing himself, helps the aspiring new star Sophia Loren put on a dress in the film *Era lui . . . si! si!* (*It was him . . . yes! yes!*), directed by Mario Girolami, Marcello Marchesi, and Vittorio Metz. In 1955, Antonioni filmed *Le Amiche*, in which Clelia, the protagonist, is a fashion manager of a Roman atelier that opens a branch in Turin, and in the film, we see a parade of dresses, models, and actresses.

Other US cinema stars followed, and Italian fashion designers capitalized on the presence, fame, and glamour of their clients—Audrey Hepburn, Ingrid Bergman, Ava Gardner, Gregory Peck, Cary Grant, and others—and used them as vehicles to elevate the increasingly international status of Italian fashion. The Fontana Sisters created a dress called "Roma antica" (Ancient Rome) for Ava Gardner, one of the American ambassadors of Italian fashion, who was invited to Grace Kelly's wedding in 1956.

The increasingly hegemonic role played by Rome and the city's designers in dictating what was fashionable also led to changes in men's fashion. In the early 1950s, along with women's fashion, men's fashion—whose sartorial elegance was epitomized by Brioni's "Roman style"—was also presented at the Sala Bianca. Launched as a brand in 1952, Brioni's "Roman style" was, in the early 1960s, given even greater exposure by the continental suit that had first made its appearance in the late 1950s worn by Marcello Mastroianni in *La Dolce Vita*. Italy has had an important role in tailoring men's fashion the world over, following a well-established sartorial male tradition in Naples, Milan, and especially Rome. The Neapolitan suit was to bring about a sartorial revolution insofar as its cut had the effect of softening the male jacket, as we can see in a recent documentary, *O'Mast*, made by Gianluca Migliarotti in 2011.

In fact, a different image of masculinity was taking shape at this time, thanks to a suit that was gradually dispensing with its armorlike stiff edges and now embraced the body with soft fabrics and sartorial fineness of detail. In addition, a color revolution in men's wear put an end to what John Carl Flügel had defined as the "great male renunciation," by which he meant the abandonment of sartorial display and decoration in men's clothing around the beginning of the nineteenth century. Brioni, for instance, introduced red for men's evening wear, and Angelo Litrico created a purple dinner jacket in 1956 and borrowed from women's wardrobes for his experimentation with color for men's wear.[28] One of the most innovative colors in men's wear was "ottanio," a mix of green and light blue created by the Trading Tex and wool firm Cerruti. The color was the unifying theme in a fashion show featuring men's wear organized in Rome on April 23–24, 1959, at the Excelsior Hotel.[29] Several American and British customers appreciated the Italian style revolution in men's wear. And, of course, cinema powerfully publicized it.

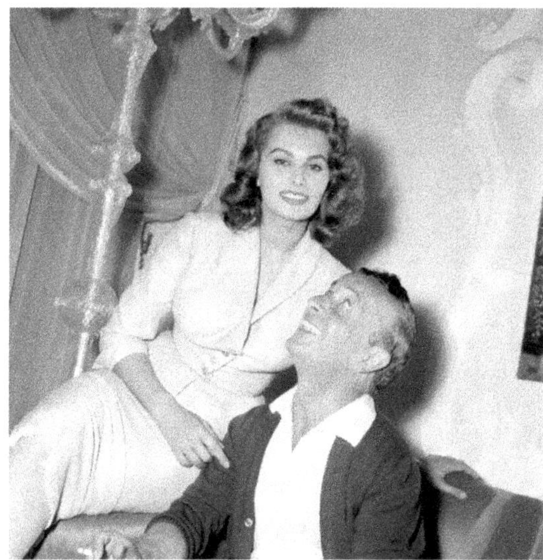

Fig. 6.2 Sophia Loren at Emilio Schuberth's atelier in Rome, June 6, 1955. Photo by Giuseppe Palmas. Image courtesy of Roberto Palmas and the Giuseppe Palmas Archive, Italy.

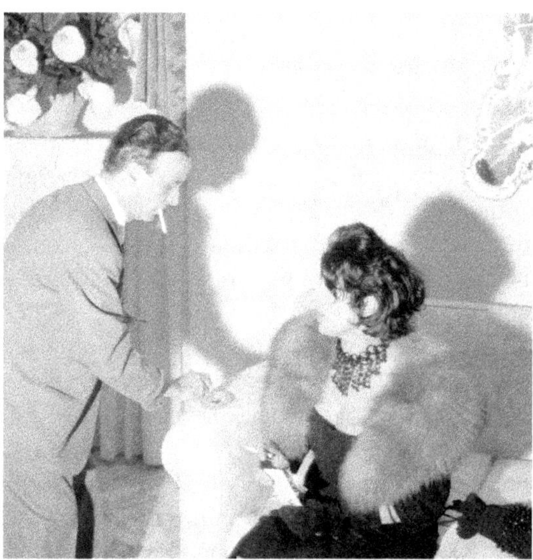

Fig. 6.3 Anna Magnani at the inauguration of Emilio Schuberth's new atelier in Rome, March 28, 1960. Photo by Giuseppe Palmas. Image courtesy of Roberto Palmas and the Giuseppe Palmas Archive, Italy.

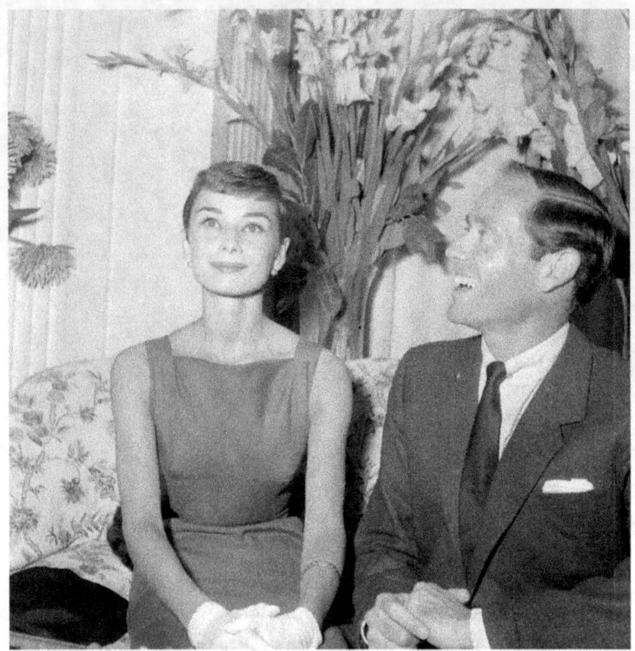

Fig. 6.4 Audrey Hepburn and Mel Ferrer in Rome, December 1954. Photo by Giuseppe Palmas. Image courtesy of Roberto Palmas and the Giuseppe Palmas Archive, Italy.

It was, then, the encounter between Italy and the United States that launched Italian fashion on a global scale, and it was cinema that provided the fashion industry with a high enough profile (an increasingly international shop window) for promoting and publicizing Italian designers' creations to the world. And it was the bodies and images of both male and female celebrities that powerfully mediated the experience of fashion and film. Through fashion and cinema, and facilitated by the movie industry and the presence of the Cinecittà Studios, Rome began to project an image of glamour, art, and beauty and gained the status of a leading fashion city. Later, the crucial 1950s and 1960s—years of the postwar "economic miracle"—were defining times for the Italian capital in the larger global economy and the identity of Rome shaped through American mediation was made possible by popular culture, fashion, film, and photography and sanctioned the idea of Italy as the place for fashion and style.[30] Fashion was in the forefront in telling this complex story of how different systems of cultural mediation (film, journalism, art, architecture, and so on) made critical contributions to our understanding and experience of Rome and Italy, whether

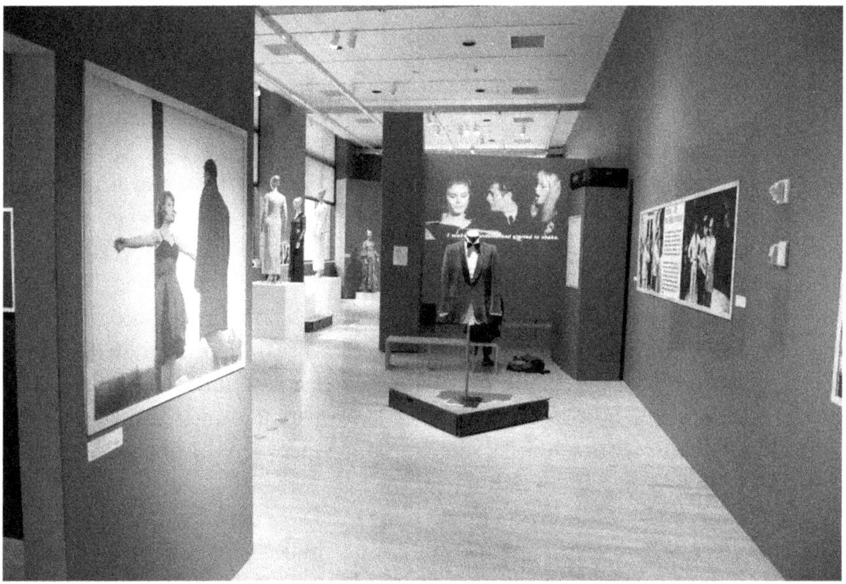

Fig. 6.5 Brioni Red Tuxedo Jacket from1952. *Fashion + Film: the 1960s Revisited* exhibit at the James Gallery, The Graduate Center of the City University of New York, 2010. Photo by Don Pollard.

of their ancient past, of their present, or of their future as a dream or destination to which to aspire.

The new Italian identity that emerged from the postwar boom and the emergence of Rome as capital of chic were epitomized most tellingly and memorably by Fellini's 1960 film *La Dolce Vita*, for which Piero Gherardi won an Oscar for his costumes. And it was the Gattinoni *maison* that made the black velvet dress that was worn by Anita Ekberg in the famous scene at the Trevi Fountain. In fact, couched in a history clearly visible in its architecture and style, Rome became the theater on whose stage some of the most influential images of Italian style and *la dolce vita*—the sweet life—were forged and transmitted to the world via the powerful medium of global cinema.

The fashion and filmic experience was more visible in Rome thanks to the numerous films that were produced there and to the synergy of fashion houses and costume designers, not to mention the media around the two industries. For the foreign press, buyers, visitors, and movie people, Italy and its cities, especially Rome, became an unforgettable sartorial, cultural, and personal experience of the type so often romanticized in literature and cinema. Wearing Italian, especially Roman, fashion meant wearing Italy's culture, its breathtaking artistic heritage. In other words, it meant wearing and embracing the country and its unique and beautiful cities.

The Hollywood stars populated the Roman fashion houses not only because this is where they got the costumes used in their films, but also because they had discovered that Italian couture was elegant and stylish. Above all, their ateliers were a uniquely warm and friendly environment. The fashion and film experience was produced and constructed through personal interactions between customers and couturiers, such as that between Micol Fontana and Ava Gardner and between Fernanda Gattinoni and Ingrid Bergman.

From a more prosaic standpoint, filming in Cinecittà was also much cheaper for American filmmakers, as they received a tax break that facilitated cultural exchange; in addition, for their film costumes American film directors relied on the expertise, know-how, and creativity of Italian ateliers and the more specialized theatre/film costume houses such as AnnaMode, Tirelli, and others related to accessories and wigs, such as Rocchetti.[31]

The 1950s and 1960s were a vibrant time to be in Rome. The city was a magnet that attracted both foreign and Italian filmmakers, a locus of a creativity that revitalized design, fashion, and the arts in general. Rome as a city—and as an idea—became an ongoing "dream spectacle," a promised land for visitors from abroad and from the Italian provinces who hoped to play a part on the city's stage. These characters can be seen in Fellini's and Pietrangeli's movies, where costume plays a key role in the process of fashioning and doubling and in the *mise-en-abyme* of identity. The doubling of identity and the suspension and tension between two different worlds—between fantasy reality, between the fast and uneven process of urban transformation and building in the cities (especially Rome) and the "backward" countryside of the South, between the center and the periphery—all these provide a background for films by Antonioni, Fellini, Pasolini, Pietrangeli, and others, such as the very successful genre of the *commedia all'italiana*. A film such as *Lo sceicco bianco* (*The White Sheik*, 1951) by Fellini proves to be far ahead of its time in grasping the impact of a growing media culture and the effect *fotoromanzo* (comic strip story) characters have on provincial young women like Wanda, the protagonist of the film.

The *fotoromanzo* was a romantic type of literature that appeared in 1947 and enjoyed a huge boom during the 1950s and 1960s. The protagonists, often women of modest means, followed their dreams and fantasies, which for the most part involved the pursuit of a male protagonist. Fellini's Wanda represents the quintessential reader of *fotoromanzi*. She goes to Rome on her honeymoon, but instead of spending time with her husband, a banal, petit bourgeois, provincial stereotype, she seeks out her real hero, a character in the *fotoromanzo* she avidly devours each week: the White Sheik (played by Alberto Sordi). Wanda is offered a role in the making of the latest *fotoromanzo*, dresses in exotic costumes, and ends up playing the part of the Sheik's love slave. Parallel to Wanda's search for a world of fantasy is her husband Ivan's quest to maintain a façade of bourgeois respectability and participate in the ritual audience of newly married couples with the Pope.

In *The White Sheik*, Fellini focuses on the nuances and meanings of dress and its emotional and social impact, relating it to the world of appearances, rituals, and religion, all the time blurring the boundary between the sacred and the profane. Later, in *La Dolce Vita*, Fellini has Sylvia (Anita Ekberg), a superstar international actress who is visiting the city, dress in a priestlike outfit (an idea Fellini got from the Fontana Sisters' 1955–1956 winter collection, from the *pretino* that was worn by Ava Gardner). Elsewhere in *La Dolce Vita*, Fellini treats "religious miracles" as media events and as pretexts for the fabrication of new heroes. In both their theatrical and everyday rituals, dress and appearance in *The White Sheik* tell the story of the development of a new Italian identity that is suspended somewhere between fantasy and glamour, on the one hand, and petit bourgeois hypocrisy and decorum on the other.

A different and tragic epilogue awaits Adriana in Pietrangeli's film *Io la conoscevo bene*, which chronicles the process of self-destruction of the female protagonist, Adriana, who has arrived in Rome from the countryside dreaming of becoming a movie star and finding herself treated as the toy of male fantasies and erotic pleasures. If Wanda in Fellini's film is an eager consumer of popular press literature but still protected by petit bourgeois provincial moralism and a husband, Adriana is the extreme opposite, with no protection on her side. Every single human being, male or female, takes advantage of her. She is even possessed by the camera. Adriana is played by a very young Stefania Sandrelli and becomes a representation of the frivolous airhead woman easily manipulated and who seems to read only *fotoromanzi* and fall for their spells. She is framed in different Roman scenes and urban sites, from center to periphery and working-class neighborhood like the Ostiense district. Her character is suspended between her peasant origins and her aspirations, in what was the messy and tricky modernity epitomized in Fellini's *La Dolce Vita*.

In crucial scenes, the urban space of the city plays a crucial role in layering and complicating Adriana's relationship to its inhabitants. The river Tiber, as in many films, acts as a divide between two different worlds that do not seem to communicate with each other. Adriana, looking out from the window in her apartment building, sees several juxtapositions of Roman landscape and sites where new construction is glimpsed against the early industrial Rome rendered by the circular gas tower, the "Gazometro," built in the early twentieth century to serve the city port in the Ostiense district. She is recurrently presented as part of an ongoing masquerade in which she changes wigs and outfits, and it is only in

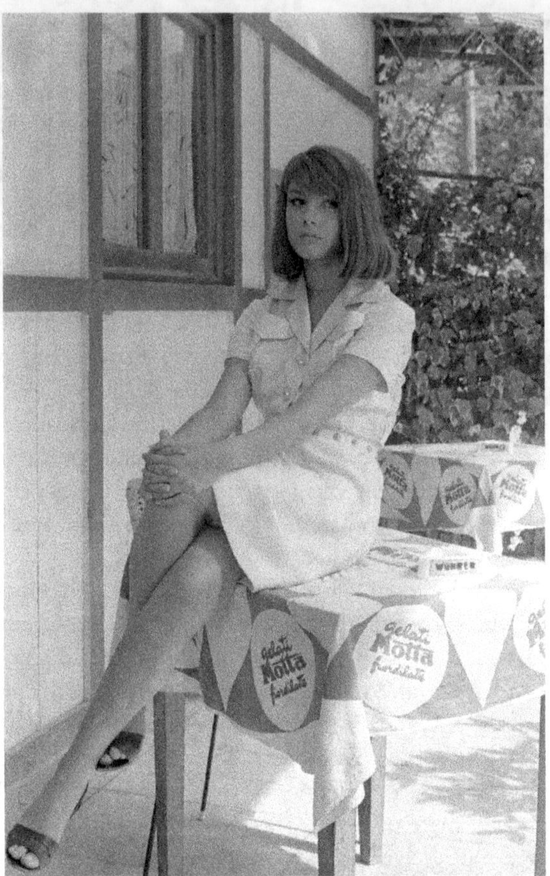

Fig. 6.6 Stefania Sandrelli in Viareggio, August 1962. Photo by Giuseppe Palmas. Image courtesy of Roberto Palmas and the Giuseppe Palmas Archive, Italy.

her moments of masquerade that she appears completely at ease, as impeccable as a model in a fashion magazine. But when the mask slips, we see that her personal life is as grim, sordid, and lonely as the urban landscape of the new developing Rome that Pietrangeli shows.

If Fellini makes Wanda the imaginative fantasizer who objectifies rather than the one who is objectified, then Pietrangeli's Adriana is the complete defeat of a problematic economic boom and miracle that began as the fantasy. There are no miracles in *Io la conoscevo bene*, and certainly not for Italy; there is only the suicide of Adriana with which the film ends. She is the embodiment of a dream for a glamorous life that went wrong, and *Io la conoscevo bene* shows the audience the stark contradictions characterizing the economic boom and a hierarchical class structure that excluded her from fully participating in the glamorous experience of Rome as the land of opportunity for success and happiness.

There is one scene in the film that says it all. Adriana is wearing one of her most elegant dresses, everything is perfect. She looks like a model on the cover of *Vogue*. She goes into the garage in her apartment building and the mechanic, who is attracted to her, sees she is driving a modest Fiat *Cinquecento*. He remarks that there is no correlation between the elegant way she is dressed and the car she is driving. If her clothes are her masquerade, her car is her reality. The tiny *Cinquecento* was the vehicle that was made specifically to be affordable for the working classes during the boom so that they could have their own part in the new dream of mobility and freedom. And while Adriana's appearance in high fashion clothes does not fit this image, the car indicates that she does not and can never fit in the world of celebrities.

Conclusions

As a tangible contemporary example of this marriage of fashion, film, and Rome as a powerful object of experience, let me turn to the recent case of Louis Vuitton, the French luxury brand that has invested in the cultural capital of the eternal city and its old film industry. A few details about Vuitton's project will be useful for a cross-cultural perspective on the subject. In 2012, Vuitton opened a new store in a building that once hosted Rome's first movie theatre, the Cinema Etoile, which opened in 1907 and had been closed for more than twenty years. The architect Peter Marino, who redesigned the 1,200-square-meter space, worked on maintaining and incorporating the idea of the movie theatre into the concept of the store. In fact, in the store itself, there is a screening room where movies are regularly shown.[32]

But the relationship between fashion and cinema goes well beyond the restoration of a cinema and the site of a store located in a square in Via del Corso, a street that has become a fashion hub for global brands such as Burberry and Christian Louboutin. Vuitton's project, in fact, is more far-reaching and includes a three-year collaboration with Centro Sperimentale di Cinematografia, the Rome-based school of cinematography. The first result of this collaboration is the documentary *Handmade Cinema* (2012), funded by Vuitton, which highlights the savoir faire of Rome-based Italian artisans such as wigmakers, tailors, make-up artists, builders, costume and set designers, and all the others who made possible the magic of film and performance. This is a film that documents what is behind the screen, and in celebrating the artisanal bravura of Italian craftsmanship, it touches on something that is crucial for any study that focuses on fashion and film: the process of making the performance happen.

"Handmade cinema" is entirely parallel to handmade luxury fashion, whose art and skills are at risk of disappearing in the fast-paced production of the global and mass-market fashion industry. The film, narrated by *figlia d'arte,* Chiara Mastroianni, daughter of Marcello Mastroianni and French actress Catherine Deneuve, was screened at the opening of Vuitton's store in Rome. The French luxury brand has, then, capitalized on the cachet Rome possesses as a city of film and a city of fashion. In Vuitton's official statement, a correlation is established between the art of cinema and the art of fashion based in the cultural heritage, history, and craftsmanship of both, and it is here where the "natural" link between the French brand and film can be found. But this also calls attention to the fact that both fashion and film can be seen as crafts whose end result is due to the various skills and labor of the people involved in the making of a film (or an object of fashion such as a dress, a pair of shoes, or a bag). The documentary parallels the craftsmanship of the artisans and artists working in Cinecittà with the world of fashion in a sort of a romanticized image of labor, but one that tends to efface the "true cost" of glamour and the real conditions of labor.[33]

What is interesting about Vuitton's commercial operation is how a quintessential French brand communicates its message of chic and distinction by way of "Italianness." This combines the seductiveness of the objects on display and the recreation of a store as if it were still a palace of spectacle and performance where the history of film and the city of Rome collide. On the one hand, then, Vuitton has bought into tradition, both Italy's national history and that of the city of Rome, its fashion and film heritage and architecture. Yet, on the other, his project reveals how a contemporary and globally recognizable French fashion brand with all its French chic and heritage is making use of the local cultural capital of a foreign city like Rome and its cinematic flair. [34]

Or is Rome here transformed into a paradigm of universal history, "a site of origin of European culture, religion and power, as a central node (with Athens and Jerusalem) in millennial history"?[35] Vuitton's commercial and cultural enterprise translates local cultural capital into global terms. This complex operation, at once commercial, cultural, and emotional, is both illustration and confirmation of the fact that fashion, film, and screen media as object of experience are more than ever intertwined, just as they were at the beginning of cinema, although in a revolutionized time and space relation. It is as if the intersection of fashion, film, and the city has come full circle, even after the digital revolution.[36]

EUGENIA PAULICELLI is Professor of Italian, Comparative Literature, and Women's Studies at Queens College and The Graduate Center of the City University of New York. She is author of *Fashion under Fascism.*

Beyond the Black Shirt; Writing Fashion in Early Modern Italy: From Sprezzatura to Satire; Fashion is a Serious Business: Rosa Genoni, Milan Expo 1906 and the Great War; and *Italian Style: Fashion & Film from Early Cinema to the Digital Age.*

Notes

1. This chapter is part of a larger study of the relationship between fashion, film, and the city experience contained in my book *Italian Style: Fashion & Film from Early Cinema to the Digital Age* (London and New York: Bloomsbury Academics, 2016). I would like to thank the anonymous reader at Indiana University Press for the useful comments and feedback on the earlier version of the chapter and also to thank Francesco Casetti for his comments and suggestions, as well as Giuseppe Palmas for his willingness to help in making available the photographic archive of his father, Giuseppe Palmas.

2. Pamela Church Gibson, "New Stars, New Fashions and the Female Audience: Cinema, Consumption and Cities, 1953–1966," in *Fashion's World Cities*, ed. Christopher Breward and David Gilbert (Oxford: Berg 2006), 93.

3. Francesco Casetti, *Relocation* (Milan: Editrice il Castoro, 2009), 7–8.

4. Francesco Casetti, *The Lumière Galaxy: 7 Key Words for the Cinema to Come* (New York: Columbia University Press, 2015), 5.

5. Robert Gordon, "Hollywood and Italy. Industries and Fantasies," in *The Italian Cinema Book*, ed. Peter Bondanella (London: BFI/Palgrave Macmillan, 2014), 129.

6 Angelo Restivo, *The Cinema of Economic Miracles: Visuality and Modernization in the Italian Art Film* (Durham, NC: Duke University Press, 2002), 46.

7. See Kate Abnett, "Can Neuroscience Unlock the Luxury Mind?" *Business of Fashion*, April 22, 2015, http://www.businessoffashion.com/articles/intelligence/can-neuroscience-unlock-the-luxury-mind, accessed June 15, 2015.

8. Roland Barthes, *The Language of Fashion*, trans. Amy Stafford, ed. Andy Stafford and Michael Carter (Oxford and New York: Berg, 2005), 28.

9. Casetti, "Filmic Experience," 9

10. See Nick Rees-Roberts, "Single Men: Aesthetics of the 60s and Vintage Style in Contemporary Cinema" in the present volume.

11. See, for instance, *Rome in Cinema: Between Reality and Fiction*, ed. Elisabetta Bruscolini (Rome: Centro Sperimentale di Cinematografia, 2000).

12. Robert Gordon, *Bicycle Thieves* [*Ladri di biciclette*], (London: BFI Classics, 2008), 62.

13. In my longer study, *Italian Style,* through an analysis of several exemplary films and directors, I provide a historical and theoretical framework within which to understand the different typologies and meanings of costume in film. Attention is given to the way dress, fabric, and mise-en-scène contribute to the creation of a new cinematic language. In more historical terms, the project looks into the different ways fashion is embodied and manifested in film during periods of great transformations and how it is connected to Italian fashion capitals.

14. In *Fashioning the City*, which explores how different media supported the image of Paris as a fashion city, Agnès Rocamora has emphasized the importance of both the imaginary and the lived dimensions of the city (*Fashioning the City: Paris, Fashion and the Media* [New York: I. B. Tauris, 2009], 123). See also Christopher Breward, *Fashioning London: Clothing and the Modern Metropolis* (Oxford: Berg, 2004).

15. David Gilbert, "From Paris to Shanghai: The Changing Geographies of Fashion's World Cities," in Breward and Gilbert, *Fashion's World Cities*, 6.

16. See Pamela Church Gibson's work on the topic of celebrity culture and its relations with fashion and film in "New Stars, New Fashions and the Female Audience" and *Fashion and Celebrity Culture* (London and New York: Berg, 2012).

17. Cinzia Capalbo, *Storia della moda a Roma: Sarti, culture e stili di una capitale dal 1871 a oggi* (Rome: Donzelli, 2012), 142.

18. Giulio Andreotti recounts the international context of this crucial period of Italian national history in a book emblematically titled *1949: L'anno del patto atlantico* (Milan: Rizzoli, 2006).

19. Guglielmo Pescatore, "Hollywood/Cinecittà: andata e ritorno," in *Hollywood sul Tevere: Anatomia di un fenomeno*, ed. Stefano Della Casa and Dario E. Viganò (Milan: Mondadori Electa, 2010), 29.

20. See Gian Piero Brunetta, *Identità Italiana e Identità Europea nel cinema italiano dal 1945 al miracolo economico* (Turin: Edizioni della Fondazione Giovanni Agnelli, 1996) and *Storia del Cinema Mondiale*, vol. 1, *L'Europa* (Turin: Einaudi, 1999). See also *Hollywood in Europa: Industria, Politica, pubblico del cinema 1945–1960*, ed. David W. Ellwood and Gian Piero Brunetta (Florence: La Casa Usher, 1991); Lorenzo Quaglietti, *Ecco I nostri: L'invasione del cinema Americano in Italia* (Rome: ERI, 1991); *Il cinema italiano degli anni '50*, ed. Giorgio Tinazzi (Venice: Marsilio, 1979); and Casa and Viganò, *Hollywood sul Tevere.*

21. Although it is true that Italian fashion's distinct style gained the nation international recognition during the postwar years, prior to this period, there had been a long and complex history of Italian fashion, textile manufacturing, and clothing and accessories that goes back to the Middle Ages. A comprehensive history of Italian fashion that connects the different domains of production with a parallel creation of a fashion culture and discourse has yet to be written.

22. *The Glamour of Italian Fashion*, ed. Sonnet Stanfill (London: V & A Publishing, 2015), 12.

23. Stephanie M. Amerian, "'Buying European': The Marshall Plan and American Department Stores," *Diplomatic History* 39.1 (2014): 21.

24. Catherine Rossi, *Crafting Design in Italy: From Post-war to Postmodernism* (Manchester, UK: Manchester University Press, 2015).

25. David Harvey, *Spaces of Capital: Towards a Critical Geography* (London and New York: Routledge, 2001).

26. It is interesting to consider in this context the Italian production of the so-called peplum genre that reenacted the Greco-Roman past. See Frank Burke, "The Italian Sword-and-Sandal Film from *Fabiola* to *Hercules* and *The Captive Women*," in *Popular Italian Cinema. Culture and Politics in a Postwar Society*, ed. Flavia Brizio-Skov (London and New York: I. B. Tauris, 2011), 17–51.

27. See Eugenia Paulicelli, "*Cronaca di un amore:* Fashion and Italian Cinema in Michelangelo Antonioni's Films (1949–1955)," in *New Perspectives in Italian Cultural Studies*, ed. Graziella Parati, (Madison, NJ: Farleigh Dickinson University Press, 2013), 107–31.

28. In 2010, an exhibition entitled *Fashion + Film: The 1960s Revisited* was held at the James Gallery at the City University of New York Graduate Center. On view was a red velvet morning jacket (1952) by Brioni.

29. Capalbo, *Storia della moda a Roma*, 139.

30. Guido Crainz, *Storia del miracolo italiano: Culture, identità, trasformazioni fra anni cinquanta e sessanta* (Rome: Donzelli, 2005).

31. See the documentary by Guido Torlonia entitled *Handmade Cinema* (2012).

32. The architect Peter Marino, who was responsible for the rebranding of Barney's NY in the early 1990s, is an interesting and important case study for the reconceptualization of space in concept store and branding. See, for instance, the spring 2013 travel issue of the *New York Times Magazine* (March 24, 2013) that dedicated a profile to his accomplishments (pp. 38–39). One of his latest projects has been the restructuring of the Bulgari flagship store in Via Condotti in Rome to celebrate the 130th anniversary of the brand. The store was originally opened by Sotirio Bulgari in 1905.

33. *The True Cost* (2015) is the title of a recent documentary directed by Andrew Morgan that looks at the exploitation of workers in the globalized fashion industry and the real cost of jeans that retail for eight US dollars.

34. "Experience" is one of the most recurrent words in fashion market strategies and discourse. The official Vuitton site proclaims specifically that a consumer or visitor can share the Vuitton experience and join a larger community. See also "Dubai Hosts Middle East's First *Vogue* Fashion Experience" in the digital edition of *Vogue Italia*, certainly one of the most influential among the different Vogue editions. What is interesting to note is that fashion on screen, online shopping, and store shopping are linked to a distinct gestural quality of individuality and taste. Thus, choices are materialized in the experience we establish with them.

35. Gordon, *Bicycle Thieves*, 62. See also Peter Sloterdijk, *L'ultima sfera: Breve storia della globalizazzione* (Rome: Carocci, 2002), and Salvatore Settis, *Futuro del classico* (Turin: Einaudi, 2002).

36. See Marketa Ulhirova, "100 Years of the Fashion Film: Frameworks and Histories," *Fashion Theory* 17.2 (2013): 137–58; Ulhirova, "The Fashion Film Effect," in *Fashion Media: Past and Present* ed. Djurdja Bartlett, Shaun Cole, and Agnès Rocamora (London and New York: Bloomsbury Academics, 2013), 118–29; and Natalie Khan, "Cutting the Fashion Body: Why the Fashion Image is No Longer Still," *Fashion Theory* 16, no. 2 (2012): 235–50.

7 Contexts, Contradictions, Couture, and Clothing: Fashion in *An American in Paris*, *Breakfast at Tiffany's*, and *That Touch of Mink*

Pat Kirkham and Marilyn Cohen

Culture does not respect decades. In this chapter we begin by considering a film made in the United States in the 1950s, *An American in Paris* (Vincente Minelli, 1951), and its historical contexts as a means of better understanding central issues at stake in two American films of the early 1960s in which fashion plays an important role. Although there is a veritable industry of publications on *Breakfast at Tiffany's* (Blake Edwards, 1961), and, surprisingly for the first film to draw over a million dollars in one theater alone, far less on *That Touch of Mink* (Delbert Mann, 1962), we here explore aspects of both films that have hitherto been neglected or ignored. They include the ways in which clothing, both couture and noncouture, raises issues of Frenchness, Americanness, age, class, "classiness," morality, sexual mores, successful romantic heterosexual coupling, and star personas. We conclude by considering the varied connotations of fur in *Breakfast at Tiffany's* and *That Touch of Mink* (the very title of which invites a reading through fur) as a microcosm of some of the larger issues mentioned above.

Americans in Paris and American and French Fashion

Paris was the main European tourist destination for vacationing US citizens in the postwar period, as middle-class Americans became wealthier, transatlantic transportation costs fell, and the US government encouraged tourism to Western Europe as part of broader anti-communist initiatives. In 1950, France was visited by 264,000 Americans, and after the expansion of jet travel, the number grew to 792,000 by 1960 and 1.35 million by 1970.[1] The cultural power of Parisian fashion in an increasingly consumer-orientated American culture was such that, in 1951, the year in which *An American in Paris* was released, most American women answered "fashion" to a Gallup Poll question asking them their first thoughts on hearing the word "Paris."[2]

At the beginning of the twentieth century, Paris, and therefore France, was the leading center of Western fashion and remained so during the first half of the century. The near cessation of the French fashion industry, however, during both world wars had greatly stimulated the growth of the US fashion industry, especially the ready-to-wear trade and more casual clothing known as "sportswear."[3] When many of the French fashion houses were forced to close or relocate after Germany occupied France during World War II, American manufacturers and politicians made great efforts to supplant Paris's lucrative role as fashion leader at a time when New York was consolidating its place as the sportswear capital of the world, with designers such as Claire McCardell specializing in this type of clothing.[4] Although the American fashion industry expanded rapidly after the war ended in 1945, Christian Dior's famous 1947 "New Look" reconfirmed and reestablished Paris as the main fashion center.[5] Throughout the 1950s and into the early 1960s, French fashion still set the standards, and, not surprisingly given that the United States was France's rival in the fashion world, American attitudes towards French fashion were as contradictory as they were complex.

Those complexities and contradictions were reflected in the popular culture, including films and television, as more informal lifestyles, burgeoning youth cultures, and greater commercial competition moved clothing, and references to it, in new directions that challenged the near hegemonic position of Paris.[6] Some Hollywood films played to American women's desire for and appreciation of French couture fashion, but others problematized such things. The lighthearted romantic drama *Sabrina* (Billy Wilder, 1954), for example, offers Paris fashion as transformative in a positive sense through a dramatic change of the heroine's class position: from the daughter of an American chauffeur to the wife of a rich American businessman.[7] By contrast, the comedy *Gentlemen Prefer Blondes* (Howard Hawks, 1953), in which Marilyn Monroe and Jane Russell arrive in Paris and shop, shows the desire for such clothing as representative of the gold-digging persona of Lorelei (Monroe). The desire for French fashion was also satirized in the 1956 episode of the *I Love Lucy* television program entitled "Lucy Gets a Paris Gown" when Ricky (Desi Arnaz) and Fred (William Frawley) trick their wives, Lucy (Lucille Ball) and Ethel (Vivian Vance), into thinking they have bought them Paris gowns by sewing a French label into burlap-bag dresses that the men had created themselves.[8]

An American in Paris and *Breakfast at Tiffany's*

An American in Paris best reveals the ambivalent American attitudes toward French fashion in the 1950s. Although the film serves to introduce viewers to the beauty and delights of Paris as a tourist destination, there is no message to buy French goods, least of all French couture fashion, which is revealed as morally dubious through the behavior and intentions of the American woman who wears it. In both *An American in Paris* and *Breakfast at Tiffany's*, released a decade later, issues of couture versus more casual clothing (that viewers are meant to assume is ready-to-wear) play out alongside issues of Frenchness and Americanness. The ways in which this was done indicates both continuities and differences in attitudes not only toward couture and ready-to-wear clothing (and the various points along the continuums between them) but also toward formal clothing, on the one hand, and casual clothing, on the other.

The two main female characters in *An American in Paris* are Lise Bouvier, an impecunious young French woman/gamine with short dark hair, played by the nineteen-year-old French actress and dancer Leslie Caron, and Milo Roberts, an "older" rich, blonde American woman residing in France, played by Nina Foch (then only twenty-six), who, although born in Holland, grew up in the United States from a toddler with her mother, the American actress Consuela Flowerton. Both Lise and Milo desire the love of the leading man, Jerry Mulligan, a poor American artist living in Paris, played by American actor Gene Kelly, but only the "older" Milo (Foch), rich (from inherited money) and sexually-knowing, is able to financially support Mulligan, her younger lover who is not in love with her.

The couture clothing designed for Milo (Foch) by the Australian-born but Hollywood-employed costume designer Orry-Kelly (who won an Academy Award for his work on this film) are among the sartorial pleasures of the film, and many women viewers in the United States must have admired the expensive "French" clothes (i.e., clothes designed for the film to look as if they were French couture) worn by the morally dubious Milo, who, at the end of the day, is the "loser" in love. In short, the film strongly suggests that French couture clothing, despite its allure, offers American women nothing in terms of achieving the gender-normative societal goals of true love and romance: only immorality and unhappiness ensue if such clothes are desired or worn. In contrast, it is the young virginal Lise (Caron) who wears informal clothes, cares little about money, has a mobile body, and gets the man; Milo, with her stiffer, less mobile body, fails to hold him, despite her money and her expensive clothes.

The starkness of the message can be related to the film being made only four years after Dior's "New Look" and Paris's reaffirmation as the center of fashion. When considered within this context, the positive light shed on the casual type of clothing worn by Lise/Caron and akin to the "sportswear" and "casuals" for which the US fashion industry was known, can be read as promoting American fashion against French.[9] Because the casual clothing is worn by the young French woman who ultimately wins the man, the clothing takes on an added importance that further problematizes the relationship between Frenchness and Americanness in the film. In the two films from the 1960s that we consider below, however, these more casual types of clothes are worn by characters clearly coded as American.

This paradigm can be similarly identified in *Breakfast at Tiffany's* and related to cultural ideas attached to Frenchness and Americanness and youth and age. Audrey Hepburn, the Belgian-born British actress with a cosmopolitan upbringing who plays the lead in *Breakfast at Tiffany's*, offered both Broadway and Hollywood an Anglicized gamine, and one more luminous and youthful looking on screen than Caron. Indeed, in 1951, at age twenty-two, Hepburn played the schoolgirl *Gigi* in the eponymous Broadway play. (Ironically, Caron, at age twenty-six, played the role in the film version [Vincente Minnelli, 1958]). In *Roman Holiday* (William Wyler, 1953), a modern fairytale with a twist, Hepburn was both gamine and gaminely royal, while the more conventional transformation narrative of *Sabrina* (Billy Wilder, 1954) advances her social standing courtesy of French couture.[10] Each of these performances, albeit in different ways, led to close associations between Hepburn, "Frenchness," and style despite the fact that she was not actually French.

In *Breakfast at Tiffany's*, this British-accented actress, now aged 32, was required to play Holly Golightly, a young American woman of *lumpenproletarian* "hillbilly" origins, formerly known as Lula Mae, who had married at "going on fourteen" but now, apparently single, was working in New York City as a paid "hostess," or escort.[11] Only two years older than Hepburn, American actress Patricia Neal played Mrs. Emily Eustace Failenson, the rich American "older woman" who has a "kept man"—Paul Varjak, a writer played by George Peppard, who falls in love with Holly during the course of the film.[12] It is a credit to both actresses, the costume designers, and the makeup and hair experts, as well as to Hepburn's model-like slimness, that many people think that she comes across as no more than twenty, while the Neal character seems much older than Neal actually was at the time.

There was no need for Hepburn to wear French couture clothing in *Breakfast at Tiffany's*, and the studio resisted her requests to do so, but she insisted. By then a close friend and admirer of the French couturier Hubert de Givenchy, Hepburn used her enormous box office appeal to force Paramount to agree to her selecting some garments by Givenchy, with Hollywood stalwart Edith Head remaining in overall charge of costume.[13] In the "battle" of clothing in the film, Hepburn's garments (some designed by a French couturier and some not) "won" against the high-quality tailored wool suits, coats, and dresses created especially for Neal by French-born Pauline Trigère (1912–2002) who had trained as a cutter in the French tailoring trade before working in the American fashion industry from 1937.[14] Yet, within the diegesis of the film, as in *An American in Paris*, expensive bespoke clothing was equated with an older American woman who "keeps" a younger man financially but does not win his love. In addition, this older woman is clearly an adulteress (we hear about her rich husband and even see his pinky-ringed aged hand in order to emphasize her dubious morals). While the Trigere outfits offered many delights for viewers keen on fashion, and Neal wore them with an admirable elegance and sense of style, the character she plays she is far more formal in taste, clothing types, and manners than the quirky emblem of youth and vivacity, Holly. In this film, the tensions are between older and newer attitudes toward clothing that also marked wider generational and cultural differences. Ironically, in a film that validates the expression of individuality through style and the more casual, youthful, and "everyday" type clothing that helped bring about the end of the preeminence of the French fashion houses, some of the more desirable clothes were still from one of those houses (Givenchy).

Although young, gaminelike, and American, Holly is a far more complex creature than either Lise in *An American in Paris* or the characters Hepburn played in *Roman Holiday* or *Sabrina*. As Holly Golightly, she wears "kooky," "swinging" attention-catching clothes and accessories, and her apartment betrays a similar youthful "Pop" sensibility.[15] Given this, the garments designed by Givenchy help viewers understand her as having "class" and cultural capital when it comes to style and fashion in spite of her morally suspect profession, acquaintances, and background. Edith Head skillfully costumed the scenes in which Givenchy clothes did not feature and collaborated with Hepburn, the director, the scriptwriter, art directors (Roland Anderson and Hal Pereira), and set decorators (Sam Comer and Ray Moyer) in order to create a joyous sense of cosmopolitan flair.

Furthermore, by setting the movie in the present (1961), as opposed to Truman Capote's choice of World War II in the 1958 eponymous novella on which the film is based, the director was able to foreground contemporary fashionable dress. One reviewer remarked that, "*Breakfast at Tiffany's* is like an entire year of *Vogue* come to life," and it certainly paraded a range of up-to-the-minute clothing to viewers—from French couture that passes for American flair and individuality to a range of "hip," chic clothing designed by the Paramount studio team to show Holly as a trendsetter and to the last scene that shows that Holly can look beautiful and sophisticated, if a little mysterious, in a simple, ubiquitous trench coat..[16] But it was more than a "year of *Vogue*" on screen: the film also featured "kooky" and casual clothing as "fun" and, in the end, coded the seemingly simple trench coat as morally superior and romantically advantageous.

Hepburn's squeaky-clean persona, on and off the screen, helped viewers distance themselves from the thoroughly unrespectable background of the character she plays (which we glimpse when her former and much older husband arrives) and from the nature of her paid work. At the same time, however, the fact that she is in some way sullied by the exchange of money for social favors, and probably sexual ones too, brings her closer to the other central female character, thus narrowing the gap between them that the film works so hard to emphasize. In the early 1960s the gap was also narrowed by the public awareness of Givenchy's role in designing Hepburn's wardrobe, both on and off screen. More importantly, perhaps, within the film, the gap is narrowed between couture of any kind and more casual sportswear and accessories as represented by Holly (Hepburn)'s trench coat, sweatshirt, pedal-pusher-length denim jeans, jeans-like trousers, and oversize sunglasses. The use of denim and jeans, regarded as an archetypal American material and clothing type respectively, in particular emphasizes the Americanness of Holly (Hepburn)'s choice of casual wear, while the other clothing she wears suggests a US fashion industry geared toward young women and modern lifestyles.

At the end of the day, this morally questionable young American woman with a wide array of clothing types, both costly and inexpensive, and a great deal of flair, wins the man and seemingly perpetual happiness. She does so, however, by leaving behind couture clothes of any variety. Indeed, the clothing that viewers are led to imagine Holly (Hepburn) might wear in her new life are represented by the trench-coat-style raincoat that she wears in the final scene. It stands in for the types of ready-to-wear "casuals" for which the American fashion industry was by then renowned, and which we have seen her wear in scenes that seem to show the more "authentic" side of her character. It is no coincidence that she is clad in denim jeans and a soft sweatshirt-style top when she sings the hauntingly wistful Henry Mancini song *Moon River* while seated on the supposedly "authentic" fire escape attached to her New York apartment.[17]

Breakfast at Tiffany's suggests, therefore, like an *American in Paris*, that, in the final analysis, there is something morally suspect about couture fashion per se.[18] While the movie offers the pleasures of high-end fashion on screen, in the end it validates the pleasures of the more casual types of clothing that were increasingly popular with young girls and women and understood as designed and made in America.

Contexts: Grace Kelly, Jacqueline Bouvier Kennedy, and French and American Couture

Something of the same ambivalent attitudes embodied and reflected in Hollywood representations of French and American couture in the 1950s and early 1960s were evident in the clothing choices of key public figures in the United States who could afford to buy bespoke clothing of their choice, no matter where it was designed or made. In the wider culture, French couture was often represented as "classy" or adding "class" to the wearer, and two important American style icons of the period, Grace Kelly and Jacqueline Bouvier Kennedy, shifted between "French" and "American" fashionable dress.

The elegant blonde model-turned-film-star Kelly's star persona was closely associated with Americanness, from her role as an Eastern Quaker in *High Noon* (Fred Zimmerman, 1952) to wealthy East-Coast types in *Rear Window* (Alfred Hitchcock, 1954) and *High Society* (Charles Walters, 1956). On and off screen, her clothing was associated with a sophisticated simplicity that, like her, was presented to the public as quintessentially American. At the end of *Rear Window*, socialite Lise Fremont (Kelly) wears more casual clothes—slim denim jeans and leather loafer shoes—in order to show that she can fit in with the lifestyle of obsessive, truth-seeking, American photojournalist "Jeff" Jefferies (James Stewart).

Costume designer Edith Head commented on Kelly's exceptional understanding of the role of clothing in films, and Kelly was certainly familiar with couture clothing. Indeed, during her love affair with the Russian American couturier and film costume designer Oleg Cassini, she wore a stunning Cassini gown when she accepted her Academy Award for *The Country Girl* (George Seaton, 1954). It is perhaps surprising that for her much publicized 1956 "fairytale" wedding or the "wedding of the century" to Monaco's ruler Prince Rainier, she did not wear a couture gown, but entrusted looking her very best on that special occasion to the American film costume designer Helen Rose. Thereafter, however, as Princess of Monaco she patronized the couture houses of nearby Paris, especially the House of Dior, in part because, as she explained, she needed to dress to fit her new role.[19]

It was difficult to upstage Princess Grace, but part of the visual classiness of Jacqueline Bouvier Kennedy, a Francophile proud of her Bouvier French heritage whose study year abroad in Paris overlapped with the making of *An American in Paris*, was her passion for Parisian couture.[20] When she married into the wealthy Kennedy family in 1953 she wore a gown designed by Ann Lowe, an African American designer who ran a small custom salon in New York (but was not credited with the design at the time of the wedding), but after becoming Jacqueline Kennedy she could afford to wear clothes by the Parisian couturiers she so greatly admired, including Givenchy.[21]

During the campaign leading up to the November 1960 presidential election in the United States, in which her husband, John Fitzgerald Kennedy, was the Democratic candidate, however, she was criticized for both the cost of her wardrobe and the fact that she did not wear clothes created by American designers and made by American workers. Buckling under Democratic Party, union, and Kennedy clan pressure, she shifted her sartorial allegiances. The pressure to patronize American designers and makers continued throughout her time as First Lady of the United States, such that she mainly wore clothes by such leading American designers as Oleg Cassini and Norman Norell, some of which were inspired by French designers such as Givenchy and Chanel.[22] These transatlantic influences meant that she wore American clothes that closely resembled the types of clothes that she might have ordered from French couture houses.

Before the presidential election, Jacqueline Kennedy was featured in *Life* magazine looking at dress designs by Norell, and as First Lady she wore a Norell design in denim (a material already noted as considered to be quintessentially American) on a visit to Greece with President Kennedy in 1961.[23] Such clothing and materials pleased those Americans who felt ambivalent about her Francophile tastes.[24] It was Cassini, however, who became her official style guru as First Lady, and upon his appointment to design her personal wardrobe, he commented, "We are on the threshold of a new American elegance thanks to Mrs. Kennedy's beauty, naturalness, understatement, exposure and symbolism."[25] As a film costume designer of note, as well as a couturier, Cassini approached dressing the First Lady as if she were a film star. He later recalled, "Suddenly it came to me, this is like a film and you have the opportunity to dress the female star. This was not so different from my old job in Hollywood, designing for motion pictures. . . . I was thinking about the role she was going to play and my sketches started filling up the empty sheets."[26] Thus Cassini blurred the distinctions between film costume and couture as well as between French and American fashion design.

Jacqueline Kennedy's blurring of barriers between French and American couture and her determination to wear things as "French" as possible within the rubric of being "American" are perhaps best shown by the lengths to which she went to have a pink suit in boucle wool as near to a Chanel original as possible. Justine Picardie's 2010 authorized biography of Chanel revealed that the fabric and trimming (including gilt buttons) came directly from Chanel in Paris and that the suit was made and fitted for the First Lady at Chez Ninon in New York using Chanel's approved "line for line" system.[27] Effectively, it was as near a Chanel suit as possible in the circumstances. The now blood-stained suit became famous because the First Lady was wearing it when her husband was assassinated in November 1963.

It was alongside the public perception of the First Lady's clothing as "American," stylish and youthful, that both *Breakfast at Tiffany's* and *That Touch of Mink* were made and first circulated. At the same time as Jacqueline Kennedy's forced abandonment of French fashion for American fashion was a matter of public debate, French couture remained her preferred clothing, just as it did for Audrey Hepburn. And, as if to make her position clear, the newly widowed Jacqueline Kennedy wore French couture (designed by Givenchy) to her husband's state funeral, which was shown on television to millions around the world. It was as if she was asserting her right to wear what she liked because she no longer had to try to please the Kennedy family, the Democratic Party, the labor unions seeking to protect US jobs, or the American public.[28] At the time the two films discussed below were made and released, however, she was playing her role in promoting

American couture to perfection and, together with her husband, represented a more youthful outlook on life and lifestyles.

Breakfast at Tiffany's and *That Touch of Mink*

Both *Breakfast at Tiffany's* and *That Touch of Mink* treat the viewer to the pleasures of watching stylish, fashionable dress set against equally fashionable backgrounds. Both female leads are single and live in New York City. In *Breakfast at Tiffany's* Holly Golightly rarely works and the Doris Day character (Cathy Timberlake) in *That Touch of Mink* is unemployed, yet they both get to wear a range of fashionable clothes, A particular dress type worn in both films and featured in film posters for each links the female stars and the two movies in the popular imagination. A long slim black evening dress on each actress serves as a signifier of elegance. The *Breakfast at Tiffany's* black dress (designed by Givenchy and worn in the opening scene) was such a smash hit that the one worn by Doris Day playing Cathy Timberlake in *That Touch of Mink* was surely an attempt to bring Hepburn-style elegance to Day. When she wears the long black dress, Day's hair is also upswept like Hepburn's, further supporting a reading of this film as indebted to Hepburn and *Breakfast at Tiffany's* for the glamour of Day's persona.

Although Givenchy designed some of Holly/Hepburn's wardrobe for *Breakfast at Tiffany's*, those clothes were not conveyed to the film audience as "Givenchy" or even as French. Some young women who saw the film upon release read both Hepburn *and* the clothing as "American." "I was over sixty years old before I realized that Audrey Hepburn was not American!" said Deborah Sussman, a young designer in the 1950s and 1960s who was always at the forefront of youthful, fashionable styles.[29] Audiences could read Hepburn's clothing in the film as American—or at least as not French—because Givenchy garments were mixed with non-Givenchy in the film and because Jacqueline Kennedy and others had so greatly personalized and Americanized French couture by the very act of wearing it and establishing a signature "American" style around it. Through Jacqueline Kennedy as First Lady, Givenchy-influenced coats, suits, and dresses, together with small boxy hats, long gloves (a fashion "hangover" that continued to add glamour to ensembles), casually tied headscarves, and dark glasses were codified as "American" and embedded within American culture. When those particular items appeared in *Breakfast at Tiffany's* as markers of Holly (Hepburn), therefore, they were recognizable as fashionable within American contexts and not necessarily as French.

One of the visual appeals of Doris Day in the earlier film *Pillow Talk* (1959) was that this unequivocally all-American film star was restyled in a "sensational wardrobe" by costume designer Jean Louis without any sense of her or the clothing being French.[30] (Louis, or Jean Louis Berthault, was French-born but worked with American fashion entrepreneur Hattie Carnegie in New York before moving to Hollywood.) In *That Touch of Mink*, Day wore clothes designed by Norell, as did Jacqueline Kennedy. There is less tension between character, female star, dress, location, and plot in *That Touch of Mink* than in the other two films considered here, and, in part at least, this was because everything was unequivocally American, except perhaps Cary Grant's oft-forgotten British origins. Furthermore, in *That Touch of Mink,* the female lead is not played off against any another woman, suggesting perhaps a new confidence about American women and US fashion. At the same time, however, the film makes it clear that the clothing bought by Philip Shayne (Grant) for Cathy (Day) in the hope of her becoming his "kept woman" was couture or, at the very least, consisted of costly upscale garments. This information was conveyed to viewers by the time-honored cinematic device of presenting these clothes through a fashion show at Bergdorf Goodman, an exclusive Manhattan department store, and by using leading New York fashion models, as opposed to actresses, to display them in the show.[31]

The immoral associations of expensive clothing spelled out in *An American in Paris* and *Breakfast at Tiffany's* recur in *That Touch of Mink*. In the latter two films, it is notable that men to whom the main women protagonists are not married underwrite expensive clothing for them. In *Breakfast at Tiffany's*, the clothing of the adulterous older American woman is paid for by her rich cuckolded husband, and Holly's are subsidized by men she escorts and a gangster whom she unwittingly helps. Furthermore, as noted, in *Breakfast at Tiffany's* and *An American in Paris*, the older American women who wear couture clothing "keep" their male lovers in a financial sense. Thus, in what was the largest capitalist economy in the world, women with money are represented as immoral and as failures at holding on to the men they most desire. Additionally, when *Breakfast at Tiffany's* was made, French dominance of world fashion was still seen as threatening to the US fashion industry, both to its increasingly respected couture trade and to the ready-to-wear sector thriving alongside it. The film presents the couture clothing as a commodity that is morally dubious and potentially destabilizing. At the end of the day, the message is that only the more casual, ready-to-wear garments (or the American ones) are morally worthy and get you the man of your dreams.

At the same time, fashionable clothing represents a step toward "classiness" in both *Breakfast at Tiffany's* and *That Touch of Mink*. In the former, Holly acquires a more stable social status by the end of the film because viewers assume she will become the wife of a writer. In *That Touch of Mink* a temporarily unemployed working girl marries a rich businessman and makes a major leap up the economic and social scale. Clothing is also closely linked to "authenticity" or Americanness in the two films. Day exudes her quintessentially American star persona in the role of Cathy Timberlake, and Holly Golightly's most "real" moments happen when she is dressed not in the height of fashion but, rather, in simpler, more "all-American" clothing. At the end of *Breakfast at Tiffany's*, she wears a trench-coat style raincoat in the rain, thus allowing the coat to function as it was meant to, namely a garment that protects one from the rain, and she no longer hides behind her dark glasses. It is as if, having accepted love, the character no longer needs her clothing to be about fashion statements, performance, or a comment upon social status or taste.[32]

More assertively American than any of the other films discussed here, *That Touch of Mink* features a Doris Day groomed to look like a cross between a blonde Jacqueline Kennedy and a blonde Audrey Hepburn. Like *Breakfast at Tiffany's*, the film is set in New York City, but the plot revolves around whether Cathy (Day), an unemployed American office worker, will consummate a relationship prior to marriage with Shayne (Grant), an American businessman with international interests. Clothing and fur are made key to both Cathy's (near) seduction and the visual pleasures of the film. Indeed, the plot is set in motion by an incident involving clothing: Shayne's taxi splashes muddy rainwater on Cathy's beige dress and raincoat with its touches of leather (as opposed to mink) somewhat in the manner of noted American fashion designer Bonnie Cashin.[33] Although fully prepared to harangue him when she later meets him, she is instantly smitten—after all, he is Cary Grant! She winds up accompanying him to a meeting of the United Nations, where he gives a speech, and to a Yankees baseball game, where she sits in the dugout with Mickey Mantle, Roger Maris, and Yogi Berra, iconic ballplayers of the period making cameo appearances in the film. Thus, New York is presented at its most seductively American through a major national sport and at its most cosmopolitan through the United Nations.[34]

Shayne then invites Cathy on a trip to the island resort of Bermuda and sends an emissary (played by William Lanteau) to take her shopping and be outfitted appropriately for her sojourn among the wealthy elite. If Holly (Hepburn) had Tiffany's in *Breakfast at Tiffany's* (and in the novella, Mainbocher, an American couturier who designed and sold in both Paris and New York), in *That Touch of Mink*, Cathy (Day) has the Bergdorf Goodman department store. Both films feature obvious references to consumerism through their use of actual stores, suggesting that high fashion clothing is available to "all" American women.

In *That Touch of Mink*, Cathy (Day) and viewers watch a fashion show at Bergdorf Goodman that adds considerably to the film's spectacular appeal and privileges both the beauty and the temptation of glamorous clothing and luxurious fabrics. Both she and the spectators are seduced through the double allure of travel and fashionable clothing—or triple allure, if we factor in Cary Grant. Although Helen Gurley Brown's influential *Sex and the Single Girl* was published in 1962, the year that the movie premiered, the Cathy character raises issues related to mainstream social mores. She is a small-town girl from Sandusky, Ohio, who is supposed to be married before she has sex. Her family name, Timberlake, with its associations of timber and lake, suggests solid or upright American stock.[35]

One particular outfit Cathy wears, a black dress with a white collar, is redolent with references to the Pilgrims, the beginnings of the new nation, and puritan values. She wears this—the most demure of all her outfits—when viewing the fashion show. It symbolizes her sexual purity and, while remaining within the parameters of what was considered fashionable, serves as a partial shield against the seduction of fashion itself. Nation and national values are again invoked when Shayne, wrestling with his own conscience over the proposed Bermuda trip, states "to take a girl like that to Bermuda is a desecration of everything the Minutemen fought for at Concord," thus linking protection of Cathy's virginity to a masculine moral code of Americanness and the values for which ordinary Americans fought the War of Independence.

The finale of the Bergdorf Goodman fashion show features a mink-lined silk or satin coat, the outer shell of which is available in an array of rich jewel tones, reminiscent of Christian Dior's fur-lined couture raincoats.[36] Cathy opts for the more restrained but ultrafashionable beige—the new "jewel tone" of 1962. Here, the color spelled both a "good girl" cautiousness of choice (after all she was wearing her "puritan" outfit when making her selection) and Jacqueline Kennedy–style taste. At her husband's inauguration as president in 1960, Kennedy studiously avoided the bright colors that were then popular (and also decided against a fur coat, a sensible and conventional choice for January in Washington, DC), preferring instead to make a fashion statement by appearing in a greige tweed ensemble by Cassini with just a small touch of fur (sable—considered the most noble of furs) at the neck.[37] Thus, the beige mink-lined coat links Cathy (Day) to both French couture, via Dior, and to First Lady taste, as well as to the luxurious associations of fur, with a degree of restraint suggestive of social and personal respectability, which Jonathan Faiers also connects to a new simplicity in 1960s fashion.[38]

The mink-lined coat in *That Touch of Mink*, therefore, was intended to reek of "class" to viewers. The lining is never completely hidden, but the conceit of using such an expensive material as mink simply as a lining, not as the main material, is an example of how such conspicuous understatement draws even more attention to both the cost of the garment and the wearer. Through the mink-lined coat, the film plays with the ambiguities attendant to fur, and to mink in particular, as a signifier of wealth and status, on the one hand, and "fallen" morality on the other—in this case the pressure on Cathy (Day) to have sex before marriage. Safe within the generic conventions of romantic comedy, the film plays with these anxieties through "that touch of mink."

Touches of Fur in *Breakfast at Tiffany's* and *That Touch of Mink*

From the beginning of the US film industry, fur epitomized glamour both on and off the screen. Indeed, Adolph Zukor, founder of Paramount Pictures, was originally a furrier, and fur featured in Cinderella-style or other transformation narratives (characteristic of several films starring both Audrey Hepburn and Doris Day) in early cinema.[39] Historically, fur has signified power and status, and the (upper) class connotations of fur remained strong in Europe and North America into the twentieth century.[40] This changed dramatically, however, in the United States after World War II, as spending power rose and fur coats came within the reach of middle-class and better-off working-class women. Sable and fox were the most popular furs before World War II, but thereafter, mink (which is very soft, silky, and dense) was the most popular.[41]

By the 1950s, sales of mink were estimated as worth three to four times as much in terms of money as all other furs put together,[42] and in 1960 and 1961, advertisements for the Eastern Mink Breeders Association featured mink-coated women photographed at internationally famous tourist sites, thus associating such coats and such women with luxury and jet-age lifestyles.[43] Those advertisements also identified mink as an essentially American product, in contrast to furs of African, Persian, or Brazilian origin, in an attempt to link mink with patriotism.[44] In the 1950s and early 1960s, mink coats were desired and worn by all manner of American women: society matrons, respectable middle- and working-class women, *nouveaux riches* women, kept women, and prostitutes. In *Butterfield 8* (1960), released shortly before *Breakfast at Tiffany's* and *That Touch of Mink*, for example, Elizabeth Taylor plays a model and sometime escort who steals the mink coat belonging to one of her client's wives and is pictured as sexually predatory when wearing it.

Such was the instability of the fur coat by the early 1960s as object type, material, and metaphor that fur was introduced notably only in touches in both *Breakfast at Tiffany's* and *That Touch of Mink*. Neither Holly nor Cathy wears a conventional fur coat. Holly wears a mink hat in a simple modern form that suggests good taste and classiness in a key romantic scene, while in an earlier scene, a black hat form adorned with what looks like a giant ermine powder puff and long delicate black feather suggests the more frivolous, "funky" side of her taste spectrum before she falls in love with someone who appreciates her for herself. Cathy (Day)'s stunning coat with the mink lining places her closer to women who wore conventional mink coats at the time than to Holly (Hepburn). The coat also symbolized the silver lining behind the disastrous beginning to her relationship with Shayne (Grant). Having Cathy (Day) wear a touch of tasteful mink, as well as partnering her with Cary Grant, linked her with the desires of thousands of women across the United States at that time. (While Cary Grant might not be within reach of all women such desirable clothes were available for purchase at high-end department stores.)

Fur, with its soft, sensual, luxurious qualities, touches us, writes Julia Emberley, and is a material we love to touch.[45] In fact, fur *invites* touch. In the 1950s and early 1960s, advertisers played on the idea that mink was irresistible to women (and made women irresistible to men), as if it had talismanic powers in and of itself. Indeed, the power and allure of mink and fur in general was so entrenched in the culture that it constituted a source for humor. In "The Fur Coat," a 1951 episode of *I Love Lucy*, for example, Lucy, annoyed at her husband's refusal to buy her a fur coat, cuts up a fake mink one, to the horror of her unsuspecting husband, who thinks it is real, while in "The Commuters and The Fur Coat" episode of Sid Caesar's *Your Show of Shows* (1954–1957), a husband is brought to tears at the thought of parting with a substantial amount of their joint savings to buy his wife a fur coat.[46] Such programs reified the status of fur coats, particularly mink ones, as gendered objects steeped in patriarchy and capitalist exchange and portrayed women wanting a fur as scheming and beholden to men to own one.

This link between men and women and mink coats was exploited in the sexual innuendo of advertising copy for high-end Buick automobiles in the November 1, 1960 issue of *Vogue*. The copy read: "Every Buick upholstery fabric passes a mink test! And in all ways, Buick is a gentleman when it comes to a lady. Doorways are wider, lower, seats are roomier, thicker in the middle, and because Buick is trimmer on the outside, handling is easier. . . . It looks simply elegant; it looks like mink. Try on a Buick for size. We think you'll like the way it fits".[47] Given the obvious associations between real fur and vaginal "fur," comments such as "you'll like the way it fits" take on multiple meanings, relating mink and automobiles in a form of heterosexual foreplay. Such play can be related directly to *That Touch of Mink*, where the fur lining of the coat may refer metonymically to Cathy (Day)'s genitalia, virginal and private up until now but perhaps to become no longer so in Bermuda. We see, for example, how fiercely protective Cathy (Day) is of her mink-lined coat, refusing to relinquish it to a flight attendant even though there are no other passengers on the Pan Am jet taking her to Bermuda to meet Shayne (Grant)—he purchased all the seats! By embodying and encasing herself in clothes purchased for her by Shayne (both literally and figuratively), and especially with the mink-lined coat secure in her lap, she appears to be giving herself over sexually to Shayne before she has even gone to bed with him.

The "immoral" connotations of the mink-lined coat are clearly spelled out when Cathy (Day), standing next to Shayne (Grant) in the hotel elevator in Bermuda and wearing the coat, is alongside an obvious "gold digger" and her "sugar daddy." Enveloped in what looks to be a silver fox coat (the allusion was probably deliberate), the "gold digger" looks directly at Cathy (Day)'s hand to see if she is wearing a wedding band in an attempt to discover whether she too has been "bought." Suddenly, Cathy (Day) views her own coat and herself in a different, more problematic, light. In that moment, the mink lining is recontextualized and she no longer feels comfortable—not in her own skin or in the coat that stands in for her skin, a coat that now symbolizes her predicament as a potential kept woman.

Thus, the mink-lined coat as a marker of class or status in the film is compromised in much the same way as the French and American couture clothing discussed earlier in this chapter. Indeed, it is questionable even as to why mink is necessary at all in Bermuda, where the average temperature is between sixty and seventy degrees even during the winter months. Furthermore, the play between what is public and what is private (the coat and the partly visible lining) is expanded cinematically by a recurrent disturbing fantasy that Cathy has in Bermuda (albeit meant to be humorous to the film viewer) in which everyone on the streets, at the hotel pool, or in the elevator, sees her occupying the canopied hotel bed with a man to whom she is not married. At least one contemporary reviewer clearly understood the phrase "that touch of mink" as a euphemism for a kept woman.[48]

That Touch of Mink and *Breakfast at Tiffany's* were made when sexual and moral codes were changing in American life and in Hollywood. The Hays Production Code, which had monitored movies since the early 1930s with regard to what was acceptable in relation to sex on screen (and other matters), was losing its power. Needing to draw people away from television and to compete more effectively with foreign films, Hollywood filmmakers increasingly turned to more overtly adult themes. In the early 1950s, for example, producer and director Otto Preminger famously ignored a Motion Picture Production Code edict to remove words such as "virgin" and "seduction" from *The Moon is Blue* (1953), a romantic comedy that dealt with virginity, but the code was not fully abandoned until 1968.[49]

The availability of the birth control pill also had an impact on sexual activity and attitudes toward it. By 1957, "the pill" was approved in the United States for the treatment of extreme menstrual discomfort, and by 1960 in all but eight states as a contraceptive device. After 1960, the numbers of women using the pill increased rapidly, and thus, when *Breakfast at Tiffany's* and *That Touch of Mink* were being made and first seen, young American women (particularly the wealthier and more highly-educated ones) had greater options open to them to prevent pregnancy or were learning about them and were somewhat freer to have, or consider having, sex outside marriage.[50] But it was the early days of "the pill," and most young women continued to worry about unwanted pregnancies and being left to raise a baby alone (fears this film does not address). These anxieties and contradictory feelings about what would become known as the "sexual revolution" were given expression through dress in *That Touch of Mink*.

Like the mink-lined coat, the black evening dress Cathy (Day) wears in Bermuda with a short white capelike jacket over it for "protection" reads as somewhat contradictory. While the front of the deeply V-cut, fitted, and thin-strapped evening dress displays the curves of Cathy (Day)'s body alluringly, as well as her back (which Shayne (Grant) first begins to kiss once the jacket is off), the stiffer white silk jacket stands away from her body and covers it. As Jeanne Thomas Allen commented about the film *Fig Leaves* (1926), women's clothing is often the grounds of struggle, both literal and figurative, for control of their bodies.[51] Cathy (Day)'s evening dress and jacket, although black and white, is not so "black and white" after all. Like "that touch of mink" on the coat, it speaks to ambiguities or ambivalence around sexuality, display, virginity, respectability, and the conventions of both courtship and seduction, as well as the blurred lines between attraction or desire, and love.[52] Indeed, Day's casting as a virgin when she was thirty-eight years old, the mother of a grown child, and divorced three times (as recounted on the cover of the June 20, 1961, issue of the popular magazine *Look* well before *That Touch of Mink* premiered) epitomizes how movie stars can broker social and cultural contradictions through fashion.[53]

By the time *That Touch of Mink* was made, fur coats, like couture—whether French or American—had multiple, complicated and ambivalent meanings related to sexuality, morality, and nationhood. Cary Grant, known to take a great deal of interest in the clothes Day wore for this film, reputedly did not want to call the movie *That Touch of Mink* because he thought that mink was already passé. And for many people, it was. In 1964, the older of us (Pat Kirkham), as a British undergraduate, remodeled her mother's mink marmot fur coat (with a pair of leather shears) out of all recognition from what had gone before, getting rid of the wide collar and cuffs and slicing the length to mid-thigh (shades of Lucy cutting up the fur). Because she could not sew the skin, she secured the now collarless coat with a pin at the neck, secured it loosely around the waist with a soft leather belt, and wore it Cossack style, with jeans and long boots. Thus, a working-class woman's coat that was passé not long after she had finally been able to afford to buy it found a new life as part of the younger more casual styles influenced by, among many things, American casuals and sportswear, the creativity of British fashion in "Swinging London," the flair of film characters such as Hepburn, and slim silhouettes influenced by body shapes such as Hepburn's. The younger of us (Marilyn Cohen), as an American preteen, remembers watching *That Touch of Mink* and rooting for Cathy to hold off having sex until she was married to Shayne. Even before seeing the movie, she recalls saving coins to buy her mother a mink coat; she knew from watching reruns of such television programs as *I Love Lucy*—and her mother's playful but frequent hints to her father—that a mink coat was a precious, fashionable, and very desirable commodity.

Conclusion

We hope to have shown in this chapter some of the various ways in which the Hollywood movies discussed here used fashionable clothing, along with accessories, materials, color, characterizations, actors, and personas, to represent ideas of "difference" and inscribed them into notions of femininity, nation, age, class, "classiness," morality, respectability, and heteronormative romantic outcomes. *An American in Paris* and the contextual discussions related to America in the 1950s indicate that, at particular moments in the postwar period, France's hold over world fashion was hotly contested in the United States, and French couture designers and garments were regarded with some ambivalence in Hollywood movies.

Holly (Hepburn) in *Breakfast at Tiffany's*, despite her gamine style and perhaps because of her affected use of French phrases, was presented as a thoroughly modern and fashionable young American woman working through issues that would remain relevant throughout the 1960s as was Cathy (Day) in *That Touch of Mink* (1962.) Both films Americanized French-influenced clothing, as the US fashion industry had done, and offered viewers, particularly women viewers, many sartorial pleasures. Only, however, in *That Touch of Mink* were those sartorial pleasures offered without worrying about the national origin of the couture clothing or the character. As if to make the national question absolutely clear, any lingering associations of foreignness in Hepburn's persona, on or off the screen, were replaced by the certainty with which audiences identified Doris Day as an all-American girl with all-American values, including even her penchant for a "touch" of mink.

MARILYN COHEN teaches in the Masters Program in the History of Design and Curatorial Studies offered jointly by Parsons School of Design/The New School and Cooper Hewitt, Smithsonian Design Museum. She is author and curator of *Reginald Marsh's New York*, and she has published on the subject of popular/material culture in relation to film and television.

PAT KIRKHAM is Professor of Design History, Kingston University, UK, and Professor Emerita at Bard Graduate Center, New York. Her many publications on design, film and gender include *Charles and Ray Eames: Designers of the Twentieth Century*, *The Gendered Object* (ed.) and two volumes (coedited) on masculinity and movies.

Notes

We are extremely grateful to Rebecca C. Tuite for her help in completing this chapter.

1. Christopher Endy, *Cold War Holidays: American Tourism in France* (Chapel Hill, NC: University of North Carolina Press, 2004), 8. See also, Harvey Levenstein, *We'll Always Have Paris: American Tourists in France since 1930* (Chicago: University of Chicago Press, 2004).

2. George H. Gallup, *The Gallup Poll: Public Opinion, 1935–1971* (New York: Random House, 1972), 2:990. It was not just French fashion that interested Americans: food, literature, and wine were also among the attractions. In *To Catch A Thief* (1955), John Robie (Cary Grant)

eats quiche on the French Riviera and asks what it is called. By 1961, he could have found a recipe for it in *Mastering the Art of French Cooking*. The latter was published by the American-born Julia Child, who, together with her French friends Simone Beck and Louisette Bertholle, began teaching cooking to American women in Paris in 1951, the year *An American in Paris* was released.

3. Richard Martin, *American Ingenuity: Sportswear 1930s–1970s* (New York: The Metropolitan Museum of Art, 1998), and Rebecca Arnold, *The American Look: Fashion, Sportswear and the Image of Women in 1930s and 1940s New York* (London: I. B. Tauris, 2009).

4. For details on the French fashion industry during World War II, see Dominique Veillon, *Fashion under the Occupation*, trans. Miriam Kochan (New York: Berg, 2002).

5. Diana De Marly, *Christian Dior* (New York: Holmes & Meier, 1990); Colin McDowell, *Forties Fashion and the New Loo*k (London: Bloomsbury, 1997), 154–89; Valerie Steele, *50 Years of Fashion: New Look to Now* (New York: Yale University Press, 1997), 1–16.

6. For a list of 1950s films dealing with fashion, see "The Fifties at the Grand Action Cinema," Palais Galliera, accessed online March 9, 2015, http://www.palaisgalliera.paris.fr/en/news/fifties-grand-action-cinema. Also, the clothing emerging from Mary Quant and others during Britain's "swinging sixties" was especially challenging to the position of Paris in terms of fashion; see: Christopher Breward, *Fashioning London: Clothing and the Modern Metropolis* (London: Berg, 2004), 151–76; Mary Quant, *Quant by Quant* (London: Cassel, 1966); Alwin W. Turner, *Biba: The Biba Experience* (Woodbridge, UK: Antique Collectors Club, 2004); and Steele, *50 Years of Fashion*, 49–78.

7. The transformative clothing designed for the film by French couturier Hubert Givenchy in dialogue with Edith Head, head of film costume at the Paramount film studio, and by Head and her staff team helped establish several aspects of Audrey Hepburn's sartorial star persona that reverberate in *Breakfast at Tiffany's*. For more on this relationship between Head and Givenchy, see Jean-Pierre Dorléac, "Edith Head and the 'Sabrina' Dress,'" in *Los Angeles Times*, October 24, 2010, accessed online, March 3, 2015, http://articles.latimes.com/2010/oct/24/image/la-ig-edithredux-20101024. In his discussion of Paris as a center of American tourism, Harvey Levenstein also used this film to back his claim that, for American women in the 1950s, Paris was "the place whose style, culture, and sophistication can turn one into an attractive new woman" (See Levenstein, *We'll Always Have Paris*, 162-163), but as we show, cinematic representations of Paris fashion and American women were more complex.

8. "Lucy Gets a Paris Gown," episode 147 of *I Love Lucy*, aired March 19, 1956 (Michael McClay, *I Love Lucy: The Complete Picture History of the Most Popular TV Show Ever* [New York: Warner Books, 1995], 290).

9. See Martin, *American Ingenuity*, and Arnold, *The American Look*.

10. See Gabrielle Finnane, "Holly Golightly and the Fashioning of the Waif," in *Fashion in Fiction* (Oxford and New York: Berg, 2009), 137–48. Finnane explicates three "types": the waif, the gamine, and the ingénue. See also Sam Wasson, *Fifth Avenue, 5 A.M.: Audrey Hepburn, Breakfast at Tiffany's, and the Dawn of the Modern Woman* (New York: HarperStudio, 2010).

11. According to Truman Capote, "Holly Golightly was not precisely a callgirl." In a 1968 interview with Eric Norden, Capote is quoted as saying that Holly was the prototype of today's liberated female and representative of "a whole breed of girls who live off men but are not prostitutes. They're our version of the geisha girl" (Eric Norden, "Playboy Interview: Truman Capote," in *Truman Capote: Conversations*, ed. M. Thomas Inge [Jackson: University Press of Mississippi, 1987], 141).

12. Truman Capote, *Breakfast at Tiffany's: A Short Novel and Three Stories* (New York: Random House, 1958).

13. For confirmation that Hepburn's clothing would be provided by Givenchy, see "Production Memo," in Clippings File (*Breakfast at Tiffany's*), Performing Arts Division, New York Public Library.

14. Eleni Sakes Epstein, "Trigère," in *American Fashion: The Life and Lines of Adrian, Mainbocher, McCardell, Norell and Trigère*, ed. Sarah Tomerlin Lee (New York: Quadrangle, 1975), 409–96; Jack Alexander, "New York's New Queen of Fashion," in *Saturday Evening Post*, April 8, 1961, p. 30 and pp. 88–90.

15. For interiors see Marilyn Cohen, "*Breakfast at Tiffany's*: Performing Identity in Public and Private," in *Performance, Fashion and the Modern Interior from the Victorians to Today*, ed. Fiona Fisher, Trevor Keeble, Patricia Lara-Betancourt, Brenda Martin (Oxford and New York: Berg, 2011), 159–68.

16. *Saturday Review*, September 30, 1961, in Clippings File (*Breakfast at Tiffany's*) Performing Arts Division, New York Public Library.

17. Of the fire escape where Holly/Hepburn sings, James Sanders writes: "No one should (or could) confuse this moment with the reality of apartment life in New York—even in a former row house. Indeed, the setting itself is a complete invention: a fire escape lifted off the front of an old-law tenement, then moved around the side to an implausible 'air court' placed in what should be the unbroken party wall of a row house" (*Celluloid Skyline: New York and the Movies* [New York: Alfred A. Knopf, 2001], 212).

18. For a discussion of couture clothing and sexuality in film, see Stella Bruzzi, *Undressing Cinema: Clothing and Identity in the Movies* (London and New York: Routledge, 1997), 3–34.

19. H. Kristina Haugland, *Grace Kelly: Icon of Style to Royal Bride* (New Haven, CT: Philadelphia Museum of Art in association with Yale University Press, 2006); Haugland, *Grace Kelly Style* (London: V&A, 2010); Donald Spoto, *High Society: The Life of Grace Kelly* (New York: Three Rivers Press, 2010).

20. Alice Kaplan, *Dreaming in French: The Paris Years of Jacqueline Bouvier Kennedy, Susan Sontag and Angela Davis* (Chicago: University of Chicago Press, 2012); The Metropolitan Museum of Art Exhibition Catalogue, *Jacqueline Kennedy: The White House Years: Selections from the John F. Kennedy Library and Museum* (New York: Bullfinch, 2001).

21. For Lowe, see Pat Kirkham and Shauna Stallworth, "'Three Strikes Against Me': African American Women Designers," in *Women Designers in the USA 1900–2000: Diversity and Difference*, ed. Pat Kirkham (New York: Bard Graduate Center, 2000), 123–44.

22. A notable exception took place in France. Having worn a Cassini gown to a dinner given by the French President at the Élysée Palace, she wore a Givenchy gown to an official dinner at the Palace of Versailles, carrying it off to great acclaim as an homage to French design (Sarah Bradford, *America's Queen*, rev. ed. (New York: Penguin 2013), 264–65; for more on her relationship with Givenchy, see pages 182, 196, and 281). Metropolitan Museum of Art Exhibition Catalogue, *Jacqueline Kennedy*, 126–31; Kaplan, *Dreaming in French*, 60–68.

23. See *Life* magazine, September, 1960 (reference in Clippings file [Norman Norell], Costume Institute Library, The Metropolitan Museum of Art, New York).

24. Nevertheless, it was due in large part to that "taste" that she added "class" to the presidency and to the White House. See, James A. Abbot and Elaine M. Rice, *Designing Camelot: The Kennedy White House Restoration* (New York: Van Nostrand Reinhold, 1998).

25. Ed Gold, "'Friendless' Cassini Says He Got First Lady Nod on Merit Alone: Oleg Cassini Captures the Press," *Women's Wear Daily*, January 13, 1961, p. 1.

26. Oleg Cassini, *A Thousand Days of Magic: Dressing Jacqueline Kennedy for the White House* (New York: Rizzoli, 1995), 15.

27. Justine Picardie, *Coco Chanel: The Legend and the Life* (London: HarperCollins, 2010), 304–07.

28. John S. Major, "Givenchy, Hubert de," in *The Berg Companion to Fashion*, ed. Valerie Steele (Oxford: Berg, 2010), 371.

29. Deborah Sussman, Letter to Pat Kirkham and Sarah Lichtman, December 1999, Los Angeles.

30. Ross Hunter (producer), quoted in Deborah Nadoolman Landis, *Dressed: A Century of Hollywood Costume Design* (New York: HarperCollins, 2007), 216. See also Tamar Jeffers, "'Under All Those Dirndls': *Pillow Talk*'s Repackaging of Doris Day," in *Fashioning Film Stars: Dress, Culture, Identity*, ed. Rachel Moseley (London: British Film Institute, 2005), 50–61. For further discussion of Day's perceived "Americanness" (and her invitation to the Moscow Film Festival in 1961 precisely because of this all-American image), see David Kaufman, *Doris Day: The Untold Story of the Girl Next Door* (New York: Virgin Books, 2008), 302.

31. See Charlotte Herzog, "'Powder Puff' Promotion: The Fashion Show-in-the-Film," in *Fabrications: Costume and the Female Body*, ed. Jane Gaines and Charlotte Herzog (New York and London: Routledge, 1990), 134–59. See also Adrienne Munich, "The Stars and Stripes in Fashion Films," in *Fashion in Film*, ed. Adrienne Munich (Bloomington and Indianapolis: Indiana University Press, 2011), 260–80.

32. Cohen, "*Breakfast at Tiffany's*," 166–67.

33. According to Doris Day, Cary Grant was very involved in all details related to production values and costume design in *That Touch of Mink*. Grant saw an ad for a raincoat that he thought would work well for Day in the pivotal scene where she is splattered by mud from Shayne (Grant)'s cab, so he called the owner of the New York company that made the coat, Norman Zeiler, to discuss using it (Kaufman, *Doris Day*, 304). In the early 1950s, Bonnie Cashin worked for Zeiler making coat design illustrations, and her designs for him are in her archives (Norman Zeiler Rainwear Designs, Box 21, Folder 1; Box 22, Folder 2; Box 35, folder 6; Box 77, Folder 2, Bonnie Cashin Collection of Fashion, Theater and Film Costume Design [Collection 440], Library Special Collections, Charles E. Young Research Library, University of California, Los Angeles).

34. Filmgoers would have connected Grant and the United Nations to Alfred Hitchcock's *North by Northwest* (1959), in which Grant, playing a New York advertising executive, has a scene at the UN building.

35. Helen Gurley Brown, *Sex and the Single Girl* (New York: Bernard Geis Associates, 1962).

36. Joseph Wechsberg, "Haute Couture," in *Remembrance of Things Paris: Sixty Years of Writing from Gourmet*, ed. Ruth Reichl (New York: Modern Library, 2005), 57; Marie-France Pochna, *Christian Dior: The Biography* (New York: Duckworth, 2008), 145.

37. In the reign of King Henry VIII of England, for example, it was announced, "By the Statute of Apparel . . . it is ordained that none under the degree of an earl shall use sables" (cited in Ebenezer Cobham Brewer, *The Wordsworth Dictionary of Phrase and Fable* [Ware, UK: Wordsworth, 2001], 949). Also, for the inauguration coat, see Metropolitan Museum of Art Exhibition Catalogue, *Jacqueline Kennedy*, 60–61, and Cassini, *Thousand Days of Magic*, 36–41.

38. Jonathan Faiers, *Dressing Dangerously: Dysfunctional Fashion in Film* (New Haven, CT: Yale University Press, 2013), 77–80. (See also note 48.)

39. For Adolph Zukor and his furrier background, see: A. Scott Berg, *Goldwyn: A Biography* (New York: Knopf, 1989; New York: Riverhead Books, 1998), 15, 22, and 44; Carol Dyhouse, *Glamour: Women, History, Feminism* (London: Zed Books, 2010), 37. For fur and transformation narratives, see Faiers, *Dressing Dangerously*, 80.

40. There were sumptuary laws regarding wearing fur in the medieval period. For example, in 1363, English sumptuary legislation forbade the wearing of sable fur by the wives and daughters of knights and all those below them in the social order (Aileen Ribeiro, *Dress and Morality*

[New York: Holmes and Meier, 1986], 12–22). See also, Ken Albala, *Food and Faith in Christian Culture* (New York: Columbia University Press, 2011), 60, and Andrew Bolton, *Wild: Fashion Untamed* (New York: Metropolitan Museum of Art, 2005).

41. Carol Dyhouse, "Skin Deep: The Fall of Fur," *History Today* 61.11 (November 2011), accessed February 22, 2017, http://www.historytoday.com/carol-dyhouse/skin-deep-fall-fur.

42. Dyhouse, "Skin Deep: The Fall of Fur."

43. For these advertisements, see *Vogue* and *Harper's Bazaar* throughout 1960 and 1961.

44. *Vogue* and *Harper's Bazaar*, 1960–1961.

45. Julia V. Emberley, "Venus and Furs: The Cultural Politics of Fur," *Fashion Theory: The Journal of Dress, Body & Culture* 52 (May 2001): 221–23. See also Freyja Hartzell, "The Velvet Touch: Fashion, Furniture, and the Fabric of the Interior," *Fashion Theory: The Journal of Dress, Body & Culture* 13.1 (March 2009), 51–82. Hartzell draws on the work of Valerie Steele, who wrote that, in the nineteenth century, women and courtesans often wore the same fashionable clothing and that "Luxurious materials such as silk velvet and sable, reinforced the image of woman as an expensive and desirable object. Exclusivity created degrees of value, as did the style and sensuousness of particular fabrics and furs" (Valerie Steele, "Figures of Ill-Repute," in *Fashion Theory: The Journal of Dress, Body & Culture* 8.3 [September 2004]: 326). We must also bear in mind that both velvet and fur carried other connotations and were also worn by children and men.

46. "The Fur Coat," episode 10 of *I Love Lucy*, aired December 10, 1951 (McClay, *I Love Lucy*, 273). The television series *Father Knows Best* also had an episode devoted to a mink coat: "The Mink Coat," episode 20 of season 1, aired February 13, 1955.

47. *Vogue*, November 1960, p. 23.

48. Pat Kirkham and Marilyn Cohen, "*Breakfast at Tiffany's*: Fashion, France, Costume and Class" (paper presented at "The 1960s Revisited: Fashion, Cinema, Urban Space," City University of New York, March 12, 2010. One reviewer wrote, "The initial reels of this naughty-nice picture reiterate the tedious cliché that 'that touch of mink' is the reward a nice girl receives for being naughty" (unmarked clipping, Clippings File [*That Touch of Mink*], Performing Arts Division, New York Public Library). For sexual implications of the mink-lined coat, see also Faiers, *Dressing Dangerously*, 78.

49. See Pat Kirkham, *Saul Bass: A Life in Film and Design* (London; Laurence King, 2011), 115, and Thomas Doherty, *Hollywood's Censor: Joseph I. Breen and the Production Code Administration* (New York: Columbia University Press, 2007), 302. The code ended in 1968.

50. The numbers of women using the pill increased so rapidly in the early 1960s that the Pope convened the Commission on Population, the Family, and Natality in 1964 (Elaine Tyler May, *America and the Pill: A History of Promise, Peril, and Liberation* [New York: Basic Books, 2010], 128; Lara V. Marks, *Sexual Chemistry: A History of the Contraceptive Pill* (New Haven, CT: Yale University Press, 2010), 224–35.

51. Jeanne Thomas Allen, "*Fig Leaves* in Hollywood: Female Representation and Consumer Culture," in Gaines and Herzog, *Fabrications*, 122.

52. See Anne Boultwood and Robert Jerrard, "Ambivalence and Its Relation to Fashion and the Body," *Fashion Theory* 4.3 (August 2000): 301–21.

53. Tamar Jeffers McDonald, "Carrying Concealed Weapons: Gendered makeover in *Calamity Jane*," *Journal of Popular Film & Television* 34.4 (Winter 2007): 179–87, and "'Under All Those Dirndls,'" 50–61. Richard Dyer has discussed the complex nature of movie stars as social constructs mirroring cultural contradictions in his seminal work *Stars* (London: British Film Institute, 1979; 2nd ed., 1998).

PART III
Gender: Modernity and Tradition

8 The Fashioning of Julie Christie and the Mythologizing of "Swinging London": Changing Images in Sixties Britain

Pamela Church Gibson

No account of the relationship between fashion, film, and urban space in this most scrutinized of all decades could possibly leave out a consideration of actress Julie Christie, whose stardom was created by her two-minute stroll, skip, and canter through a nameless northern city in the film *Billy Liar* (John Schlesinger, 1963). This sequence dominated contemporary reviews of the film and endeared her instantly to audiences everywhere. Men, of course, were attracted by her youth and good looks: an Oxford University student poll instantly proclaimed her "The Most Beautiful Woman in the World." But she was equally popular with young women, perhaps in part for being what Kenneth Tynan described as "blazingly nice"—and most certainly for her mode of self-presentation.[1] The particular visual components of her style—the simple bob, wide smile, muted makeup, and short skirts—when combined with her seeming independence, made for an immediate appeal to younger women, then without a contemporary screen icon of their own.

Since she exemplified the emerging look of a decade when London was, however briefly, the most important of fashion capitals, she was instantly interviewed and photographed for magazines that ranged widely across demographics of class, age, and income. She was enthusiastically profiled in both the new teenage publications like *Honey* and *Petticoat* and the "colour supplements" that were fast becoming a staple of broadsheet journalism. Her appeal as fashion icon extended to the august tastemakers at *Vogue*, and she appeared in its pages on both sides of the Atlantic.

She moved seamlessly from publicity shots and film reviews to fashion spreads, unusual for actresses at that time, and she was photographed for several years after *Billy Liar* by the leading names in fashion. Early in her career, she was picked up by mainstream American journalists, fascinated as they were by the new and increasingly sexy "look" of young London girls.[2] *Time* magazine profiled Christie some weeks before the infamous issue in which "swinging London" was celebrated and dissected; so too did writers for *Life*. The release of John Schlesinger's *Darling* in 1965 would see her on the cover of the conservative US magazine *Parade*, which, in that same week (July 11) carried a message to America's youth from J. Edgar Hoover. When *Doctor Zhivago*, one of the top-grossing films of all time, was released in December that year, *Newsweek* devoted four pages to a consideration of the film, while its cover featured Christie, christened the "new darling of the movies." She appeared on magazine covers across Europe and behind the Iron Curtain, while specialized fashion publications would continue to use her until her final flight from Hollywood to a self-imposed solitude on her Welsh farm in 1974. Only recently, she granted an interview to a journalist writing for the incredibly chic *AnOther Magazine*. Interest in this star does not diminish.

However, here we will focus on the years when she was first in the spotlight and on the two films that created so much interest and attention. The fascination of the general public with Christie at the time was a result of the particular part she plays in *Billy Liar* and her subsequent, sharply contrasting role as the manipulative heroine of *Darling* two years later. Somehow, these two very different characters served to complement one another in the popular imagination, for in these two films, she seemed to epitomize in very different ways the much discussed new modernity of Britain, to embody perceived contemporary changes in sexual behavior, and lastly, to be an integral component in the new mythologizing of the metropolis. Significantly, these two roles also entwined her on- and off-screen appearance with the new youthful fashions that were taking over; she became seen as a key player in the cast of "swinging London." In fact, her image was construed as being so completely contemporary that her later forays into period drama generated some criticism for her apparent lack of fit with the historical periods portrayed.[3] She was also an interesting early variant within the problematic configuring of the 60s "dolly bird."[4] From the start, Christie, unlike the fashion models of the time who were usually featured in the pages of print devoted to the "dolly," had a forceful off-screen persona and a highly publicized nomadic lifestyle, telling the eager interviewers of her student days when, as she said, "I just dossed down in the flats of my friends."[5] When *Life* magazine later featured the actress on April 29, 1966, the caption beneath a sizeable photograph read "Julie Christie in motion, which she ever is," as she was shown running along a London street swinging a straw basket and sporting a gingham headscarf like those then on sale in the new London boutiques. In addition to her perceived independence and this desire to be on the move, she had strong, serious political views that set her apart. While still an aspiring starlet, she had posed handcuffed to black actor Cy Grant in order to publicize Human Rights Day in 1962. Lastly, she had an impeccable middle-class background, which the media dissected straightaway. This not only inflected her first two roles but also served to highlight the tensions around class and gender both in contemporary cinema and in the salacious consumption of the new "dolly bird" image, even of the "dolly bird" herself.[6] All this extradiegetic information that saw Christie featured so prominently across the media after the release of *Billy Liar* affected the reception of her performance in *Darling*, making its selfish heroine infinitely more appealing.

The "swinging London" to which she was seen as integral would later be coolly dissected by documentary filmmaker Peter Whitehead. *Tonite Let's All make Love in London* (1967) was constructed in part of interviews with those seen as central to the phenomenon of the new London, one of whom was Christie herself. Whitehead's particular style of interviewing here seemed at times intended to undercut both subject matter and interviewee, and arguably, only Christie and artist David Hockney hold their own, somehow triumphing over both director and context. Both are cheerful, unpretentious, and lacking in arrogance and emerge with credit, unlike some of the actors, models, musicians, and artists we hear in the film. Whitehead also found and featured an anonymous "dolly bird," whom he interviewed while she swung back and forth on a child's swing, musing on her own status and function. Here, questions around class, gender, and sexuality are raised, highlighted, and then left unanswered.

Darling has been discussed within the academy, while *Billy Liar* has been, by comparison, sidelined.[7] What is of importance to this chapter is that, in all the understandable focus on Christie's casting and persona, no one has actually noted the quite extraordinary difference and discrepancy between the two heroines she portrays. Liz in *Billy Liar* is cheerful, straightforward, honest, and utterly lacking in ambition or desire for material gain. As Billy tells his friend Arthur when they (and the audience) first spot Liz in the cab of a lorry on her arrival in the city, "She just goes wherever she likes." Liz supports this nomadic existence by working at a series of odd jobs. She does love Billy and in fact suggests that they should finally sleep together. Unlike his other girlfriends, she does not demand an engagement ring, and she tells him, "You know, there have been others." She says she would like to marry him one day, but first they must escape to London. Billy, trapped by cowardice and fantasy, contrives to miss the train. But Liz has her independence and will doubtless survive alone in the metropolis.

Diana Scott, the heroine of *Darling*, seen by some feminist critics as showcasing the new independence of young women, is also, as they are of course aware, selfish, manipulative, dishonest, and mercenary.[8] Despite her conscious attempts to advance her status, she ultimately does not fare well in the complicated "London" that the film depicts. Most tellingly, she can see only one way to advancing her career and altering her life—through the use of her sexuality as she moves from man to man. Although she too is seen moving throughout cities, and even across national borders, she is always, until the final sequence, escorted and seemingly guided by a man.

Interestingly, the line of dialogue that is so telling, in which she admits to Mal, the gay photographer, that she could easily do without sex—"I don't even like it all that much"—has been completely ignored by critics. There are also two important shots of her face at separate moments of intense sexual activity with two of the three lovers she takes in the film that seem to have escaped critical scrutiny. In the first of these, Robert (Dirk Bogarde) kisses her passionately after a quarrel, and as he unbuttons her shirt to fondle her breasts, she watches herself in a mirror with a kind of horrified fascination. In the second, suave Miles (Laurence Harvey) bends over her naked body in bed, and the camera closes in on her face as she winces with a mixture of pleasure and possible distaste. Diana's sexuality may indeed have presented on film the new freedom of 60s women, but she uses it for the most part as a bargaining counter. And her forceful seduction of Robert has also been overlooked, for it is she who takes the physical initiative that will move their affair on from a series of snatched romantic encounters and, so, free her from her stultifying marriage.

In the 1980s, Sara Maitland edited a volume of essays that looked back at the 60s, where her contributors—all women, including a novelist, a journalist, and a leading politician—reflected on what they had achieved. Maitland herself chose to interview Christie and called her essay, inevitably, "Everybody's Darling," describing the Christie of the 60s as "the embodiment of all my adolescent yearnings."[9]

It is, of course, Christie herself, rather than Diana, who is the "darling" in question and who made that problematic character so attractive. She herself describes Diana as "a new kind of heroine . . . who didn't want domesticity, didn't want to be tied down," not unlike Christie herself, who had stressed her own unwillingness ever to marry from the start.[10] And she also preempts academic writing on the film: "Of course at the time this was seen as greedy promiscuity and she had to be punished."[11] To this anthology, Maitland gave the title *Very Heaven*, quoting Wordsworth seemingly without irony.

Instead, it was Christie herself, so central to the iconography of the period, who was to sound a cautionary note about the 60s, speaking here with great honesty of her own self-doubt and insecurity in that period, when there were very prescriptive rules about what constituted a fashionable appearance. It is perhaps the tensions Christie herself notes that, combined with her increasing dislike of fame and her growing political involvement in different campaigns, in fact served paradoxically to reinforce her status and influence. Jean Shrimpton, one of the first supermodels, now describes herself as having been "a waif astray" for most of the 60s, and at their close, she fled from the city to a commune in Wales.[12] Her fellow model, the Biba poster girl Ingrid Boulting, also left London and now teaches yoga on America's West Coast.[13] Christie's flight from London and then from stardom reinforces the way in which she epitomizes both the decade and its repercussions.

Radical and Stylish: A Heroine for Changing Times

Christie had appeared in small starring roles before her success in this film. The actress originally meant for her role dropped out, and she was cast as Liz, the only girl to understand Billy and to share his dislike of their claustrophobic lives in this anonymous northern city. If "Liz" escapes by hitchhiking and visiting other cities on a whim (she has tried to persuade Billy to go with her to France in the past and failed) Billy, by contrast, escapes into an elaborate fantasy world. The film follows a single day in Billy's life when Liz appears in the city halfway through the morning. We—and Billy—spy her in the cab of the lorry as she arrives. While he moves off, the camera chooses instead to follow Liz as she clambers down and strolls nonchalantly through the city, seeming to command the grim industrial landscape around her. Of course, to move through urban space is not necessarily to command it; the flâneur of Baudelaire's poetry has no female equivalent, for the only woman who shares his nocturnal exploration of the city streets is the *passante*. But Liz, unlike Diana in the following film, actually does give the audience the impression that she can move happily through this city (and others) alone and unchallenged. She skips along a pavement, pulls a face at herself in a shop window, jumps across puddles, and trails her hand along a railing, all the while swinging her small shoulder bag.

What is as important as her command of her surroundings are the clothes she is wearing, the effect they would have had on contemporary audiences, and the sharp visual contrast with Billy's other girlfriends. Liz is seemingly set up here to represent, in every way, a new and different kind of life. She passes a wrecking ball as it demolishes a Victorian building, calls in at a record shop where the Top-Ten list is displayed in the window, and ends up at the official opening of a supermarket, that dubious symbol of the modern city. In her movement and her dress she looks forward, whereas Billy's two fiancées in this momentous year that brought so many changes seem to be looking back to the 50s. Middle-class Barbara has carefully set semi-pageboy hair with regulation "kiss curls," while her A-line skirt and white blouse with its Peter Pan collar evoke the middle-class styles of the 1950s. His other girlfriend, Rita, a waitress in a coffee bar, has heavily outlined eyes and the fiercely backcombed "beehive" hairstyle popular in the first years of the decade. Rita's skirts are tight, her heels are high, and she evokes a different kind of 50s look, the "glamour" of its British film stars. The J. Arthur Rank "charm school" had produced indigenous variants on Hollywood styles, homegrown answers to Marilyn Monroe and Liz Taylor in the opposed styles of Diana Dors and Joan Collins. Rita is styled and presented throughout to look as if she might well be an avid reader of British magazines such as *Picturegoer*.

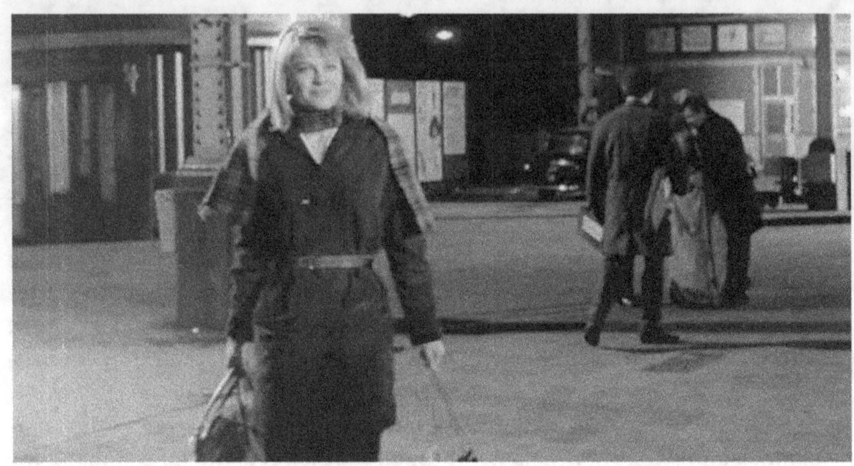

Fig. 8.1 Liz waits at the station—behind her, the train to London and the chance of escape.

Liz, however, looks radically different. Many iconic stars of cinema, in their most memorable fashion moments, look as if they could step from the screen, move across the fashion pages, and then go out to command the streets around them: James Dean in his jeans and leather jacket and Steve McQueen astride his motorbike in combat trousers and T-shirt. Like Liz as she is presented here, they have an instant contemporary appeal. Here, as throughout the film, Liz wears a long black jacket belted over a simple white shirt and straight skirt, while the bag that she swings is small and on a long strap. In the closing moments, when she waits for Billy on the station as they prepare to leave for London, she has added a checked muffler—a look forward, perhaps, to Bob Dylan's *Blonde on Blonde* album cover of 1966—and she now waves a tartan duffle bag. Billy, who carries an old-fashioned suitcase, loses his nerve and gets off the train on the pretext of getting them something to drink. Liz, the girl who is experienced, free, and above all likeable, is whirled away, alone, to a London that, though not yet swinging, was changing swiftly.

This particular year, 1963, was famously celebrated by poet Philip Larkin as an *annus mirabilis*, the year in which he suggests "sexual intercourse began." This he locates as being "somewhere between the Lady Chatterley ban . . . and the Beatles' first LP." He has in mind the "Profumo affair," a very British scandal involving two high-priced call girls, a member of Parliament, and a "society osteopath," in which some of the key events had taken place at Cliveden, the home of Lord Astor. The other momentous event of 1963 was, of course, the assassination of President Kennedy in November, along with the sense of instability it generated. Cinematic character Liz—like Christie herself, as interviews revealed—was moving forward, both aware of and part of the tumultuous changes taking place in the country around her. Paradoxically, it is the would-be mobile Diana who shows in her behavior and costuming the difficulties of adjusting as British society tried both to accommodate change and to shake off the legacy of the 50s.

It is important to note that the "Liz" of the novel on which the film is based was far less photogenic. Its author, Keith Waterhouse, was involved in the screenplay here, but he helped to transform his original "Liz"—plump, indifferent to her appearance, her green suede skirt slightly scuffed—into this visual emblem of modernity. British *Vogue* swiftly responded to her radical and stylish appearance by featuring both "Billy" (Tom Courtenay) and Christie-as-Liz posed on what looked like one of the Yorkshire dales seen in the film, with Christie wearing one of the newly fashionable smock dresses. The photographer here was the leading Paris-based American, William Klein.

During the years to follow, Christie would be photographed by Richard Avedon, Irving Penn, and David Bailey for fashion magazines, rather than for publicity purposes. In her former incarnation as a starlet, she had earlier posed for Bailey's friend Terence Donovan, a fellow member of London's "terrible three." This was the nickname given to the triumvirate of new working-class photographers (the third being Brian Duffy) who were to dominate British fashion pages across the next decade.[14] Donovan had portrayed her in 1962 naked except for a bed sheet, deliberately evoking the famous "last session" in which a naked Marilyn Monroe posed for Richard Avedon on an enormous double bed, her modesty protected by judicious rearrangements of the sheets. Significantly, after *Billy Liar* had defined Christie's on-screen and off-screen persona, there were no more shoots like this. She was now in more control and, for the most part, in fashionable dress rather than a state of undress, whether or not the pictures were for a fashion shoot.

Costume, Character, and Complexity in *Darling*

The most notable costumes for Diana in *Darling* were the designs of Julie Harris, who would be rewarded with an Oscar. She created the formal gowns and smart clothes that the successful model acquires as she moves onward and upward. But it is important to note that the Diana of the early sequences has a style of her own, rather as Hepburn does in the pre-Givenchy frames of her transformation films. Some of the clothes the young Diana wears were, in fact, purchased by Christie herself. There were trips with Harris, but she also went shopping alone.[15]

Barbara Hulanicki, who co-owned the new boutique Biba and created its clothes, tells us in her autobiography of watching a "tiny, beautiful blonde girl" trying on several outfits and discovering that it was Christie "choosing her wardrobe for *Darling*."[16] Her choice of boutique was significant. The clothes here were edgier and, above all, more affordable than those designed by Mary Quant for Bazaar, which had now been open for nearly ten years. Even though Quant wrote in her own autobiography that she dressed "dockers' daughters and dukes' daughters," her prices would have excluded many young girls.[17]

Quant has frequently claimed, too, that she was mainly responsible for the invention and the appearance of the miniskirt, though she has had to admit that couture designer Andre Courrèges played his part: his "space age" collection of 1964 featured short tabards and flat boots.[18] In fact, we see in this film these very same boots, worn by Diana on her trip to Paris with Miles. Obviously, no one designer could take the credit for the appearance and popularity of the miniskirt. There are a multitude of other factors to be considered, one which is surely the highly publicized appearance of Jean Shrimpton in January 1965 at the Melbourne Gold Cup in a skirt three inches above her knees. The many press photographs of the model were speedily beamed around the world, as the Gold Cup was a highly formal event and her appearance—without hat, gloves or stockings—was deemed both provocative and sensational.

The costuming of *Darling*, of course, took place in the previous year, but Christie, who swiftly adopted the new fashion, became linked in the public imagination with very short skirts. Two years later, when she presented an Oscar at the Academy Awards, her abbreviated dress attracted an extraordinary amount of press attention. There is an apocryphal suggestion that she was personally responsible for the edict that would follow and that is still in place: all women who attend the Academy Award ceremonies are required to wear long dresses.

Diana in *Darling* (ironically, since she becomes a fashion model) leaves her Biba smock dresses, trouser suits, and kilts behind as she progresses onward and upward. Her first lover, Robert, is a journalist, television pundit, and presenter of a new programme on the arts, and they meet when he is conducting interviews with passersby about changing social conventions. Her young, casual clothes are perfect in Robert's world, and she simply leaves her modest marital home for a larger flat in Chelsea.

But the particular milieu that she later enters, under the subsequent patronage of suave advertising tycoon Miles, requires her attendance at a series of very formal events. The social world of the 50s and its codes of dress and behavior have not disappeared, and Diana, far from symbolizing 60s independence in her search for self-advancement, seems instead to become trapped, as the narrative progresses, in a lifestyle redolent of the previous decade. The charity ball where we first see her perform as Miles's protegée is attended by businessmen, by one or two young "image makers" like the film director she fails to charm, and by the "old order," here represented by duchesses and a member of Parliament. She wears, here, the first of a series of increasingly formal evening gowns. For the premiere of her only film role, she wears a very low-cut evening dress that makes her look the epitome of a 50s starlet, an interesting contrast to the gold halter-neck

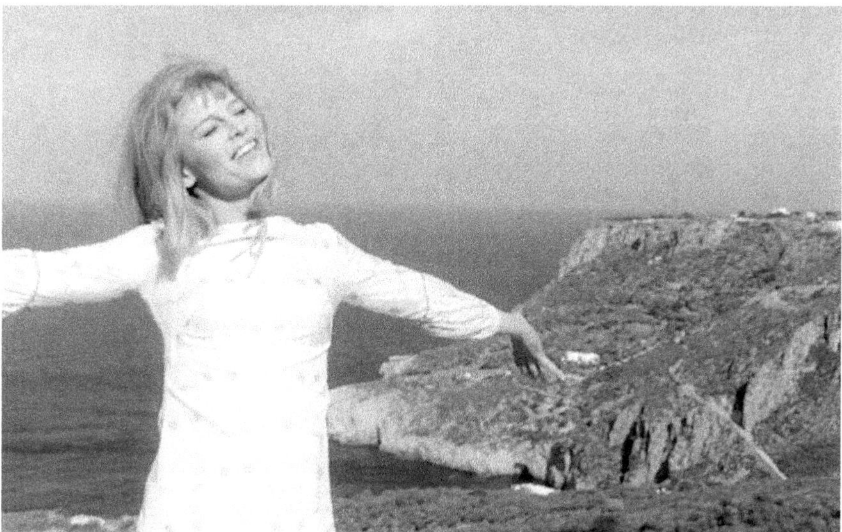

Fig. 8.2 Diana, youthful and relaxed once more during the holiday on Capri.

garment with its wide trousers that Christie the actress wore to collect her Oscar for *Darling.*

In fact, it is only on Diana's holiday in Capri with her friend and ally Mal, the gay photographer, that she is seen once again in truly youthful apparel: smocks, a striped T-shirt, white trousers, and a bikini. Otherwise she becomes more and more elegant in her dress: the Courrèges boots we see her wearing in Paris and the Cardin hat that she dons on her return for a gallery opening are attempts at Parisian chic and couture rather than a reflection of the style of "swinging London." And, by her marriage to the Italian prince, she finally removes herself from London, even from youth itself, and certainly from the new and rapidly changing fashions she wore and modelled earlier in the film.

Significantly, Diana divests herself radically of all her formal accoutrements at the film's close. We see her incarcerated alone in a vast palace as the result of this shrewd, loveless marriage to a prince old enough to be her father. After a lonely dinner with elderly servants looking curiously on, she rampages through her rooms, ripping off first her jewels, then her sumptuous evening gown with its embroidered train, and then her silk slip, until finally she stands, naked, before the glass in her bedroom. Her resplendent couture clothes are seen as symbolising the catastrophic choices she has made.

Academic Frances Tempest interviewed Julie Harris on September 16, 2010, after her appearance as the guest of honor at a special British Film Institute screening of *Darling* sponsored by *Elle* magazine. Leading British designer

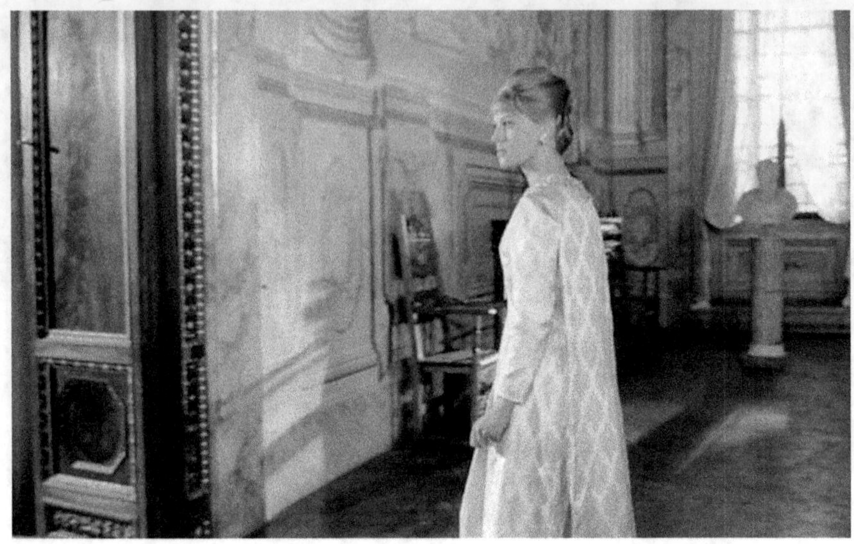

Fig. 8.3 Diana's splendid gown reflects the grandeur and formality of the palace where she is immured—far away from London, from youth, and from change.

Roland Mouret had chosen this as his favorite film and one that had a lasting influence on him. Harris, however, declared to Tempest that "it was just another contemporary film—I had no idea then that it would become such an iconic portrayal of the time." She goes on to say that, with hindsight, she can see exactly why that happened: the Americans, as she tells us, "fell in love with the whole swinging London image at that time."[19] Harris and Tempest discussed neither the contradictions I have noted within Diana's character nor the conflict between two decades, both of which, as I have suggested, are reinforced by the costume narrative.

These tensions, however, were lurking within that interview room, for Tempest noted that Harris "was more comfortable with the expensive, elegant outfits that Julie Christie wore when she became the Principessa della Romita than she was with the now iconic headscarves, caps and knee-socks of Sixties London." Harris explained that those accessories and all the youthful outfits Diana wears in the first half of the film were the result of "a quick shop with Julie Christie on the high street." But, when Tempest observed that the gingham and the headscarves reminded her of the early Biba "look," Harris was quick to say, "No, not—we didn't get anything from there."[20] Hulanicki's reminiscences, however, are obviously correct, for if we inspect her designs for 1964, we recognise several of the outfits that Diana wears. Harris was, however, happy to remember buying the elegant mink hat that Diana wears on her last unhappy trip to London. She tells

Tempest, "We bought that in Woollands," a very smart department store that has long since closed its doors.[21]

Diana's problematic progress and contradictory desires can, then, be charted clearly through her choice of clothes. We first see her in a deliberate reprise of her famous entry in *Billy Liar*: Robert spots her on the street as she walks confidently past a billboard swinging her handbag and wearing a simple trouser suit. He thinks she is just the right person to answer his onscreen questions as to why young people want to dispense with conventions. Diana tells him that "you just have to break away." But, although the film shows her managing to "break away" from her dull marriage, her fledgling career as a brassière model, and (briefly) from a dull if privileged middle-class background, what is interesting is her ultimate failure here.

Her on-screen appearance in the early scenes, of course, not only reflects Christie's own personal style, followed so eagerly in the press, but also shows off the new clothes then being created by young London designers she modeled in the growing number of fashion features in which she featured. These early images and their contemporary resonance show exactly how Moya Luckett could have constructed an argument designed to prove that both 'Diana' and Christie epitomized female mobility and independence. It is, of course, Christie herself, as she is inflected here, who is in fact the "key icon of female mobility in 1960s Britain."[22]

But Luckett's attempt to configure Diana in the same way is much less successful, and she has to admit that "Diana's agency is ultimately erased by men."[23] Diana certainly does not have any real control over her changing environment. Husband Tony is soon replaced by arts journalist Robert, but she finds life with an aspiring writer claustrophobic. She embarks on a sexual liaison with Miles, who has made her the "Honeyglow Girl" for a very lucrative advertising campaign and goes on to secure for her a small part in a horror film and then to make her the "Happiness Girl" in a second advertising campaigns. But, for all the emphasis on what Diana wants, what she achieves is only a modest modeling success, and it is in fact while filming a commercial for chocolates that she meets the Prince who offers her the chance of an advantageous marriage.

The world of advertising and high finance into which she moves with Miles is, as I have suggested, not at all the world of "swinging London." Miles—like Robert, rather older than Diana—may work in a very modern office block flanked by contemporary sculptures, but he travels to and fro in a series of 50s cars. We see him driving Diana across Paris in an American convertible, and he takes her to a supposedly "swinging" party in what seems to be an expensive brothel. He lives in a tasteful modernist flat complete with a set of Fornasetti plates, but his clothes are the smart clothes of a Fifties "lounge lizard," well-cut suits for the most part, with one glimpse of Italian "casual wear." His companions, with whom he takes Diana to a very sedate disco, are middle-aged, and in their company, Diana seems to be cut off completely from the London that reviewers and academics suppose her to embody. Robert leaves her, Miles turns out to be completely unreliable in every way, and she flees in panic into the twofold patriarchal embrace of the Prince and of the Catholic Church.

Interestingly, she can be "rescued" in this way only because of her middle-class credentials. Carrie Tarr twins her case study of *Darling* with that of a slightly earlier film centred around a sexually active young woman specifically to raise issues around social class.[24] Sapphire, the mixed-race heroine of that earlier film, is stabbed to death and her body left on Hampstead Heath, but Diana can be rehabilitated. The 60s have been configured as a decade when, supposedly, class barriers in Britain were lifted, but Diana's narrative suggests the opposite.

The cinematic heroine, like Christie herself, is a middle-class girl from a comfortable, affluent background: we glimpse a crocodile of convent girls, see her elegant mother proudly smiling at a school play, and finally attend a stifling dinner party hosted by her sister from which our heroine escapes, travelling across England in her nightdress. This rebellion is short-lived. Diana—and perhaps Liz, too—is cloaked in the protection of Christie's middle-class persona. Liz is clearly marked off from Billy's friends, fiancées, and family in both accent and demeanor.

All this is vital if we are to see Liz, Diana, and Christie herself as part of the supposed plethora of young, sexually active women in Britain so eagerly profiled within contemporary American journalism. Part of the problem around the figure of the "dolly bird" is that her sexual activity and her presumed availability raise questions around social class and gendered power.[25] Diana calls herself a "breakaway" in Robert's television interview, but as I have argued, her breaking away, motivated by a mixture of impulse and material ambition, is both unsatisfactory and short-lived.

Christie herself was quite different and later became increasingly identified with both counterculture and radical politics. This particular rebellious streak, one facet of her star persona, was celebrated in American *Vogue* of February of 1966, after the release of *Darling* and its many Oscar nominations. She was the model chosen for the main fashion feature that month, *The Breakaway Girl*. Here she wore dresses by British design duo Foale and Tuffin, which were now stocked, significantly, at Paraphernalia, the New York boutique where Edie Sedgwick shopped. The fashion copy stressed the particular way in which Christie was perceived: "With her thick pale hair worn just as it pleases her to wear it, her easy vitality and her level-eyed spill-the-beans candour, Julie Christie is the Breakaway's Breakaway."[26]

US *Vogue* was embracing the young, the new, and the British, and Christie represented the socially acceptable face of nonconformity, both on the screen and off. Her off-screen persona, in fact, had managed to erase completely the petulance, selfishness, and narrow ambition of Diana Scott, and what was celebrated instead was the cheerful nomad, "Liz," the explorer of urban space seemingly inextricable from the actress who created her. For the extradiegetic awareness of Christie herself, about whom so much information was swiftly made available after her instant popularity in *Billy Liar*, immediately became, in an extraordinary and perhaps unprecedented way, indelibly interwoven into the reception of her subsequent appearances on screen. Liz and Christie were, in fact, merged into one and the same person, her later screen incarnations would all be imbued with the perceptible warmth of that first character and fashion icon. Christie, like Liz, was seen as the stylish drifter to emulate: in May 1968, young girls across England bought *Petticoat* magazine for its free gift of a "Julie Christie tote bag." Drifters and nomads need a few essentials on their travels, and Christie/Liz had demonstrated new possibilities for young women.

PAMELA CHURCH GIBSON is Reader in Cultural and Historical Studies at London College of Fashion. Her publications include *Fashion and Celebrity Culture,* various edited anthologies, and numerous articles. She edits the journal *Film, Fashion and Consumption.*

Notes

1. Kenneth Tynan, review of *Darling*, *The Observer*, September 19, 1965.
2. See Christopher Breward, "The Dolly Bird," in *Fashioning London: Clothing and the Modern Metropolis* (London: Berg, 2004), 151–77, and Pamela Church Gibson, "The Deification of the Dolly Bird," *Journal for the Study of British Cultures* 14, no. 2 (2007): 99–111.
3. See Alexander Walker, *Hollywood England; The British Film Industry in the Sixties* (London: Michael Joseph, 1974), 272.
4. See Breward, "Dolly Bird," and Church Gibson, "Deification of the Dolly Bird."
5. Interviews with Julie Christie, quoted in Christine Geraghty, "Women and 60s British Cinema: The Development of the 'Darling' Girl," in *The British Cinema Book*, ed. Robert Murphy (London: BFI Publishing, 2001), 317.
6. Breward, "Dolly Bird," and Church Gibson, "Deification of the Dolly Bird."
7. See: John Hill, *Sex Class and Realism: British Cinema 1956–1963* (London: BFI, 1986); Carrie Tarr, "Sapphire, Darling and the Boundaries of Permitted Pleasure," *Screen* 26 no. 1 (1985); Geraghty, "Women and 60s British Cinema; Moya Luckett, "Travel and Mobility: Femininity and National Identity in Swinging London Films," in *British Cinema Past and Present*, ed. Justine Ashby and Andrew Higson (London: Routledge, 2000), 233–47.
8. See Geraghty, "Women and 60s British Cinema," and Luckett, "Travel and Mobility."
9. See Sara Maitland, "Introduction," in *Very Heaven: Looking Back at the 1960s*, ed. Sara Maitland (London: Virago, 1988), 4.
10. Maitland, "Everybody's Darling: An Interview with Julie Christie," in *Very Heaven*, 166–72.

11. Maitland, "Everybody's Darling," 167.
12. Jean Shrimpton and Unity Hall, *An Autobiography* (London: Ebury Press, 1988), 10.
13. Pamela Church Gibson, *Fashion and Celebrity Culture* (London: Berg, 2011), 167.
14. Elliott Smedley, "Escaping to Reality: Fashion Photography in the 1990s," in *Fashion Cultures: Theories, Explorations, Analysis*, ed. Stella Bruzzi and Pamela Church Gibson (London: Routledge, 2013), 143–57.
15. Frances Tempest, "Interview with Julie Harris," accessed September 13, 2013, Costume-onscreen.com 2011/06.
16. Barbara Hulanicki, *From A to Biba* (London: Hutchinson, 1983), 80.
17. Mary Quant, *Mary Quant by Quant* (London: Cassell, 1966), 75.
18. Caroline Evans, "Post War Poses 1955–1975," in *The London Look: Fashion from Street to Catwalk* (New Haven, CT: Yale University Press, 2004), 117–39.
19. Tempest, "Interview with Julie Harris."
20. Tempest, "Interview with Julie Harris."
21. Tempest, "Interview with Julie Harris."
22. Luckett, "Travel and Mobility," 140.
23. Luckett, "Travel and Mobility," 139.
24. See Tarr, "Sapphire, Darling and the Boundaries of Permitted Pleasure."
25. See Breward, "Dolly Bird," and Church Gibson, "The Deification of the Dolly Bird."
26. US *Vogue*, "The Breakaway Girl" [fashion shoot], February 15, 1966, 120, 121.

9 Women in White: Femininity and Female Desire in 1960s Bombay Melodrama

Anupama Kapse

White as a Fabric and Architectural Frame

Clothes have served as a visual shorthand for representing the class or moral stature of popular characters in Bombay cinema since the time of its inception. The hero, heroine, villain, and others could be recognized as stock characters quite simply by what they were wearing: the heroine in a simple, demurely draped sari; the vamp with an "ostrich feather fan, gold wig studded with rhinestones, and leggings under a dark blue bikini bedecked with shiny doodahs";[1] the Anglicized hero in a black suit, shirt, and tie; the poet or artist in a pristine white *kurta* pajama; a rich father in a pipe and dressing gown; a poor father in a tattered *dhoti* and vest; and a villain (often acting as a buffoon) with hair dyed red, bow tie, and bright checked jacket. In the formulaic cinema of the 1960s, narrative patterns were established according to the easy recognition of this stock cast. Characters were simple and bordered on the stereotypical: the virtuous heroine, the sexualized vamp, the rich and overbearing father, and the lascivious villain were standard characters who stood for specific social types with well-defined moral values or, sometimes, lack thereof.

Indeed, Bombay cinema mobilizes clothing as the primary sign of dramatic enunciation in highly coded and spectacular ways. If, as Peter Brooks has argued, melodrama is a form structured by the extreme polarization of good and evil, then, Bombay cinema is unapologetically melodramatic in its unfailing reliance on costume as an immediate and pervasive sign of this Manichean, black and white universe.[2] Christine Gledhill's *Home is Where the Heart is: Studies in Melodrama and the Woman's Film* was the first collection to foreground melodrama's significance as a form that mobilized women to signify wider cultural values.[3] Linda Williams has shown us how melodrama shapes dominant ideologies by exploiting conventions of realism to generate pathos through scenarios of victimized racial suffering.[4] Seemingly innocuous, melodrama feminizes and pushes the boundaries of pleasure and fantasy to articulate a wider social history of everyday life. It is why actresses repeatedly vouch for costume as the primary site for "stepping into character" to create a meaningful, realistic performance. Indian actresses turn to costume designers not only to look good but also to find the essential gestural key that charts an "arc" of identity and social frame for the character in question.

Helen (Helen Ann Richardson, known popularly her first name), the quintessential vamp of 60s Bombay cinema, describes how much effort would go into designing costumes for her spectacular dance numbers, which constituted a majority of the screen time accorded to her. Film magazines of the decade described her as "naughty-eyed" and would often carry stories of her trips to Europe.[5] The actress would shop in far-flung places in London to find buttons or sequins like the ones described above. She would bring them back for her tailors to create a unique costume for each of her films, which always featured a nightclub or cabaret style dance number with vigorous pelvic movements in elaborate gowns, bikinis, or strip tease items designed specifically to orchestrate a seductive dance number.[6] Helen's colorful clothing and Westernized looks have often served as the definitive imaginary for the 60s as a decade marked by bobbed hair, blonde bouffants, and flamboyant, tight clothing associated with luxury, leisure, and air travel in the jet age.

Jane Gaines has argued that, in American cinema, "the body was used in acting to express emotional complexities and to enunciate subtle gradations of feeling [but] costume was expected to simplify. Costume detail was 'fixed' in the Panofskian sense in that it stood, again and again for the same thing . . . it typified . . . [and] provided iconographic cues . . . [that] function[ed] as a substitute for speech."[7] The iconographic fixity of costume performs an important function in melodrama, where typification is necessary for staging action that presents familiar characters who embody conflicting social and moral values in a drama of extreme polarization. Yet, melodrama's negotiation of the quotidian requires it to interrogate and disturb its complacency, which is why Helen's costume must differ according to the specific milieu of each film, even though she repeatedly plays the vamp. While the vamp's sexuality was conceived as threatening, it could also function as a pairing for the heroine's alluring femininity: they belonged to the same moral schema, in which the one was good and the other bad. But neither was watertight: the vamp could be redeemed by an act of sacrifice, or the heroine could fall from grace because of a small indiscretion. It is in the pushing of boundaries that melodrama investigates the difficulty of conformism and the oppression of being "normal." Indeed, in the domestic melodramas of this time, the heroine's sari was embedded in an iconographic framework based on traditional values and a sense of community and much of the actress's performative labor consisted of fine facial expressions, subtle hand gestures, body movements, and poses. Scenery, setting, camerawork, and musical effects could test the stability of social codes by embedding them in costume design to play out scenarios that renewed the codes of naturalism and recalibrated acting style and performance.

As a color, white was usually associated with widowhood in Hindu culture, but Mahatma Gandhi's sartorial innovations—all of which challenged British colonial exploitation of Indian textiles, cotton in particular—transformed white into a color of social reform, independence, and progress during the 30s and the 40s, into a highly desirable "color" that expressed sobriety, political awareness, and moral fervor, with white acting profoundly as a colorless color, present by its very absence, waiting to be embellished by the body and accouterments of the actor. While dress has been used to configure and/or reinforce caste and class hierarchies since ancient times in India, the social and cultural meanings of white cotton garments originate in Gandhi's political campaigns. As a loosely draped, unstitched, and undyed garment, the white cotton sari and its male counterpart, the white dhoti, displaced the trousers, hats, shoes, and tailored coats of English manufacturers. They were also able to overcome distinctions of region, gender, and rank to strengthen and unify freedom as a cause anchored in dress reform that depended on labor and forms of manufacture that (literally) touched an Indian body politic. So popular was khaddar/khadi that tours and demonstrations of how to produce it "transformed [Indian] visitors into tourists of the nation" in the 30s and 40s.[8] Such exhibitions, organized as museum displays, featured an array of charkhas, yarns, and variations that conveyed enormous diversity in the texture, look, and feel of khadi, so much so that the sight of white homespun cotton became a heady and enticing one, something that spelled fortitude, liberation, and authority.[9]

Khadi's appeal lay in its ability to signify the twin ideals of *swadeshi* and *swaraj* (economic independence and self-rule) through a renewed semiotics of leisure and consumption that would be exploited by a range of popular media in the twentieth century. The cultural value of the white sari in cinema and public life hinges on khadi's value as a signifier of modernity and affective power in twentieth-century India. Dress is constantly reimagined and reconfigured by Bombay cinema and its film stars,[10] and it is for this reason that Indian film stars have often worn and designed their own clothes on film.[11] Such choices subvert the consumerist economy of what Roland Barthes has called a fashion system characterized by "obsolescence and rapid turnover:" [12] Indeed, cinema pushed the limits of the acceptable by pinning pleasure, desire, fantasy, and rebellion, as well their containment, to the body, dress, and performance of female stars. Further, Bombay cinema defines costume as a corporeal frame that synchronizes gesture and pose with lighting, music, and camerawork in an architecture of emotion and desire. Actresses and filmmakers alike made expedient use of this easily recognizable material and affective surplus. My interest in this essay is in the subtle, apparently "secondary" cultural value of the white sari in an era dominated by technicolor and cinemascope, which privileged overt displays of the female body against picturesque backdrops and sensational images of travel.

Costume shares an intimate relationship with performance in the black and white melodramas of 1960s Bombay cinema, one that has rarely been given serious consideration. Subtle alterations of dress reflect changing social mores in a rapidly modernizing India that was caught between new forms of consumption and the austere socialist ideology of the state. One particular slogan became a byword in government offices and public places after Jawaharlal Nehru became India's first Prime Minister (1947–1964): *Araam haraam hai* ("Resting is cheating"). The slogan foregrounded work over leisure and echoed the Gandhian ideal of selfless service for a free nation.

The present chapter turns to the white sari as a cultural marker, prop, and performative vehicle for orchestrating a range of expressive effects that were anchored in the social experience of dress in independent India. I argue that the white sari played an especially significant role in crafting some of the most sophisticated films of the 1960s, films shot in black and white in an era of color.[13] In particular, I focus on Meena Kumari as the actress most associated with wearing the white sari and with reinfusing it with a sensuality pervaded by female desire and rebellion. The actress Dina Pathak notes that postindependence cinema found exciting ways to drape the sari's flexible *pallu* (border or loose end) in increasingly creative ways for a range of expressive possibilities (shyness, eroticism, anxiety, female caregiving, fearlessness), and it brought fluidity and delicate grace to the actress's body movements.[14] However, Meena Kumari's moblization of white differs in many ways from Pathak's generic description of the sari. Key here is the privileging of stillness over movement such that the iconographic value of the white sari foregrounds its individual formal and political properties.

Drawing on films like *Duniya na Mane/The* Unexpected (V. Shantaram, 1937), Meena Kumari used the white sari in ways that recalled female political activists who wore white cotton to express their commitment to social service. As such, the white sari, often accompanied by props like a watch, umbrella, purse, or pen, signified the new, modern face of Indian femininity (with the bicycle accompanying the white dhoti wearer as the modern man). As a garment, the white sari was at once formal and informal, something that women could wear inside as well outside the home. Thus, it extended the woman's traditional association with the home outward into new public spaces such as the doctor's clinic or lawyer's office. As women became more visible and sought positions of authority in the fight for social equality and justice in the 1930s, the white sari—formerly a sign of the widow's sexual undesirability and a prison for her sexuality—reemerged as an attractive symbol of female emancipation just when the movies began to talk.

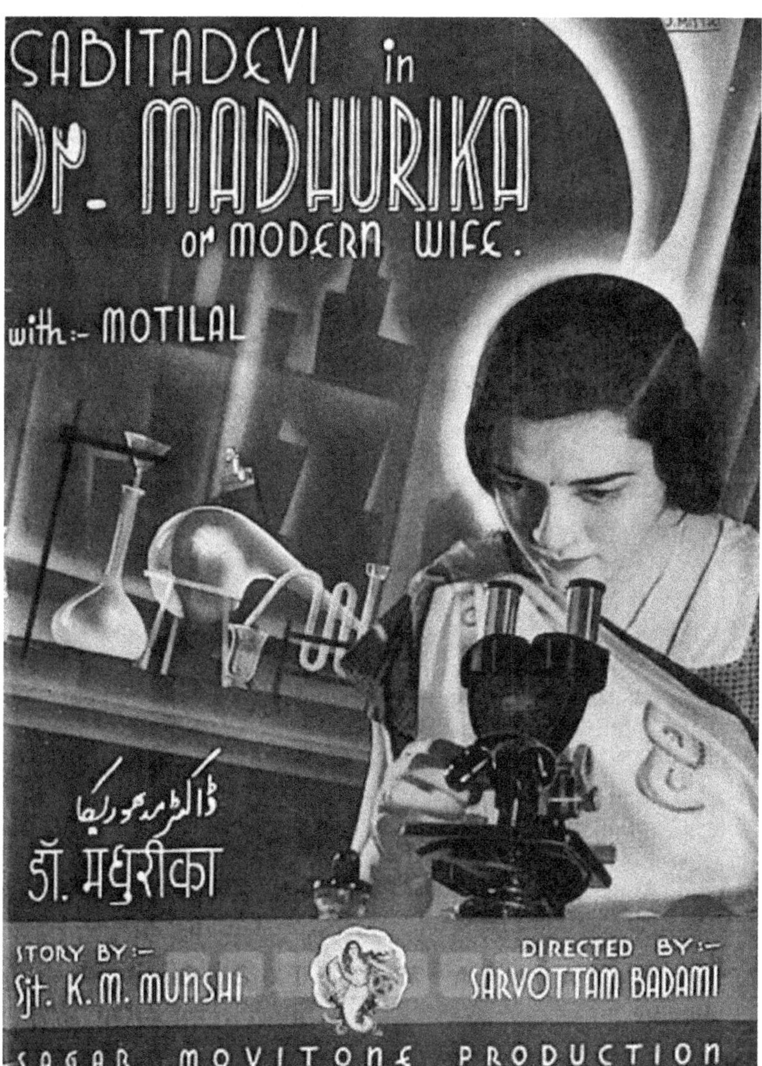

Fig. 9.1 Sabita Devi in Sarvottam Badami's 1935 *Dr. Madhurika* (*Modern Wife*).

Take, for example, the booklet cover of *Dr. Madhurika* (Sarvottam Badami, 1935), also known as *The Modern Wife*. The film revolves around a lady doctor who agrees to marriage on the condition that she will be allowed to practice birth control after marriage. While such films often punished their female protagonists for desiring independence, the demonstration of female empowerment and desire far exceeds its eventual containment. The heroine's white sari emphasizes her progressive outlook and doubles as a doctor's proper attire as she stands in a lab peering over a microscope, away from home, surrounded by the symbols of modernity. This, however, was primarily a desexualized image, and Meena Kumari would recharge this pre-independence figure with an aura of sensuality that threw the woman's immobility, fixity, and entrapment into sharp relief.

Raj Kapoor and the Erotics of White

In postindependence India, the iconography of the white sari was housed in a melodramatic configuration that materialized new star bodies and texts in the films I turn to below. Some of its most potent and generative embodiments occurred during the 1960s, both on and off the screen, even as color became an object of cinematic play and experiment. Prominent examples include the well-known playback singer Lata Mangeshkar, who lent her voice to the top heroines of the 1960s, including Meena Kumari, Waheeda Rehman, and Nutan, who lip-synced their song performances to her "golden" voice. Mangeshkar, known popularly as just Lata consolidated her status as a deglamorized star singer in the 1950s, a persona that became extremely significant in the context of the rapidly changing social mores of the 1960s. Not visible on the screen, the plain, off-screen, unadorned, unmarried, and virginal Lata often "buried her face in her notebook" when she appeared for public performances.[15] Her favorite attire was a white sari with a colored border. It bespoke the purity of her voice and drew attention to the face rather than the body, representing her simplicity and morally upright manner.

Neepa Majumdar summarizes the ensuing split between Mangeshkar's "pure" voice and the female actress's sexualized body thus: "Because of the decadence ascribed to the world of cinema and the logic of the split between pure voice and eroticized body, fan discourse stops just short of denying Lata's connection with cinema."[16] Thus, Mangeshkar's public persona focused attention on her voice over and above her body. Just as Mahatma Gandhi had mobilized these qualities to involve women in the freedom struggle, Mangeshkar deployed white to set herself apart from the blemish attached to film actresses. On the screen, the aural intensity of her voice was now available to the film actress, who could remediate it in a variety of ways. These developments are crucial for understanding the white sari's cultural value, which far exceeds its traditional linkage to widowhood in ways that conflate the history of the freedom movement with the new expressive possibilities of film as a medium. Further, Victorian novels like Wilkie Collins' *The Woman in White* (1859) were adapted in films such as *Woh Kaun Thi*/Who was She? (1964), which exploited the ethereal, Gothic qualities of white. As a color, white could express a highly desirable sobriety and moral fervor, as well as asceticism and purity.

The "postcard" imaginary of the 60s remained in tension with older modes of narrativization and cinematography. It relied on the heady possibilities of air travel to destabilize older moralities by foregrounding new modes of personal enjoyment, sexual expression and experimentation. In Ranjani Mazumdar's words:

> While the train and the automobile were mobilized for travel across India earlier in the decade, by the mid 1960s, we see the emergence of a cluster of films that showcased travel to foreign cities like Paris, London, Tokyo, and Rome. The most well-known of these films are *Sangam* (Raj Kapoor, 1964), *Love in Tokyo* (Pramod Chakravarty,1966), *An Evening in Paris* (Shakti Samanta, 1967), and *Around the World* (Pachi, 1967). These were box office successes which inspired other lesser known films remembered today only for their songs, including *Night in London* (Brij, 1967) and *Spy in Rome* (B.K. Adarsh, 1968) . . . [which] brought jet age aviation, tourism, consumerism, color film stock, fashion, and music into a distinct cultural configuration.[17]

In contrast, films like *Ek Hi Raasta/ Only One Way* (1956), *Sharada* (1957), *Ardhangini/The Ideal Wife* (1959), *Aarti* (1962), *Main Chup Rahungi/I will Be Silent* (1962) and *Bhabhi Ki Chudiyan/My Sister-in-Law's Bangles* (1962) stand out as black and white melodramas that uphold older aesthetic practices and moral values that predate color. Shot in tightly confined studio interiors (eschewing outdoor scenes that would require new kinds of color stock) these films are primarily addressed to a family audience. They emphasize traditional ideals while foregrounding femininity and female desire, and many starred Meena Kumari, who came to be known as a female tragedienne par excellence because of her portrayal of lonely, neglected, and beautiful female characters.

Other films such as *Dhool Ka Phool*/Blossoms in the Dust (1959) and *Gumrah*/The Lost One (1963) starred the actress Mala Sinha, who excelled in representing the "the unfortunate girl who faces the disastrous consequences of illicit love."[18] Unwanted pregnancies are recurring elements in films in which Sinha stars, a trope that is a symbolic expression of anxieties surrounding the arrival, easy availability, and sometimes failure of low-cost birth control in the 60s. *Dhool Ka Phool* and *Gumrah* do not contain any direct references to birth control, however, they dramatize the fear of sex without contraception, as well as heterosexual relationships that exceed marital norms, just as they echo the new nation's regulation of sexual practices through family planning agendas aimed at controlling an "exploding" population.

Public debates on birth control can be traced back to the 20s and 30s, preoccupations that were centrally addressed in *Dr. Madhurika*. They came into sharper focus during the 1960s and drew attention on the easy availability and convenience of the pill, preferred over other methods of contraception such as male vasectomies and the female loop. Newspaper and magazine articles that identified "developing countries" as the worst culprits of the population explosion come to mind immediately here. An article in the November 24, 1963, issue of *The Times of India* singles out "birth control pills as scientifically feasible for countries facing the problem of over-population," such as India. Indeed, the pill brought family planning into the center of a middle-class public discourse of sexuality that situated birth control as a new item of consumption and cultural progress in the changing social mores of the 60s.

While Sinha's star persona explored the consequences of sexual rebellion in ways that simultaneously gave vent to and reign in female desire, one cannot overstate director Raj Kapoor's overt pin-up style eroticization of the white sari in films like *Jis Desh Mein Ganga Behti Hai*/A Nation where the Ganges Flows (Radhu Karmakar, 1960) and *Sangam*/The Confluence (Raj Kapoor, 1964)—an aesthetic that reworks painter Raja Ravi Varma's voluptuous turn-of-the-century oil paintings of fair-skinned, mythical Indian women into a mass-cultural idiom of calendar art. Indeed, Kapoor frequently eroticizes the politics of Gandhian dress reform by playing off the white sari against states of undress and Westernized forms of costume design.

Kapoor's fetishization of the white sari began early in his career, going back to his creative collaboration and partnership with costar Nargis (Dutt) in *Barsaat/Rain* (1949) and *Awara/The Vagabond* (1951). His banner R. K. films featured the young lovers on the studio logo. The Nargis–Raj Kapoor duo introduced "an entirely new idiom of love" to postindependence India during the 1950s.[19] It was an affair based on a frank declaration of love and creative collaboration both on and off the screen, one that openly defied cultural prohibitions against romantic love, particularly because Kapoor was married to a girl of his parent's choice (Krishna). While Nargis's on-screen persona was feisty and rebellious, the white sari became necessary to manage her off-screen persona. As Neepa Majumdar points out, "In descriptions of Raj's influence on her choice of clothing, we see the literal whitewashing from Nargis's persona of the negative associations of her cinematic career [as an actress]. After her relationship with him, she came to be known as 'the woman in white' because she wore only white saris, and the 'poise, dignity and sophistication' associated with this image were attributed . . . . [to] 'Raj . . . who really groomed her.'"[20] The white sari played a crucial role in transforming Nargis' star persona from that of a free-spirited symbol of love to the fearful icon of *Mother India* (Mehboob Khan, 1957), facilitating a dramatic switch to the red, muddy hues of a rural peasant's burnt sienna, filmed in spectacular Gevacolor in the 1950s, the first of its kind. As I have argued elsewhere, Mehboob combined Nargis' simple off-screen image with that of her as a sexual, procreative *shakti* or force to be reckoned with, as *bharat mata* or *Mother India*.[21]

Nargis retired soon after *Mother India*, but the white sari continued to exercise authority as a signifier of power and purity. Madhu Jain writes that all the women "who came under [Kapoor's] spell switched to white . . . the roll call is long: Nargis . . . Lata Mangeshkar, his muse . . . Simi Garewal, his *cheli* [disciple] . . . Devyani, the late gossip columnist and film journalist . . . above all his elegant wife Krishna, ever draped in her crisp white organzas . . . Damoji . . . Balraj Sahni's first wife . . . all [in] white."[22] It could be said that all of Kapoor's films play out a primal fantasy built around the woman in white. *Barsaat* and *Awara* pivot around the twinning of Mangeshkar and Nargis as his creative muses. On the rebound, he replaced Nargis with the angelic, virginal Vijayantimala (Bali), a southern Indian actress who was relatively new and could be molded as a sexualized Kapoor heroine. *Sangam* is Kapoor's first color film, and he uses the white sari in an otherwise spectacular display of color to mark his hero's sexual desire and erotic fanstasies. As Surendra Miglani writes in a tribute, "*Sangam* marked . . . Raj Kapoor's [entry] . . . into [the] colour era (its technicolour prints were reportedly processed in London). This was also the first film . . . Raj Kapoor shot abroad. In fact, the picture postcard kind of foreign scenes, shot by Radhu Karmakar, had such a hypnotic effect on the viewers that shooting films on foreign soil became a fad among filmmakers in the wake of *Sangam*."[23]

Thematically, *Sangam*, which means "the union," has strong sexual overtones and rose to the demands of an era of color that portrayed exhilarating screen romances in exotic locales. Yet, the decade of the 60s was also "marginalized for its hedonistic desire for pure sensation and spectacle [and] remains [one of the] most unstable in its iconography and its mythologies."[24] Reviews of *Sangam* focus on the long drawn out, implausible triangulation of female desire as problems that color fails to compensate for.

> Impressive though it is . . . [*Sangam*] falls short of expectations. Its blurbs have compared it with "Gone With the Wind." Only where length is concerned does the comparison stand. But one wonders whether that length was necessary at all. For the four long hours it is stretched, what is spun out is a mere triangle drama. Shorn of the visual grandeur of the unfolding, the experience is disappointing.
>
> Highly reminiscent of films like "Chaudhvin ka Chand," the story told is that of two friends. . . . What is seen is hard to believe. These two pals, responsible men though they are, act irrationally in the belief that their friendship is more sacred than their love so that they may play with the life of the woman they adore. One feels that, in their hands, Radha is a pitiable victim of a "friendship-at-any-cost" fixation rather than an object of their professed, ardent love.[25]

While this review appreciates *Sangam*'s grand spectacle of color à la *Gone with the Wind*, audiences were clearly irked by the centrality of male agency, which reduces Radha (Vijayantimala) to "a mere plaything" (figures 9.2 and 9.3).

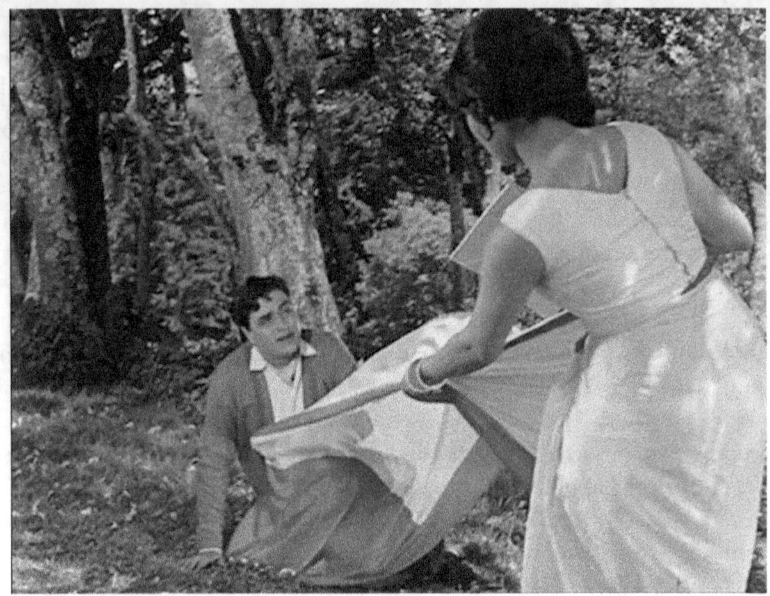

Fig. 9.2 Radha's (Vijayantimala) white sari unravels in Raj Kapoor's 1964 *Sangam* (*The Union*).

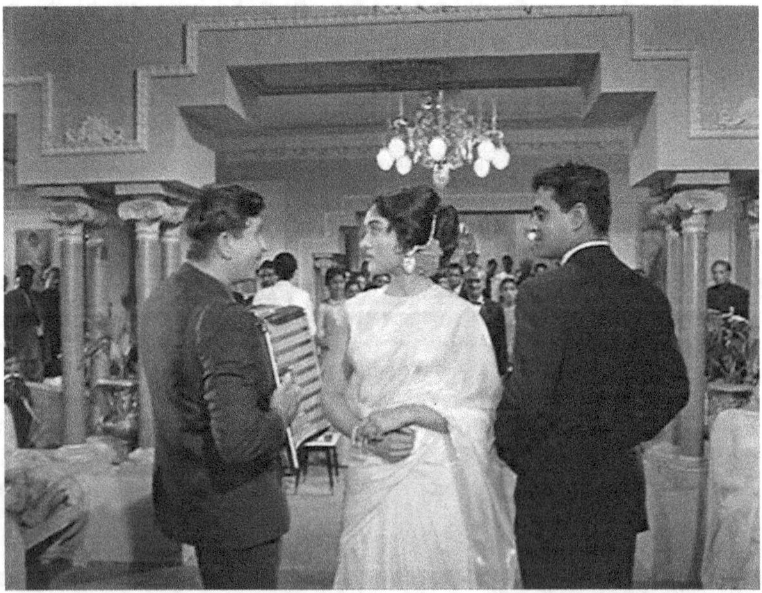

Fig. 9.3 The triangulation of desire in *Sangam*.

Indeed, Radha's entire wardrobe consists primarily of white saris and salwar kameezs with colored borders and trims that recall the Mangeshkar–Nargis duo but are devoid of their earlier gravitas. Two notable song sequences feature Vijayantimala in a red swimsuit and burlesque cabaret costumes that stand out as departures for the usually sari-clad heroine. These two sequences underscore a complicated erotic spectacle predicated on a destabilization of the iconographic fixity of the white sari by their very exceptionalism.

Sangam is reminiscent of studio melodramas such as Douglas Sirk's *Written on the Wind* (1956), which explored the pleasure and peril of male bonding by triangulating sexual desire in the baby boom era. Put simply, Kapoor turns the woman in white into a blank canvas upon which the drama of male desire can be written. *Sangam* returns to *Awara*'s oedipal father–son conflict through a homoerotic bonding and rivalry that emerges in the fraught topos of the *dosti* (male friendship) of two friends (Gopal, played by Rajendra Kumar, and Sundar, played by Kapoor) who desire the same woman (Radha).

The contest between love and friendship plays out on the woman's body, elegantly draped in white. Ironically, technicolor shows off white as the "color" that allows masculine desire to be staged upon it while emphasizing the virginal innocence and purity of a woman who is trapped within a tense and deeply contradictory relationship with her own desires and motivations. Many of the films that Kapoor directed after *Awara*, be it *Sangam*, *Mera Naam Joker* (My name is Joker, 1970), *Satyam Shivam Sundaram* (Truth, God, Beauty, 1978) or *Ram Teri Ganga Maili* (God, Your Ganges is Dirty, 1980) can be seen as variations of this key theme: all return in selective or overt ways to the trope of the woman in white. Kapoor's lurid eroticization of women in transparent, wet saris and his evacuation of political meaning from the white sari work against a pre-independence ethic that was subsumed by a sexualization of white in the era of color.

Meena Kumari and the Illumination of Desire

I have been arguing so far that Raj Kapoor's eroticization of the white sari unsettles its centrality as a core emblem of female purity and moral probity in Bombay cinema. In a majority of Kapoor's films, the point of view is structured by male desire and masculine anxiety. By contrast, Meena Kumari's star persona in *Dil Apna aur Preet Parai* (My Heart, Another Love, Kishore Sahu, 1960) returns insistently to the nurturing and feminine qualities of white, identified as the definitive attire of a doctor–nurse melodrama.

Born on August 1, 1932, Mahjabeen Ali Bux aka Meena Kumari was the daughter of musician Ali Bux. Her mother, Iqbal Begum, is believed to be a descendant of Rabindranath Tagore's family. Although she started as a child actress in mythological genres, it is only with *Baiju Bawra* (1952) that Kumari achieved recognition, standing out for the restrained sensuality of her performance. The suffering wife ready to consume alcohol to impress her wayward husband in *Sahib Bibi aur Ghulam* (Master, Mistress and Slave, Abrar Alvi, 1962) remains her best-known role, and together, her performances in *Daera* (The Role, Kamal Amrohi, 1953), *Dil Ek Mandir* (The Heart is a Temple, C.V. Shirdhar, 1963), *Kajal* (Kohl, Ram Maheshwari, 1965) and *Phool Aur Patthar* (The Flower and the Stone, O.P. Ralhan, 1966) represent a consistent body of work that showcases her exceptional ability to embody both, the limits and the possibilities of female desire in the decades following independence.

Perhaps no other actress could portray the sublimation of female desire as well as Kumari. In these films, the white sari provides an ideal architectural frame to embody not only feminine purity and strength but also a fine and intimately wrought drama of her innermost thoughts and feelings (see figure 9.5). Ira Bhaskar argues that the Indian melodramatic mode articulates specific desires that are gendered as feminine in order to negotiate the problems and pressures of modernity:

> The narratives of struggle for education and self-emancipation are shot through with other desires that do not quite square with the disciplinary regimes and ideals of modern selfhood that nationalist ideology gifted women. It is these contradictions and ambivalences constitutive of gender identities and of a modernity that was "itself not one" (Chakrabarty 1994, 87) that makes for a 'drama of inertia and entropy' (Rodowick 1987, 275) as characteristic of the particular form of the melodramatic in the films I am discussing.[26]

Turning to films like *Gopinath* (1949) and *Daera* and *Devdas* (1955), Bhaskar considers entropy as the key domain for expressing female yearning and aspiration, which is squashed at the very site of its articulation. It is here that the expressive regimes of song and dance performance and the white sari, as the "especially sensitive medium of [white] cloth,"[27] become so germane to understanding suffering and self-sacrifice as potent vehicles for signifying female desire in 60s Bombay cinema.

Like *Sangam*, *Dil Apna aur Preet Parai* (henceforward, *Dil*) also revolves around a triangulated romance, but it differs significantly from the former in its narrative and visual appeal, especially in its dramatization of the woman's sexuality and her point of view. *Dil* is best characterized as a medical melodrama that exploits the dramatic possibilities of white better than any other genre, with Kumari playing a nurse, Karuna (whose name can be translated as "the compassionate one"), and clad in a nurse's white uniform or white sari for the entire duration of the film. The cinematography was done by the German cinematographer Josef Wirsching, who started his career at Himansu Rai's studio

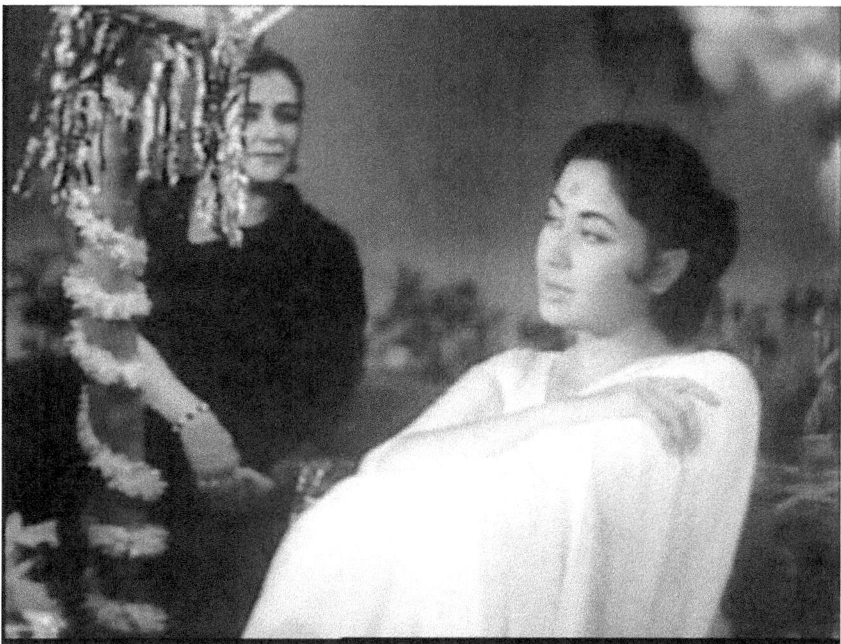

Fig. 9.4 Karuna (Meena Kumari) celebrates Dr. Sushil Verma's (Raaj Kumar) wedding by singing the title song in Kishore Sahu's 1960 *Dil Apna Aur Preet Parai* (*My Heart, Another Love*).

Bombay Talkies, which introduced German expressionistic lighting to Indian cinema during the 1930s. Wirsching's exquisite black and white photography crafts a star image that combines symbolic and textual functions: tragedienne, ethereal beauty, and poetess with seductive voice. Karuna is the ideal caregiver, helpmate, mother, wife and daughter-in-law, and her nursing work also serves the broader purpose of justifying her presence outside the home while allowing her to embody the defining features of traditional Indian femininity. Close-ups abound, drawing attention to Kumari's large, sad, kohl darkened eyes and her loose, flowing hair, while the white sari remains a diegetic signifier of her work as a nurse, functioning simultaneously as an indicator of her demure, selfless, and morally upright demeanor (figures 9.4 and 9.5).

Karuna falls in love with the hospital doctor, Sushil Verma (Raaj Kumar), who, unlike her errant, deceased alcoholic father, is devoted to his work. An ideal choice for her, Dr. Verma loves Karuna but is forced to marry a woman of his mother's choice in spite of his love for Karuna. As such, *Dil* is a film that extends the trope of suffering to its male and female protagonists through plot contrivances in order to pointedly bring to the surface the plight of individuals

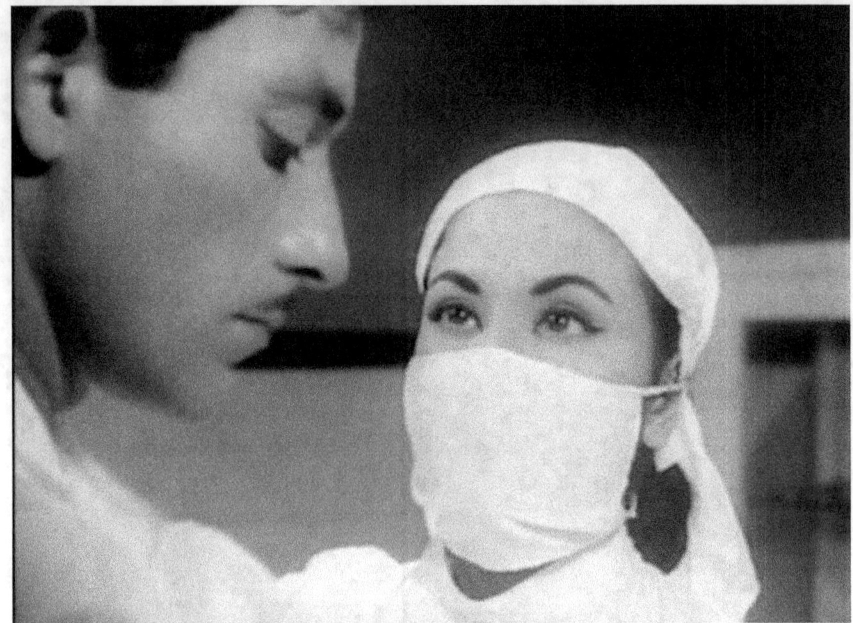

Fig. 9.5 Karuna (Meena Kumari) assists Sushil Verma (Raaj Kumar) in *Dil Apna Aur Preet Parai.*

caught up in forces beyond their control. Indeed, white becomes a key "color" that reiterates the moral legitimacy and transcendental purity of a professionally legitimized and sanctified but otherwise impermissible extramarital desire.

One cannot overstate the importance of the aural in demonstrating the urgency of such desire, which is based on a modern, professional empathy over and above loyalty to traditional family values. This urgency is enacted performatively in the song "Ajeeb dastan hai yeh, kahan shurur kahan khatam" ("This is a Strange Story, Where Does It Begin and When Will It End?"). Ironically, Karuna is asked to sing a song to celebrate the doctor's wedding. Instead, her song mourns the death of her love. The number becomes an elegy, with funereal qualities that marshal white as the color of mourning (see figure 9.4). Lighting, mise-en-scene, and the setting of the boat offset a dark night of simmering passion in a conflation of *eros* with *thanatos*, tropes that simultaneously express desire and entrapment, enveloping the principals in a shroud of immobility (see figures 9.6 and 9.7). Reviews were positive and described *Dil* as a "deeply moving drama," praising Raaj Kumar and Meena Kumari for their fine acting. [28] Expressionistic lighting highlights Karuna's unspoken, formidable attraction (Figure 9.6).

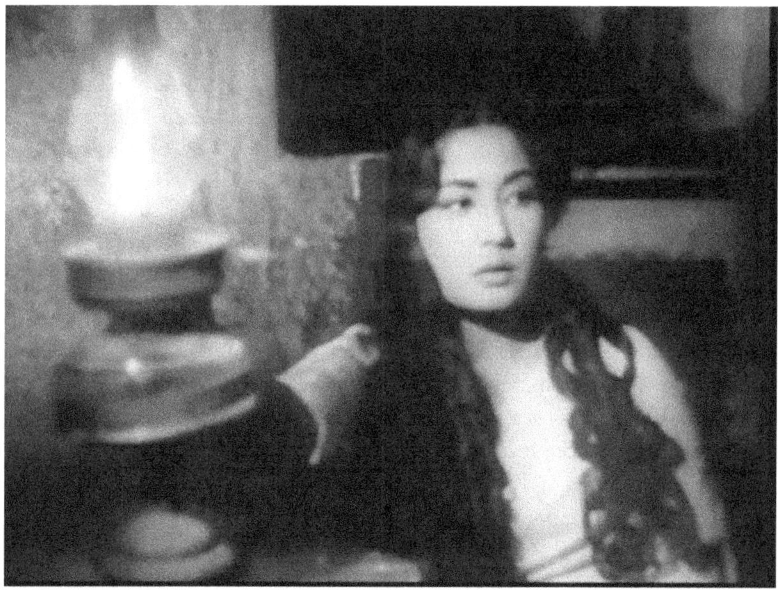

Fig. 9.6 The illumination of desire.

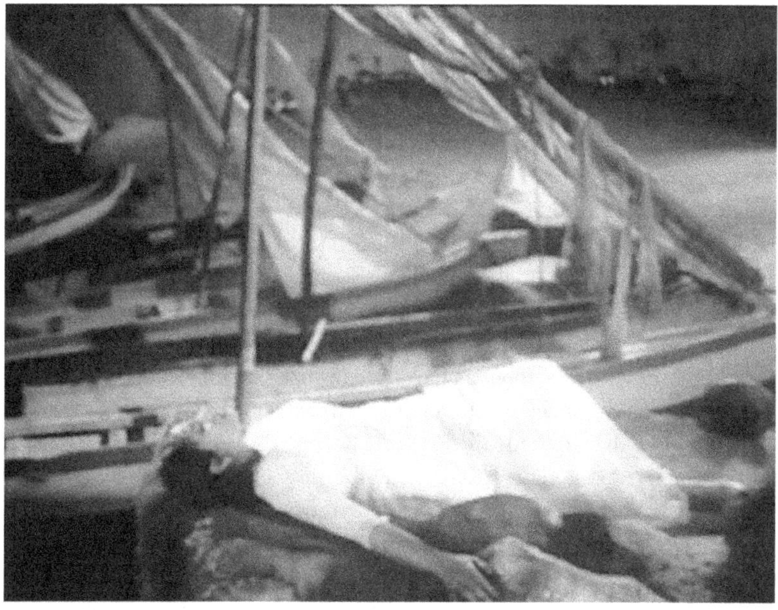

Fig. 9.7 Fixity and stasis in *Dil Apna Aur Preet Parayi.*

The beach and its flowing waters emerge as primal spaces that embody, assert, and illuminate Karuna's desire in the dark of the night. Complemented by composer Madan Mohan's soulful music, close-ups endow Karuna with a tranquility that conveys her intense beauty and sense of self. The breezy night and attractively lit boat communicate the depth and sensuality of Karuna's inner thoughts and state of mind. When Kusum, the doctor's wife inquires if she loves the doctor, Karuna has no hesitation in admitting that she does, though she will not stand in their way. The articulation of desire pervades the performative and narrative logic of the film, and thus, desire remains centrally anchored in the restrictions *Dil* imposes on movement to highlight the sensuous allure of illumination in its high contrast black and white photography.

Indeed, *Dil* amalgamates the purity of Mangeshkar's voice with visuals of Kumari's innocence and sexual desirability, which become enshrined in a mutually constitutive discourse of purity and moral transcendence. Song performances are marked by tight, still framing with soft focus lighting that is finely attuned to Kumari's economical use of gesture. Even when the camera stays on her, Kumari rarely moves. The focus remains on her face, eyes, and lip movements, and sometimes her entire body, reinfusing Lata's demure pose with the sheen of erotic allure. The camera pans and sways around Kumari to enact a rhythm of feelings while Raaj Kumar sits unmoving in a frozen posture that evokes fixity and inertia. Close-ups accentuate Karuna's inner feelings for the benefit of the audience, structuring a play of desire that unfolds from her point of view (figures 9.4 through 9.7).

The white sari reemerges as a complex signifier that returns to Victorian ideals of feminine purity in a new sexual economy where denial animates the possibility of fulfillment. Public culture is caught in the lyrical charm of white as it illuminates women's entry into a large professional workforce in spaces fraught with the possibility of redemption. Areas like the hospital were marked by an increasing freedom that also exerted pressure on the feminine by asking the woman to conform to new forms of regulation. In this, Kumari was especially sensitive to the sensual but entropic qualities of white. No other female star could conflate nobility and the thwarting of desire as effortlessly as she could. For the first *Filmfare* awards ceremony (then known as the Clare awards), Kumari appeared in a white silk sari in which the sheen of silk remained in extreme tension with the purity of white, a practice that invited "the loudest cheers" from the audience.[29]

While subsequent generations remember her as a "tragedy queen" who suffers in silence, it is important to acknowledge several press reviews that appeared in *The Times of India* applauding the appeal and finesse of her performance. Similarly, biographies and recollections written by Vinod Mehta and Hanil Zaveri remain utterly fascinated by her unconventional relationships with directors Kamal Amrohi and Gulzar, and the newcomer Dharmendra.[30] Furthermore,

Kumari's Urdu poems established her talent and artistic refinement in spite of her alcoholism, marriage and divorce from Amrohi, her husband and mentor. Amrohi and Kumari would work together on *Pakeezah* in spite of their divorce (*The Pure One)*; begun as a spectacular costume drama in color in the early 60s when they were married and released posthumously after Kumari's sudden death from liver cirrhosis in 1972 after their divorce. Needless to say, the pathos of the off-screen narrative was underpinned by intense love and loss, togetherness and separation, qualities that reappeared in the moving image version in a searing dialectic of color and noncolor. The culminating sequence has Kumari dancing with barefeet in red on a white carpet strewn with broken class, rendered crimson by the rapid and irrepressible movement of the star's bleeding feet. Put simply, the pining female star of the 1960s could not have been created without the enormous possibilities of white and its architecture of self-expression as a performative vehicle and engine of desire.

These new iterations retain the vitality and charm of Gandhian sartorial innovation while subjecting them to postindependence sexual mores as portrayed by teachers or nurses. Teaching and nursing were minor, secondary jobs that employed women to supplement a primary workforce of male doctors, lawmakers, and educators. In this mixed social universe, the nurse's white uniform stood out amid the muted color of black and white films, and then it stood out amid the spectacularization of color that arrived in Bombay cinema in the 60s. The affective meanings of white transmuted diegetically into the nurse's uniform as an ideal embodiment of the woman's commitment to serving the family and, indeed, the modern nation by joining its hospitals and schools. A number of films featured nurses as female protagonists in the 1960s. Prominent examples include *Dil Ek Mandir*/The Heart is a Temple (1963) and *Khamoshi*/Silence (1969), both of which feature doctor–nurse or nurse–patient romances.

Yet, as the word "sister" implies, nurses were expected to be chaste, refrain from sexual contact with doctors and patients, and display the "moral qualities . . . of sobriety, honesty and truthfulness." Far from reproducing this ideology faithfully, *Dil* manages to sneak a humorous interlude into an otherwise serious drama, a scene where the head nurse admonishes her nursing staff for applying lipstick while on duty and then promptly colors her lips after confiscating the lipstick. The head nurse is played by Ruby Myers (known by her screen name, Sulochana, "Pretty Eyes"), the reigning star of India's silent and early sound era, and the entire sequence underscores the performative power of white to link it to the progressive films of the 1930s.

The founder of nursing institutes in India, Florence Nightingale, recommended nursing only for "women of good character and fair ability."[31] She even suggested a penalty if nurses got married, deeming that a breach of contract if they were trainees or if they were serving in hospitals in India. In the 1960s, images of nurses played with the dramatic possibility of making money from and professionalizing what Julia Hallam calls "'the womanly' skills associated with caring for people." As such, the doctor–nurse romance foregrounded female desire by focusing attention on women who motivated narrative action and embodied new forms of social power as they "grew from innocence to experience" through a romanticized professional relationship experienced outside marriage and the traditional bounds of the family.[32]

As a fabric and color, then, the white sari is imbued with political and ideological meanings that are especially relevant for signifying the desire, agency, and increased upward mobility of female protagonists and social types in Bombay cinema. In the melodramas of the 1960s, it signified a range of meanings that were central to the cultural legitimation of women as members of a new workforce that redrew and challenged old boundaries between home and world and between public and private. Khadi's affective surplus, initially as the fabric of independence and later as an embodiment of social reform and female emancipation, played a seminal role in these ideological negotiations and became especially generative for transmuting melodrama into a cross-cultural, Indian cinematic mode with wide cultural appeal and enormous discursive power.

ANUPAMA KAPSE is Associate Professor of Film Studies at Queens College, City University of New York (CUNY). Her book *Film as Body Politic* focuses on affect, embodiment, and citizenship in early Indian cinema (forthcoming from Indiana University Press). Her areas of interest include film history, spectatorship, melodrama, and star studies in South Asian culture. Her research has been published in *Indian Film Stars; Figurations in Indian Film; Framework;* and *South Asian Popular Culture*. She is coeditor of *Silent Cinema and the Politics of Space* (Indiana University Press, 2014), which won the SCMS Best Edited Collection Award in 2015.

Notes

My sincere thanks to Eugenia Paulicelli, Drake Stutesman, Louise Wallenberg, Jane Gaines, Monika Mehta and Meheli Sen for their comments on earlier drafts of this paper.

1. Jerry Pinto, *Helen: The Life and Times of an H Bomb* (New Delhi and Mumbai: Penguin India, 2006), 88.

2. The most well-known example of the argument is found in Peter Brooks, *The Melodramatic Imagination: Balzac, Henry James, Melodrama, and the Mode of Excess* (New Haven, CT: Yale University Press, 1995).

3. Christine Gledhill, *Home is Where the Heart is: Studies in Melodrama and the Woman's Film* (London: British Film Institute, 1987), 18.

4. Linda Williams, *Playing the Race Card: Melodramas of Black and White from Uncle Tom to O.J. Simpson* (New York and Princeton, NJ: Princeton University Press, 2001).

5. *Filmfare*, "Naughty Eyed Helen." [full color spread]. April 3, 1954.

6. Take, for example, Aishwarya Rai, who describes, in a classic behind-the-scenes manner, working with her costume designer, Sabyasachi Mukherjee, to envision her character, Sofia d'Souza, in the DVD release of *Guzaarish*/ The Request (Sanjay Leela Bhansali, 2010). For an account of Helen's role in designing her costumes, see the DVD release *Bombay Talkie* (Ismail Merchant and James Ivory, 1973), which includes a detailed interview from the documentary *Helen, Queen of the Nautch Girls*, filmed in 1973.

7. Jane Gaines, "Costume and Narrative: How Dress Tells the Woman's Story," in *Fabrications: Costume and the Female Body*, ed. Jane Gaines and Charlotte Herzog (London and New York: Routledge, 1990), 187–88.

8. Lisa Trivedi, "Visually Mapping the 'Nation,: Swadeshi Politics in Nationalist India, 1920–1930," *The Journal of Asian Studies* 62 no. 1 (2003): 15.

9. Emma Tarlo, *Clothing Matters: Dress and Identity in India* (Chicago: University of Chicago Press, 1996).

10. See my "What Happened to Khadi? Dress and Costume in Bombay Cinema," in *Figurations in Indian Film*, ed. Meheli Sen and Anustup Basu (London and New York: Palgrave-Macmillan, 2013), 44–66.

11. See in particular Bhanu Athaiya's autobiography, *The Art of Costume Design*, in which she recollects such collaborations with female stars like Meena Kumari and Rekha (New Delhi: Harper Collins India, 2011). Athaiya specializes in handlooms and Indian fabrics that signify permanence and connectedness as hallmarks of traditional Indian clothing.

12. Roland Barthes, quoted in *Cloth and Human Experience*, ed. Annette B. Weiner and Jane Shneider (London and Washington, DC: Smithsonian Institution Press, 1991), 11.

13. For a nuanced account of costume design in film, see Drake Stutesman, " Costume Design, or What is Fashion in Film?" in *Fashion in Film*, ed. Adrienne Munich (Bloomington and Indianapolis: Indiana University Press, 2011), 17–39.

14. *The Sari*. ed. Mukulika Bannerjee and Daniel Miller (London and New York: Berg, 2008), 29.

15. Sanjay Srivastava, "Voice, Gender and Space in Time of Five-Year Plans: The Idea of Lata Mangeshkar," *Economic and Political Weekly* 39, no. 20 (2004): 2025.

16. Neepa Majumdar, *Wanted Cultured Ladies Only! Female Stardom and Cinema in India 1930s–1950s* (Chicago: University of Illinois Press, 2009), 194–95.

17. Ranjani Mazumdar, "Aviation, Tourism and Dreaming in 1960s Bombay Cinema," *Bio-Scope: South Asian Screen Studies* 2, no. 2 (2011): 251.

18. *The Times of India*, December 13, 1959, 3.

19. T. J. S. George, *The Life and Times of Nargis* (Chennai, India: East–West Books, 1994), 77.

20. Majumdar, *Wanted Cultured Ladies Only*, 155.

21. *Mother India* would later become the inspiration for Yash Chopra's 1975 *Deewar* (*The Wall*). For a detailed gloss on the end of the Nargis-Raj Kapoor collaboration and her return to Mehboob, her initial mentor, see my essay on *Mother India* in *The Routledge Encyclopedia of Films*, ed. Sarah Barrow, John White and Sabine Haenni (London and New York: Routledge, 2015), 356–359.

22. Madhu Jain, *The Kapoors: The First Family of Indian Cinema* (New Delhi: Viking for Penguin India, 2005), 122–23.

23. Surendra Miglani, "*Sangam* Revisted," Spectrum, *The Tribune* (India), March 28, 2006.

24. Mazumdar, "Aviation, Tourism and Dreaming," 151.
25. *Filmfare*, July 10, 1964, 39.
26. Ira Bhaskar, "Emotion, Subjectivity, and the Limits of Desire: Melodrama and Modernity in Bombay Cinema, 1940s–50s," in *Gender Meets Genre in Postwar Cinema*, ed. Christine Gledhill (Chicago: University of Illinois Press), 166.
27. See Christopher Bayly, "The Origins of Swadeshi (home industry): Cloth and Indian Society, 1700–1930," in *The Social Life of Things: Commodities in Cultural Perspective*, ed. Arjun Appadurai (London and New York: Cambridge University Press, 1986), 285–317.
28. *The Times of India*, May 6, 1960, p. 10. See also the November 8, 1959, and August 4, 1963, issues of *The Times of India*. The latter congratulates Meena Kumari and Raaj Kumar as excellent tragic actors with "an aura of impending martyrdom."
29. *The Times of India*, April 19, 1963, 10.
30. Hanil Zaveri, *Mehmood: A Man of Many Moods* (Mumbai: Popular Prakashan, 2005), and Vinod Mehta, *Meena Kumari: The Classic Biography* (New Delhi: Harper Collins, 1972; repr. 2013).
31. *The Selected Writings of Florence Nightingale*, ed. Lucey Ridgely Seymer (New York: Macmillan, 1954), 248.
32. Julia Hallam, *Nursing the Image: Media, Culture and Professional Identity* (London and New York: Routledge, 2000), 33.

10 Mago's Magic: Fashioning Sexual Indifference in Ingmar Bergman's 1960s Cinema

Louise Wallenberg

Introduction

After a rather long period of a mediocre film production, at least when seen in relation to the so-called golden age of Swedish silent cinema that lasted approximately between 1917 and 1924), the Swedish film industry would come to obtain a certain critical acclaim in the 1950s, and this "new" favored position was due to winning a few prestigious prizes at international film festivals. While this newly applauded cinema was received and talked about as something particularly "Swedish," its sudden acclaim was mostly due to the work of a single man who soon was to become synonymous with Swedish (national) cinema:[1] Ingmar Bergman. Up until his death in 2007, Bergman held an unquestioned position as the ultimate bearer not only of Swedish film but also of Swedish culture at large. If we are to believe John Orr, he even bore culture at large for the time: "The death of Ingmar Bergman . . . marked the end of an artist who defined the twentieth century as much as Joyce, Picasso, Stravinsky, Eliot or Brecht."[2]

Although Bergman managed to achieve a notable position as a director already in the 1950s, it was, however, his more somber and more modernist 1960s films—films like *Såsom i en spegel/Through a Glass Darkly* (1961); *Nattvardsgästerna/Winterlight* (1963); *Tystnaden/The Silence* (1963); *Persona* (1966); and *Vargtimmen/Hour of the Wolf* (1968), all of which are hugely successful with film critics—that would secure him a leading position as an auteur within Swedish and European cinema, a type of "art cinema" that, in the early decades of film studies as a discipline, was considered in opposition to Hollywood cinema, as if one of its arty "others."

Although Sweden had been understood as an alternative (if not queer) nation in terms of its politics and culture in previous decades, as has been argued by Daniel Humphrey, it was in the 1960s that the nation would become synonymous with its equality politics, its progressive gender politics, and its supposed sexual liberation, three phenomena that were closely aligned with, if not the very consequences of, a successful social democratic governing and guidance.[3] And, because so many of Bergman's films deal with sex and gender, and especially with the intimate relationship between the two sexes, his oeuvre lent itself to be understood as a sort of display window for this politics. It is not surprising, then, that his cinematic representation of gender would strongly contribute to and inform the notion of how Sweden and Swedes were perceived, both within and outside the country.

This is not to say that Bergman was the exclusive, nor the first, interpreter and portrayer to contribute to a distinctive perception of the nation, for as Humphrey writes, "the image of Sweden . . . predates Bergman's emergence on the world stage, and . . . that image can actually be seen as having helped Bergman's 'authority,' rather than the other way around."[4] But his impact on the preexisting image was immense, and in the early 1960s, he would be referred to as "the big Swede" and the huge popularity of his work would be labeled "Bergmania." This popularity has led to numerous articles and books, on both the popular and scholarly levels, about his extensive film production, most of which have dealt with its art cinema qualities, its often innovative technical style, and its grim and painful representation of heterosexual love, as well as of loneliness, loss, and death.

Very little attention has, however, been paid to the importance of costumes (and fashion) in his films, despite the fact that his work includes not only modern (and clearly modernist) dramas but also more historical comedies and dramas that give great prominence to costume. Queer costume designer Mago (Max Goldstein) worked closely with Bergman in most of his 1960s productions and, along with photographer Sven Nyquist, contributed to the making of the rather unique Bergmanesque vision. Dressing female film stars Bibi Andersson, Liv Ullmann, Harriet Andersson, Eva Dahlbeck, Gunnel Lindblom, and Ingrid Thulin in new and strict fashions (often in black and white slacks and jumpers), Mago helped create and sustain the notion of a uniquely Swedish womanhood as an utterly modern type from the North of the country. This modern woman constituted a complex category within Bergman's universe, always more complex than her male counterpart, who often appears as "a child with adult genitals," as Berman once described himself and several of his male on-screen characters. Refusing any simple feminine either/or stereotyping, this new modern woman was clearly struggling with her somewhat paradoxical position within a patriarchy that proudly proclaimed "advocacy" of feminism but still placed (and therefore implicitly valued) men over women.

While producing costumes and fashion for many various filmmakers active in the Swedish film industry (Arne Mattsson, Kenne Fant, Jörn Donner, and Vilgot Sjöman could be mentioned), Mago has become most known for his collaborations with Bergman. And yet, Mago's extensive work for the screen, as well as for the stage, has received little, if any, attention amongst Swedish (and international) film and/or fashion scholars. This is surprising, given that he was one of the more crucial contributors to the cinematic representations of Bergman and that Bergman has been so debated and analyzed by so many scholars—and it is also very telling. Costume designers (like many others in the film industry) seldom get much credit.

By focusing on Mago's collaboration with Bergman in the 1960s, this chapter sets out to expand the already ample academic and critical work on Bergman's film production, most of which has focused on its art cinema qualities, its grim representations of gender relations, and its representations dealing with the laborious fear of loneliness and death, which often is intimately connected to a constant questioning of God's existence.[5] Because very little attention has been paid to the role that costume, dress, and fashion play in Bergman's work, the very expansion lies in addressing these aspects, and so this chapter has one purpose: to pay a specific tribute to Mago, who, during half a century (from the early 1950s to the mid-1990s), played a crucial role within Swedish film (and theater) production, and who must be understood to have been imperative to Bergman's 1960s productions. While the focus is put on *Persona*, featuring modern fashions that helped emphasize a new Swedish womanhood understood to be at odds with any old, traditional notions of womanhood and sexual difference a as "natural" and desired, a few other films in which Mago's work appears will also be taken into account so as to provide a fuller picture of his oeuvre and his contribution to cinematic representations of gender.

Mago and Swedish Film in the 1950s and 1960s

The name Mago, of course, was an acronym for his full name, Max Goldstein, and it was used to evoke magic, giving him the aura of being a magician with his pencil and his imagery. After having managed to escape from Nazi Germany as a young boy in the 1930s, and after settling down in Stockholm with his parents and his brother, he started out as a fashion illustrator for the Swedish evening press in the early 1940s. Most of these early sketches were of famous Swedish women—or rather, of their dresses—as they frequented grand gala premiers at the theater or at the movies. By the end of the 1940s, he started to sketch costumes for theatre and vaudeville, and in the early 1950s, he started sketching costumes for cinema. When retiring in the mid-1990s, he had made costumes for some 125 theatrical plays and for some 40 films. While he clearly dominated the Swedish costume scene, it should be noticed that Mago was also productive outside of Sweden, making costumes for film and theater productions in neighboring countries such as Norway, Denmark, the United Kingdom, and Germany, as well as in the United States.

In a sense, Mago was for the Swedish film scene what Adrian Gilbert was for Hollywood, often creating somewhat excessive and impossible costumes. In many instances, his most affluent costumes were, to quote Jane Gaines, next to "impossible," that is, unwearable.[6] As unwearable garments, made to be seen and appreciated from a distance, they were not only highly inspirational as stage or screen costumes but also correlated to fashion, or to the very notion of fashion (as something intangible, untouchable, and abstract). While indeed material and tangible on the screen and stage, worn by actors and actresses to help them get into character, they were also fantasy constructions, imaginary to the audience in all of their alluring unwearability, just as fashion and the fashionable are. But, whereas Gilbert would pass over from costume to fashion production, launching his own rather successful fashion brand, Mago would never try to make it into fashion. It is interesting, however, that he would make private dresses for a few of his prima donna friends to be worn off-stage, but these dresses were made for specific performative occasions such as galas and premiers and were, thus, to some extent, more costumes than pure fashion—although they were highly fashionable.

After his death in April of 2008, Mago was referred to in the daily Swedish press as the "elegant of the Swedish stage" and as a "shameless aesthete."[7] While praising his contribution to the screen and the stage, journalists seemed to be in agreement that his skills as a tailor were next to nonexistent: it was emphasised that, although he clearly had been a magician with his pencil, drawing the most spectacular dresses and costumes, he never learned how to sew. This was a fact that Mago never had tried to cover up: he always gave an enormous amount of credit to his seamstresses, dressmakers, tailors, shoemakers, and so on, and in his memoirs, he pointed out that, without them, there would have been no Mago.[8] Just like Christian Dior, he was a *visionaire*, never having claimed to be a dressmaker. Yet, as they also did with Dior, the press noted his lack of sewing skills in order to implicitly question his talent.

As a *visionaire*, Mago was indeed without boundaries. This limitlessness became most blatant and manifest when it came to the making of women's costumes, and his strong and profound sense of glamour and his love for effeminacy were indeed his signatures, dressing the actresses (and his female friends) in the most unashamed feminine garments and accessories. And, whereas many of his film (and theater) productions would excel in using costumes to emphasize sexual difference (although clearly always constructed and performed), his costumes in the productions for Bergman seemed instead to strive for an erasure of this very difference. This visual erasure—what I argue is a fashioning of sexual indifference—is here not only in stark contrast to Mago's other productions; it also helps question the dominant view on Bergman's films as reinforcing the notion of sexual difference as natural and inevitable and, hence, as undeniably straight.

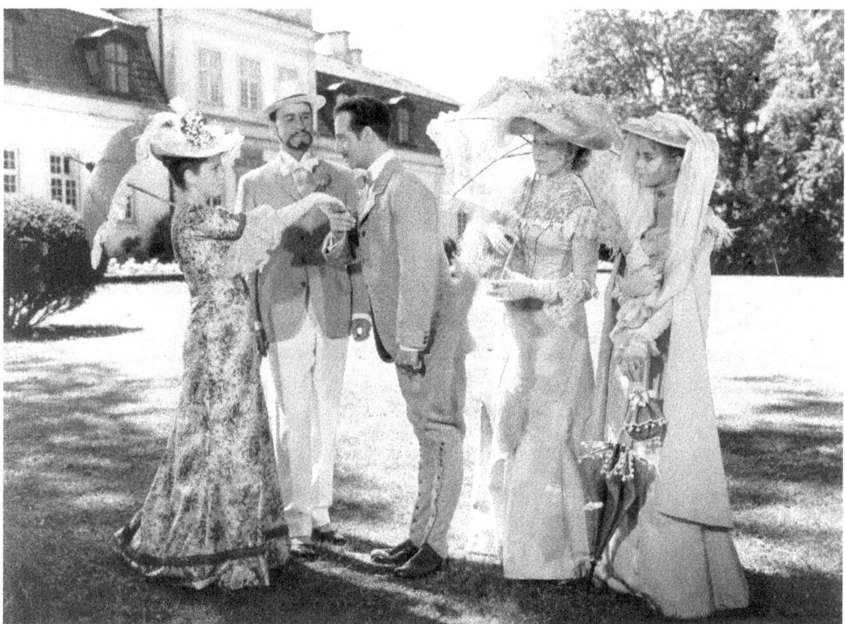

Fig. 10.1 Performing sexual difference through Mago's excessive costumes in Ingmar Bergman's *Smiles of a Summer Night* (1955). Photograph by Louis Huch. Image courtesy of Sommarnattens leende, © 1955 AB Svensk Filmindustri.

Yet, the very excess in costumes that served forcefully to inscribe a scenario in which sexual difference was law in films such as *Sommarnattens leende/Smiles of a Summer Night* (1955) and *För att inte tala om alla dessa kvinnor/All these Women* (1964)—could also serve to question and upset this difference as truth: through its very excess, sexual difference may be read and understood as a mere construction. In Mago's case, his excessive costumes served to underline a sort of unchallenged agreement between two sexed and gendered parties, a silent agreement that this difference needed to be upheld, incorporated, and expressed—that is, performed. This does not relate only to Mago's work, of course: I would argue that all costume that is excessively gender-marked can be read as a masque used to cover up a possibly failed sexual difference (i.e., a sexual difference that is not—in fact, cannot—be achieved) and, hence, as pointing at or even uncovering a possible sexual indifference. Here, indifference should be understood both as not only a lack of difference but also an active refusal of difference.

Whereas the 1910s and the early 1920s, generally known as the golden age of Swedish silent cinema, had proven to be extremely successful for Swedish film production both nationally and internationally, the following two decades were marked by a popular and local film production that clearly did not cater to the international audience. Whereas the silent period had provided fantastic epic stories based on Nordic literary masterpieces, on one hand, and charming, witty, and elegant upper-class comedies, on the other, the 1930s and 1940s offered mostly simple local comedies and a few heavy dramas, most of which were set within a working-class setting.[9] Only in the early 1950s would Swedish film again reach a critical acclamation internationally, and this acclaim was dependent on the young and upcoming Bergman. He had started out as a scriptwriter and filmmaker in the mid-1940s, writing the script for *Hets/Torment* (1944) and *Kris/Crisis* (1946), the latter of which he also directed. Between these two films and his international breakthrough film, the young love drama *Sommaren med Monika/Summer with Monika* (1953), he had already directed a total of ten films, most of which had had international screenings but did not go down well with the critics.[10] *Summer with Monika* was then followed by a string of successful films in the 1950s: *Gycklarnas afton/Sawdust and Tinsel* (1953); *Smiles of a Summer Night* (1955); *Smultronstället/Wild Strawberries* (1957); and *Ansiktet/The Face* (1958), all of which would be critically acclaimed on the international scene. In the 1960s, Bergman, like Jean-Luc Godard, Alain Resnais, Federico Fellini, Akira Kurosawa and Michelangelo Antonioni (to mention but a few), took up a leading position as an auteur filmmaker within what is often referred to as "art cinema" (or, European art cinema). This gave him the solid and unquestioned position as Sweden's most famous director, a position he would keep until his death in 2008.

As has been indicated above, the 1960s was also the decade in which Sweden as a nation gained renown for its (supposed) gender and class equality, as well as for its forward gender politics. Furthermore, this was when the nation became celebrated (and scorned) for its audacious sexual liberation, which was most vividly represented abroad through the various sexual education films that were being made with the aim to educate and "free" men and women sexually, although these films were misinterpreted to a certain extent. For instance, in the United States (where they were highly popular), they came to be classified as pornographic films rather than educational sex films. These films aside, though, it was Bergman's successful cinematic production that came to play a central role in how Sweden and Swedes were being perceived. There were, of course, other directors who managed to have their films screened abroad, a few of whom would also win prestigious film prizes at international festivals—Bo Widerberg, Mai Zetterling, and Vilgot Sjöman could be mentioned. But their impact was lesser because they were not as prolific as was Bergman, who was an extremely productive director and whose film production after 1953 was highly supported from within the industry and well-received outside of it. Philip Moseley, one of the first scholars to write on Bergman, states, "Bergman has thus been remarkably free of the pressures towards compromise which have warped so many talents in the history of the industry. He has taken maximum advantage of the privilege."[11]

Modern Women and Feminist Critique

The iconic Bergman actresses—to whom Marlene Dietrich is said to have referred as "the Bergman widows"—are central here: together they came to represent this Swedish type of woman mentioned above, a kind of northern woman who was quite distinct and quite different from other earlier representations of women. Over the years, many film scholars and critics have analyzed the role of women within his films, with a considerable number, like Constance Penley and Joan Mellen, uncovering misogyny and fear of woman as "other" inscribed in his representations or (the long-standing most dominant view) discerning an essentialist, biologist view of women as better human beings because of being closer to life: woman as nature, as a reproductive sex.[12] In 1973, Mellen argued that Bergman's women, although they are very much the focus in his body of work, "are ensnared at a much more elementary level of development [than men]. Their lives lack meaning because they are rooted in biology and an inability to choose a style of life independent of the female sexual role."[13]

Others, like Marilyn Johns Blackwell, have read these representations as more open, as more complex, and as possibly profeminist. Johns Blackwell thus places Bergman's work in a realm of *potential* feminist, reading them as feminist texts pointing at the sex and gender binary of both social construct and essentialist nature. She writes, "Although Bergman's films may not aspire to feminism, the disjunctive devices—which are the feminist strategy that the feminist avant-garde uses—that Bergman employs so frequently may nonetheless encourage a feminist experience in the spectator by deconstructing certain aspects of dominant male discourse."[14]

Especially in a film such as *Persona*, there are many instances in which a feminist experience can be said to be encouraged. The film is indeed a good example of a "feminine text," a concept linked to Roland Barthes, Julia Kristeva, and Luce Irigaray and later developed in relation to cinema by film scholar Annette Kuhn in her book *Women's Pictures* from 1982. The feminine text, as an opposing text, serves to disrupt the "malestream" narrative and to clearly reject any closure, thus refusing the dominant and traditional (and patriarchal) narrative path.[15] In a similar vein, the malestream narrative has been referred to as deeply "Oedipal" by Teresa de Lauretis, who argues that most of Western narration is indeed masculine, putting the male at the center and telling *his* story (which is a story about manhood)—never hers.[16]

There are other aspects that also make *Persona* a feminine text. Its challenge to and deconstruction of the hierarchy of traditional modes of discourse have clear similarities with feminist theory and film practice. In addition, there is also an apparent rejection of a male point of view in this film: most of the viewpoints represented are female. And although Bergman's voice is briefly on the audio track as some kind of "voice of God" when describing the new scenario for the two women, he is most often absent, as completely excluded from his own story, and it is instead Alma's voice that we hear, since she is the one who does all the speaking, in a sense also giving Elisabet a voice. Yet, the feminist critique arguing that Bergman's overall cinematic universe is one relying on sexual difference as law, with women as more tied to nature through their reproductive capacity, is one that is convincing for the most part. Although always more complex than male characters, and mentally stronger, the female characters in his films are indeed marked by their biological gender, as well as by their ascribed social and sexual role.

I believe that these sometimes conflicting feminist readings and outcomes have to do with how and whether the director, Bergman himself as auteur, is being allowed to figure in the analysis and in what way. A director who so generously has shared himself with his audience, talking openly about his own fears and phobias and his problems with women, and who has written so extensively about his childhood as an explanation of his shortcomings as an adult, is of course difficult to exclude from the reading of a text.[17] If the author obnoxiously insists on being present, it is, to say the least, difficult to see him as dead.

Bergman was once considered to be the auteur of all auteurs, and he still is, due in great part to the public's interest in his life and in his keeping his auteur position. For, as has been pointed out by Bergman scholar Maaret Koskinen, drawing on Tom Gunning and John Caughie among others, "the viewer's (pre-) knowledge of a particular director is part of the experience of watching the film," and this knowledge or recognition shapes our expectation when watching a film, positioning the us in a specific relation to the film as text, as well as to the author.[18] And, as long as there is a huge interest in Bergman as a private person and as an auteur, it will be hard to let his films stand for themselves. While I am writing this, it seems that Swedish interest in Bergman is only increasing: Bergman festivals are organized, documentary films are being made, new books and new articles are being written, and it is no question, then, that the culture is still obsessed with him, both as person and as artist.[19]

Mago and Bergman

Theater critic Leif Zern has called Mago and Bergman working together "a joyful meeting between two shameless aesthetes," explaining that, "Mago's scenography (costume design was called scenography back then) indulged in Bergman's love for the colour red."[20] Let me return to Mago and to the 1960s, the decade that proved to be the most creative and productive for the Mago–Bergman collaboration. During this period, they worked together on no less than ten films, which makes Mago the most important costume designer for Bergman, given that the latter made a total of fourteen films during this decade. Leading up to the productive 1960s, they had worked together on two films, *Sawdust and Tinsel* in 1953 and *Smiles of a Summer Night* in 1955. Their collaboration ended with Mago's death and, thus, continued through the 1998 making of the production *Bildmakarna* (*The Image Makers*) for the big stage at the Royal Dramatic Theatre in Stockholm.

It is interesting to note how Mago considered his contribution to these films, most commonly known and referred to only as "Bergman's films" by a larger audience. In his memoirs, from 1988, he writes, "Twelve films all in all I have made together with Ingmar Bergman," placing himself on the same level as Bergman, not working *for* him, but rather working *together with* him, as if these films would not have been made without him.[21] Most people who were involved in Bergman's films—actresses, actors, photographers, and set designers alike—have put it quite differently: there is an almost suffocating national admiration for Bergman as the most talented and artistic film director ever, and so, working *for* him is more often than not described as an "enormous favour."[22]

In his memoirs, Mago lovingly, yet a bit pejoratively, calls Bergman a "director in a worn out leather jacket and a beret," and Bergman was anything but fashionable himself, although I believe one must credit him with a certain style.[23] Mago, on the other hand, come across as a modern dandy for whom perfection in detail and good taste was everything, at least when it came to his own appearance. And the striving for perfection in every detail was also significant for his costume design. Everything had to be perfect, although it could, at times, be anything but moderate. His costumes were excessive when allowed, as in his costume production for numerous stage plays or for comedy films, such as Bergman's *All these women*, and it was often utterly effeminate, no matter whether it was men's or women's costumes.

According to Mago, Bergman (together with very few of the directors he worked for) took a serious and detailed interest in costume design and would have Mago involved already in the scriptwriting stage so as to have costumes and appearances present in the early design of each shot.[24] All costumes were designed by Mago, even the ones that we see, for example, in *Persona* (although some, if managing to meet his vision, probably were bought). So, even in the more contemporary films, like most of Bergman's 1960s films, Mago would never let actresses or actors wear their own clothes, nor would he himself just pick things from the rack in the department store: he would always draw his costume sketches, envisioning (and creating) the characters in and through their costumes. For *Persona*, he would have some costumes handmade, while others he would have his assistants buy (if available in the stores). To a much younger female colleague, Anna Bergman, who worked with him in the 1990s at the Dramatic Theatre in Stockholm, he would proudly claim that he would never lower himself to become a "picker," trying to prevent her from becoming one either. Almost everything, from underwear and outerwear to hairstyle and jewellery, was designed by him and then most often created and crafted by others with whom he worked very closely.[25] He drew, and others carried and materialized out his visions, which might have been quite problematic, since Mago's sketches were not very detailed, but his vision was translated in the intimate dialogues he had with his seamstresses, who came to know what he liked and how he thought about costume.

Fabric was always central to his work process, and when starting on a new production, Mago would tour the most exclusive and detailed fabric shops in Stockholm, letting fabrics inspire him in his work as he would "borrow" meters and meters of different kinds of exclusive fabrics.[26] Notwithstanding the occasional excess in his costumes, Mago was very sensitive about the role the costumes would play in the narrative and a film's (or a play's) whole, the totality. In his memoirs, he writes, "All of my costumes are made to be seen in a specific context. They must relate to their surroundings, they must be connected to it, to its physical milieu and to its atmosphere. Well, they must help reinforce and create this atmosphere while not sticking out or making themselves too noticeable, they must not break the frame. Good costume subordinates itself to the totality of the film or the stage play and does not attract the gaze."[27]

In Bergman's 1953 *Sawdust and Tinsel* (the first film the two made together), his circus costumes helped visualize and emphasize the pain and the emotional distress the characters' experience and carry as outcasts from normative society but without exaggerating it, without making the costumes excessive. Yet, costumes play a central, if not crucial, role here, as they do in many of Bergman's films. In *Sawdust and Tinsel*, the portrayal of an alternative and outcast life situation (the hard life at the circus) demands costumes (as well as *rekvisita*, props) that underscore this situation, including emphasizing the theatricality that this life involves. In this sense, *Sawdust and Tinsel* must be considered to be a costume film, just as we may think of *All these Women* as a costume film just as much as it is a comedy. Other films by Bergman that clearly fall into this category are, of course, *Smiles of a Summer Night* from 1955; *Smultronstället/Wild Strawberries* from 1957; *Det sjunde inseglet/* (*The Seventh Seal*), and 1982's *Fanny och Alexander* (*Fanny and Alexander*).

And in *Persona*, as we shall see, the costumes, consisting of contemporary clothes in black and white (costumes that I would argue are in fact fashion), were all subtle, not breaking the frame in a film in which the narrative and visual framing is broken over and over again. Here, Mago's costumes helped contribute to the visual representation of the fusion between the two women, or, if one wishes, to their transcendence. While Bergman was experiencing and "engaging with a series of dialectics," with the narrative technique and the tension between image and word, and with trying to break the frame so as to give rise to reflexivity, the costumes were the only reliable element in the film.[28]

But Mago's costumes could break the frame at times and would stick out in a way that made them so much more than just costumes. For instance, in a film like Arne Mattsson's crime film *Mannekäng i rött /Mannequin in Red* from 1958, a film that takes place in a fashion house, the excessive and affluent fashion almost constitutes a "third meaning" in a Barthesian sense.[29] While expanding or infringing on the totality of the film narrative, they also work to emphasize the double role of dressing up: on the one hand, something that is made desirable for most women by societal norms and the dominant "vestimentary system" (what Barthes would call *le système vestimentaire*) and, on the other hand, a means to hide and cover up identities and desires that heteronormative society deems unacceptable.[30] The ultrafeminine, highly fashionable dresses, made by designer women and put on model women walking the catwalks, seemingly for a male gaze, have the function of visualizing and normalizing sexual difference and, hence, of enforcing heterosexuality as normal and desirable. But these costumes (a stream of fancy outfits ranging from deep décolletages dresses with exciting cuts to velvety suits, tight shiny trousers, voluptuous chiffons, and romantic light blue and pink effeminate dresses) must also be understood as masquerading, as a means to disguise an innate desire amongst the women for sexual indifference. And this desire for sexual indifference is also to be found in Bergman's films, with Mago's costumes reinforcing or fashioning it.

Sexual Indifference in Persona

I have already mentioned how Mago worked with Bergman and Nykvist to make a specific Bergmanesque femininity in the 1960s (or "femaleness," if following some of the early feminist criticism of Bergman). Dressing the female film stars in modern and strict costume very much in line with the fashion of that era, Mago helped create and nurture the notion of a modern Swedish woman who was clearly superior and wiser to men. These women—or rather, their representations, roles, and characterizations—helped in constructing Bergman's body of work as national: they filled his screen with specific traits that, together with other Bergmanesque traits such as lighting, the use of the close-up, and a few recurrent narrative themes, made his oeuvre appear as typically "Swedish" and, hence, as national. If actresses like Sofia Loren, Claudia Cardinale and Monica

Vitti constituted and represented a certain Italian femininity (or femaleness) in Italian films made during the same era, their Swedish counterparts did the same for Swedish cinema. It is indeed interesting that it was female actresses, rather than male actors, who came to dominate the screen and its related media discourses in the 1960s and to represent and embody an imagined "national identity." And in the Swedish context, Mago's vision and creation of a new, modern femininity through his modern, strict and fashionable costumes were absolutely crucial.

And, while the "Bergman widows" came to represent a new Swedish womanhood closely tied to the nation and to the reproductive (other) body, this strong femininity must also be read as, indeed, ambiguous and paradoxical in relation to the unquestioned conception of a dominant sexual difference as the basis for everything (that is, for life). The modern, simple fashions with which these female bodies were formed and represented served to tone down sexual difference and, so, to play down women as the other sex. Sleek, streamlined, dressed in black and white slacks and jumpers, and wearing short haircuts, these women had little to do with any traditional depiction of female reproduction or female affluence. Androgynity rather than (ef-)femininity constituted the guiding and aesthetic principle when it came to the formation and display of a new, modern womanhood.

And so, while Mago would excel in using costumes to playfully emphasize sexual difference (only to serve to unveil or undress this difference as masquerade) in many of his films and theater productions, his costumes and his fashion in the 1960s productions for Bergman seemed to strive for a conscious and erasure of this difference. Besides *Persona*, films like *Nattvardsgästerna/Winterlight* (1963); *Hour of the Wolf* (1968); and *Skammen/Shame* (1968) should be mentioned as important examples of "costumary" sexual erasure—as Mago made the costumes for all three. This erasure was clearly in line with the more progressive Swedish fashion at the time and mirrored the awakening discourse on gender that questioned traditional gender roles and heteronormative constellations between men and women.[31] This visual erasure of sexual difference (what I would argue is a sort of fashioning of sexual indifference) was inscribed in the costumes by Mago, and so his costumes may help us question the dominant view on Bergman's films as reinforcing the notion of sexual difference as natural and inevitable.

In *Persona*, the film on which I wish to focus here, the very unveiling of sexual indifference through Mago's costumes, together with Bergman's narrative and cinematic techniques, is one that has to do both with an erasure of sexual difference (and hence, of a strictly heterosexual structure) and with an open embracing of lesbian desire and identification. Hence, this fashioning of indifference translates itself into an openly queer desire, a desire that can be discovered in the portrayal of identification and identifying. The film, shot in black and white, focus on the intimate and emotionally difficult, if not sticky, relationship between two women, to some degree resembling the sticky and complex relationship between the two women (sisters) in *The Silence*, filmed a few years earlier.[32] In *Persona*, Alma and Elisabet are identifying with one another, or rather, Alma is identifying with Elisabet, her patient, and it becomes apparent that her identification has to do with both the desire to be like and the desire to be with—that is, to have. This desire will lead to a fusion, or collapse, between the two, and this fusion does not takes place only on a narrative level. It is also underscored and supported by the cinematography with a few superimpositions or dissolves in which the two women's faces become one and, at one point, with the total breakdown of the film strip. In an interview with Bergman, author, film critique, and film maker Stig Björkman states, "*Persona* is almost exclusively built up around close-ups and wide long shots, and the form is entirely congruent with the content. In the relations between the women there are these strong vacillations between closeness and distance, intimacy and reserve. This narrative technique is of course consciously intended."[33]

It should be mentioned that Bergman's cultivation of the close-up as a new cinematic device—which, after *The Face* in 1958, would become one of his signatures, and which Moseley has referred to as "the awareness of the expressive potentials of the human face"—was a great disappointment to Mago. As a costume designer, he would, of course, rather have his creations in-frame, not off-frame. In his memoirs, Mago serenely complains that Bergman's use of the close-up in *All these Women* did little justice to his many frivolous and elaborated costumes, costumes with which he "via lines and materials had tried to accentuate femininity and a kind of sensual coquetry."[34] The fusion, or complete union, is foreshadowed in a few sequences that display the physical closeness of the two women, for example, the sequence in which Alma and Elisabet sit next to one another sorting mushrooms and comparing hands in the sun while humming, the sequence at the kitchen table with Alma's profile close to the camera with Elisabet facing her, making it look as though she is melting into Alma, or the dreamy sequence with both actresses looking into the camera in a close-up as Elisabet strikes Alma's forehead softly. This last sequence leads up to a total fusion in which Bergman has the two faces become one, juxtaposing their faces in a final close-up.

This fusion between the two women is also reinforced visually by the very similar clothing that the two actresses wear. Here, Mago emphasized their increasing similarity and fusion by having their dress become more and more similar, yet he did so not by letting the costume stand out, but rather the opposite. In white and black slacks, turtleneck jumpers and straight cut dresses, the two characters become interchangeable. As Alma starts "becoming" Elisabet, their similarities are emphasized, and this transformation can be understood not only as her desire for becoming and/or having Elisabet—"she tries to incorporate Elisabet into herself, to come to know her and experience life as she does…"—but also as a desire for sexual indifference.[35] Alma's honest confessions about her private life and her sexual past, especially under the influence of alcohol and in the intimacy that the two women share, reveals that heterosexuality (and marriage) is something she is just settling for and not something she desires. It is expected of her according to dominant societal norms, just as her devotion to her profession as a caring nurse is expected of her. The detailed description of the infamous orgy further adds to an interpretation of lesbian desires: the two boys in Alma's story can be read as tools used to cover up Alma's desire for her friend Katarina. The emphasis on sexual indifference is again pointed out when Alma says that they were sunbathing in the nude, wearing only identical large straw hats. These hats are of course reminiscent of the hats that Alma and Elisabet wear in an earlier sequence when they sit in the patio sorting mushrooms and comparing hands. Their fusion, the desire for becoming not the other, but the *same*, the desire for sexual indifference and the uncovering of heterosexual happiness as an ideal, yet suffocating, construction that is forced from the outside, help us read *Persona* as a lesbian story.[36]

Although Mago did not make the costumes for *The Silence*, I would like to bring it up briefly in relation to *Persona* in terms of sexual indifference and lesbian desire. Similarly to *Persona*, as I have pointed out, it narrates the story of two women (two estranged yet tightly related sisters), but here the older sister's desire for the other and for sexual indifference is doubly complicated and paradoxical, since the object of desire is a sibling, and so this is a desire that lingers on the incestuous, one of the strongest taboos in Western civilization. Here, just as in *Persona*, the costumes help emphasize the longing and desire, and, as described by Gwendolyn Audrey Foster, they can be said to help display "the performance of lesbian desire."[37] Both *Persona* and *The Silence* demonstrate the performance of lesbian looks of exchange and female bonding, and they do so in relation to heterotopic and heterosexist norms while clearly challenging these norms through the women's intimate yet complicated bonding.[38]

The two films mirror each other in their emphasis on female bonding, yet they differ in their spatiality: whereas the two sisters in *The Silence* are suffocating, restricted, and sweating away on a dark, dirty train and, later, in a stifling hotel, Alma and Elisabet are physically free on an empty island (Fårö, located off the Swedish East coast just north of the island Gotland) and live next to the forest and the open sea, far away from any intruding gazes. Clad in bathing suits, in slacks, knee-long pen-shaped skirts, turtleneck jumpers and wide hats when outside, and in loose fitting and flowing night gowns in white when inside, they are the epitome of 1960s fashionable and modern (Swedish) femininity. Yet, the

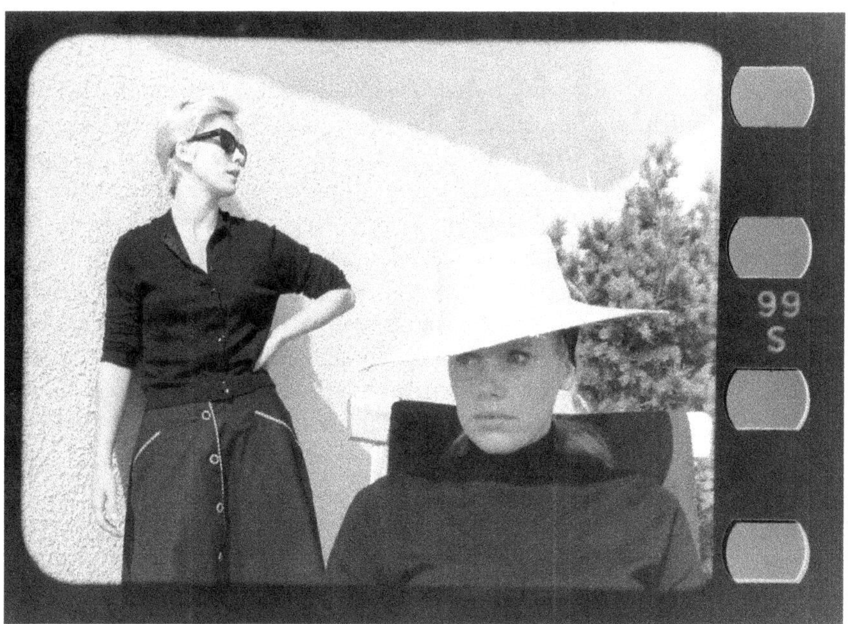

Fig. 10.2 Alma (Bibi Andersson) and Elisabet (Liv Ullmann) mirroring each other and becoming one through their similar costumes. Persona © 1966 AB Svensk Filmindustri.

simplicity of their costumes and the similarity in style make them seem ungendered and, hence, less sexed. They are not sexually differentiated as the "other," but rather, they are expressing a sameness, and that sameness is one that is sexually undifferentiated.

When Steven Meisel made a fashion spread for *Vogue Italia* in November of 2008, he revisited this all-female scenario, creating his own Fårö where two models engage in an intimate, caring, yet destructive, relationship, positioning them in poses very much the same as those of Elisabet and Alma in *Persona*. The very queer quality of Bergman's film is being relocated to the still pages of a fancy fashion magazine, transferred some fifty years forward, into the twenty-first century. While serving to emphasize the lesbian desire in the film story, these stills also serve to pinpoint the lesbian possibility that structures much of todays' fashion photography (as well as contemporary fashion film, a genre that I would argue is indeed prolesbian). So iconic is the film's representation of unhealthy, yet highly desirable, identification, painful love, and harsh nature that even an unquestioningly straight fashion film like *Archipelago Stories* (by Swedish fashion brand Boomerang for their Sring/Summer collection in 2014), focussing solely on a boy and a girl in love on an island, immediately recalls Alma and Elisabeth and their queer story.

Queer Costumes

Besides the representation of desires for sexual indifference amongst women, Bergman's films have also included other queer representations and qualities. For example, in *The Face* (1958); *All these Women* (1964); *The Winter Light* (1968), and (considerably later) *Fanny and Alexander* (1982), we find a certain questioning of the traditional, heteronormative gender binary that opens up for the possibility of a third gender. Ambiguous and androgynous characters are, within his narrative universe, often positioned as wiser and more clear-sighted than his cis-characters. This aspect or recurring trait in Bergman's corpus has been discussed in depth by Marilyn Johns Blackwell, and others have followed her line of thought in an attempt to queer Bergman's work.[39] For this chapter, this additional queer quality is central because it underpins what I label the desire for sexual indifference, yet the queer quality I am after is the one constructed through and emphasized by costume.

We have already seen how the modest costume in a film like *Persona* works to emphasize this indifference, and I will now briefly turn to a Bergman and Mago film that deviates from the pattern of *Persona* and *The Silence* by its excessive costume, all filmed in bright colours: namely, *All these Women* made in 1964. Whereas the two previous films had as their focus the complex, intimate, and unequal relationship between two women, this film encompasses and gives room to some of the most famous female (and male) actors in Sweden at the time. Hence, the film is very much like a display or a parade of Bergman's "stall" or "cabin" (both privately and professionally), with Bibi Andersson, Harriet Andersson, Eva Dahlbeck, and Karin Kavli (female) and Mona Malm, Jarl Kulle, Allan Edwall and Carl Billquist (male) all playing characters obsessed with performing their "sexed" part in a continuous war between the sexes.

The film was Bergman's first color film, and it heavily employs various nuances of red together with black and white: in one scene, most of Mago's female costumes (which vary and differ in terms of cut and look) are in dark red, in bright red, and in light pink, together creating a wonderfully excessive and colourful red palate. As in *Smiles of a Summer Night*, his costumes serve to emphasize gender construction and performativity, as well as the female characters' desire to belong while simultaneously standing out as unique, as if displaying an almost exaggerated example of Georg Simmel's understanding of fashion in terms of social distinction and belonging. The male characters are similarly being marked by their gender construction through their costumes: dressed in black tuxedos and white shirts, the construction of masculinity is emphasized as one of uniformity and conformity (and possibly, as one formed by the fear of standing out). Both male and female costumes serve to ridicule (and, I would add, to queer) the two genders as mere constructions while visually emphasizing the war that they partake in. Sexual difference is here marked and brought to the fore by Mago's costumes *ad absurdum*, and through its absurdity, it is laid bare as heavily constructed. Hence, sexual difference can be read as a mere cover-up for that which it may actually be instead—an indifference.

Many of the films made by Bergman in the 1960s also contain another queer quality, or rather, a representation of a queer desire, that is more difficult to define: the substantial number of costumes used in the films that are the fabrications of Mago's desire for the feminine (or rather, the ultrafeminine). His fascination with beautiful and extravagantly dressed women seemed to have been somewhat extreme, and reading his memoirs, it becomes clear that this fascination could easily be understood as a deep and, as it would prove, productive fetishism that was developed in very early years. Already as a child, his attraction to performative and clearly constructed femininities was obvious. In his memoirs *Klä av, klä på* (*Undress and Dress*), he recalled how he, when growing up in Berlin in the late 1920s and early 1930s, very early on was attracted to women who displayed and embodied femininity through the wearing of heavy makeup, jewellery, and perfume. Long nails with colourful and metallic nail polish, deep décolletages, furs, and high heels were heaven to the five-year-old Max:

> The fatal and the deviant carried with it an enormous attraction. The by the regime cherished new German women—without make-up, dressed in a dirndl-dress and Gretchen tails, a type of woman who now tried to dominate the silver screen, I found very, very boring. Just like did most of the audience. These blonde, untalented new stars never became popular and soon I discovered new femmes fatales covered in fur and silk. . . . The vamp had become my idol. . . . I always paid attention to, with the greatest of pleasures, women with heavy make-up and who wore plenty of perfume. The women in my family smelled of lavender and mild soap. My own mother would only very seldom wear colourless nail polish. My excitement knew no limitations when I one day discovered that there were women who wore green nail polish.[40]

As an adult, when meeting an elderly Marlene Dietrich for the first time in 1960, as she arrived to give a performance in Stockholm, he realized that she was the very origin of his desire and admiration for the femme fatale.[41] This comes as no surprise: Marlene's super femininity was often intermingled with a certain ambivalence not only in terms of gender but also in terms of sexuality. Mago explains: "That which according to me was 'the good German,' and which had been there but which had, like us (i.e., Germans that were Jewish), been excluded and expelled, had for me taken the form of this exquisite creature, this actress dressed in fantastic feathers and floating furs. Marlene was also Berlin. Whenever I had drawn sketches, I gave my women a Marlenesque look, and it was from her wardrobe that I took my first inspiration."[42] He would come to design stage and film costumes for la Dietrich at several occasions, reckons here to mention his work in the film *Just a Gigolo* (David Hemmings, 1978), in which Dietrich plays a baroness in charge of a brothel, and they would become close friends.

Dressing prima donnas like Git Gay, Sarah Leander, and the elderly Marlene Dietrich, Mago exaggerated the queer hyperfemininity that he as a young man had seen Dietrich incorporate on screen. This femininity, highly constructed like all femininities (and masculinities), was somewhat unconventionally feminine in that it clearly was drawing on masculine traits, mixing the hyperfeminine with the hypermasculine. The campy prima donna look that he created for his female friends, which was most probably based on the Dietrich look, combining traits from both genders, indeed served to upset the notion of sexual difference as natural and essential.

Within the world of the fashion industry, Mago would most probably not have been able to make it, but within the world of film and theater, his creations were fantastic, whether in their excess or in their modesty—and most fashionable. In addition, his costumes and his creations were indeed queer creations: they were the result of a desire that seemed to have exceeded any rigid, dualist structure for hetero- or homosexual desires and identities that serve to sustain heteronormative dominance together with sexual difference. And in this sense, his costumes were magic.

LOUISE WALLENBERG is Associate Professor in Film and Fashion studies and former Director of the Centre for Fashion Studies at Stockholm University. She is coeditor of *Nordic Fashion Studies*; *Modernism och mode*; and *Harry bit för bit,* and has published extensively on film, gender and fashion.

Notes

1. For the 1955 *Sommarnattens leende* (*Smiles of a Summer Night*), Bergman won the Special Jury Prize at the Cannes Festival in 1956, and the following year, he won the same prize for *Det sjunde inseglet* (*The Seventh Seal*), and in 1958, the same prize for *Nära livet* (*Brink of Life*). In 1958, he received the Golden Berlin Bear for *Smultronstället* (*Wild Strawberries*), and in 1962, the OCIC Award for *Såsom i en spegel* (*Through A Glass Darkly*). Bergman received his first Oscar for *Jungfrukällan/The Virgin Spring* (1960) for the best foreign film. All in all, he received four Oscars (for *Såsom i en spegel/Though A Glass Darkly* [1961] for best foreign film, *Viskningar och rop/Cries and Whispers* [1973]) for best photo and *Fanny och Alexander/Fanny and Alexander* [1982] for best foreign film). Other rewards and prizes that he received over the years include Golden Globe Awards, Guldbaggen, and BAFTA Awards.

2. John Orr, *The Demons of Modernity: Ingmar Bergman and European Cinema* (New York and Oxford: Berghahn, 2014), 9.

3. See Daniel Humphrey, *Queer Bergman: Sexuality, Gender, and the European Art Cinema* (Austin: Texas University Press, 2013), 14.

4. Humphrey, *Queer Bergman* , 60.

5. The literature published dealing with Bergman's work is vast and seems to be never-ending, the first books and articles coming out already in the early 1960s and a substantial number of texts coming out only as recently as 2013. See, for example: Peter Cowie, *Ingmar Bergman: A Monograph* (Loughton: Motion, 1962); Philip Mosley, *Ingmar Bergman: the Cinema as A Mistress* (London: Marion Boyars, 1981); Paisley Livingston, *Ingmar Bergman and the Rituals of Art* (Ithaca, NY: Cornell University Press, 1982); *Ingmar Bergman Revisited: Performance, Cinema and the Arts*, ed. Maaret Koskinen (London and New York: Wallflower, 2008); *Ingmar Bergman's Persona*, ed. Lloyd Michaels (New York: Cambridge University Press, 2000); Geoffrey Macnab, *Ingmar Bergman: the Life and Films of the Last Great European Director* (London and New York: I. B. Tauris, 2009); Robin Wood, *Ingmar Bergman: New Edition* (orig. 1969), (Detroit, MI: Wayne State University Press, 2011); Peter Ohlin, *Wordless Secrets: Ingmar Bergman's Persona; Modernist Crisis and Canonical Status* (Cardiff, UK: Wales Academic Press, 2011); Humphrey, *Queer Bergman*; Orr, *The Demons of Modernity.*

6. Jane Gaines, "Wanting to Wear Seeing: Gilbert and MGM," in *Fashion in Film*, ed. Adrienne Munich (Indianapolis: Indiana University Press, 2011), 171.

7. See Gaby Wigardt, "Klädskaparen Mago död," in *Svenska Dagbladet*, April 7, 2008 and Leif Zern, "Den svenska scenens elegant", in *Dagens Nyheter* April 8, 2008.

8. See Mago, *Klä av, klä på: tecknat och antecknat* (Stockholm: Författarförlaget, 1988).

9. For an overview of the "golden era" of Swedish Silent Cinema, see, e.g., Bo Florin, *Den Nationella stilen: studier i den svenska filmens guldålder* (Stockholm: Philsophical Dissertation, 1997).

10. Between 1944 and 1952, Bergman directed *Kris* (*Crisis*, 1946) and *Det regnar på vår kärlek* (1946); *Skepp till India land* (1947); *Musik i mörker* (1948); *Hamnstad* (1948); *Fängelse* (1949); *Törst* (1949); *Till glädje* (1950); *Sånt händer inte här* (1950); *Sommarlek* (1951); and *Kvinnors väntan* (1952).

11. Moseley, *Ingmar Bergman*, 19.

12. See Constance Penley, "Cries and Whispers," in *Movies and Methods*, ed. Bill Nichols (Berkeley: University of California Press, 1976), and Joan Mellen, "Bergman and His Women: Cries and Whispers," *Film Quarterly* 27.1 (1973), 2–11.

13. Mellen, "Bergman and His Women," 2.

14. Marilyn Johns Blackwell argues that many of his works can be seen as radical experiments whose goal is to disrupt the cinematic structures that reinforce patriarchal ideology while being clearly essentialist and biologist in terms of gender (*Gender and Representation in Ingmar Bergman's Films* [New York: Camden House, 1997], 11).

15. Annette Kuhn, *Women's Pictures: Feminism and Cinema* (London: Verso, 1982).

16. See Teresa de Lauretis, *Alice Doesn't: Feminism, Semiotics, Cinema* (Bloomington: Indiana University Press, 1984).

17. See Ingmar Bergman, *Laterna Magica* (Stockholm: Norstedts, 1987) and *Söndagsbarn* (Stockholm: Norstedts, 1993).

18. Maaret Koskinen, "Introduction," in *Ingmar Bergman Revisited: Performance, Cinema and the Arts*, ed. Maaret Koskinen (London and New York: Wallflower, 2008), 3.

19. In 2015, the book *Fårö and Ingmar Bergman: A Mutual Bond* (Fårö: Fårö Local Heritage Association Publishers, 2015) was published, dealing with Bergman's relation to Fårö and the inhabitants on the island. And in 2013, some five years after Bergman's death, a book dealing with his love life, by some considered interesting due to his many marital, nonmarital, and extramarital relationships, was published: Thomas Sjöberg, *Ingmar Bergman: en berättelse som kärlek, sex och svek* (Stockholm: Lind, 2013). In 2012, Swedish Public Television (SVT) produced a series, *Bergman's Video*, focusing on Bergman's many VHS cassettes kept in his

lounge in his house on Fårö, and in 2013, this series was followed by a documentary, *Trespassing Bergman*. In both *Bergman's video* and *Trespassing Bergman*, the focus is on the impact Bergman has had on internationally acclaimed actors, actresses, and directors. And, since 2003, a Bergman Week (*Bergmanveckan*) has been held at Fårö in June–July every year, inviting international scholars and film artists to engage in discussions and screenings together with Swedish film artists, scholars, and journalists.

20. Leif Zern, "Den svenska scenens elegant," in *Dagens Nyheter*, April 8, 2008, 10.

21. Mago, *Klä av, klä på*, 133: "Sometimes people ask me why we did not make any more [films]. 'Perhaps one of us is superstitious.' That is the best answer I can give them" (my translation).

22. See for example Liv Ullmann, "Prologue," in Koskinen, *Ingmar Bergman Revisited*, 9: "Now, who am I? I have been his actress. His lover. We have a child together. He built the house on Fårö for the two of us. We have been the best of friends."

23. Mago, *Klä av, klä på*, 130.

24. Mago, *Klä av, klä på*, 202.

25. At times, when the character and the story demanded it, he would not create new costumes but instead go to a length to find a specific, worn-out garment. One example would be the lamb's fur coat that Ingrid Thulin's character wears in *Nattvardsgästerna* (*Winterlight*). Here, the coat is used to signal not only her socioeconomic status, but also her specific cultural belonging: as a middle-aged teacher in a small town in the northern part of Sweden, she is practical and has a rather low income (Mago, *Klä av, klä på*, 230).

26. This information was told to me by Anna Bergman in Stockholm in October 2013.

27. Mago, *Klä av, klä på*, 196 (my translation).

28. Marilyn Johns Blackwell, *Persona: The Transcendent Image* (Chicago: University of Illinois Press, 1986), 9.

29. Roland Barthes, "The Third Meaning: Research Notes on some Eisenstein Stills" (orig. 1970), in *The Responsibility of Forms: Critical Essays on Music, Art, and Representation*, trans. Richard Howard (Berkeley: University of California Press, 1985). Barthes here discusses a third order of meaning, an inarticulable beyond, a meaning that is obtuse. The third meaning takes its shape from a "theoretical individuality" and is closely associated to the Barthesisan "punctum" discussed in *Camera Lucida* (orig. *La chambre claire*, 1980), trans. Richard Howard (New York: Hill and Wang, 1981).

30. See Roland Barthes, "Histoire et sociologie de vetement," *Annales* 12.3 (1957): 430–41. See also Louise Wallenberg, "Eleganten," in *Citizen Schein*, ed. Pelle Snickars et al. (Stockholm: Kungliga bibiloteket, 2010).

31. Fashion in Sweden in the 1960s took on a playful and disruptive character. Inspired by youth culture and by a growing awareness of a much needed gender equality, as well as by more proleftist cultural expressions and directions, Swedish fashion became more ungendered in terms of blurring the distinction between male and female. It was then that the "velour-daddy" was being introduced, and it was during this decade that fashion designer Sighsten Herrgårdh started designing his unisex jumpsuits.

32. Johns Blackwell points this resembling out in *Persona*, 29: "Although the parallels with *Persona* are not exact, they are nevertheless striking."

33. Stig Björkman, in Stig Björkman, Torsten Manns, and Jonas Sima, *Bergman on Bergman* [orig. 1970], 206, quoted in Johns Blackwell, *Persona*, 77.

34. Mago, *Klä av, klä på*, 231 (my translation).

35. Johns Blackwell, *Persona*, 40–41. Blackwell writes further: "Although the erotic ramifications of their relationship are never explicit, there is obviously an erotic element to the feelings Alma bears for the actress" (68).

36. Further, a possible lesbian desire is portrayed in the middle sequences in the film when the physical biting takes place. Here, the representation of vampirism works as a metaphor for queer desires. On vampirism as a metaphor for homosexuality, see Richard Dyer, "It's in his kiss! Vampirism as homosexuality, homosexuality as vampirism," in *The Culture of Queers* (London and New York: Routledge, 2001). See also Gwendolyn Audrey Foster, "Feminist Theory and the Performance of Lesbian Desire," in *Ingmar Bergman's Persona*, ed. Lloyd Michaels (Cambridge: Cambridge University Press, 2000).

37. Foster, "Feminist Theory and the Performance of Lesbian Desire," 130.

38. The possibility (and performance) of lesbian desire is in fact present in many of Bergman's films. Maria Bergom-Larsson describes how women in his work are often allowed to "share a playful and erotic togetherness" (*Ingmar Bergman och den borgerliga ideologin* [Stockholm: Norstedts and PAN; orig. 1976], 75).

39. See Johns Blackwell, *Gender and Representation.*

40. Mago, *Klä av, klä på*, 39–40 (my translation).

41. Mago, *Klä av, klä på*, 183.

42. Mago, *Klä av, klä på*, 184 (my translation).

11 Single Men: Sixties Aesthetics and Vintage Style in Contemporary Cinema

Nick Rees-Roberts

The use of iconic film stars in contemporary fashion advertising includes a number of examples drawn from the cinema of the 1960s, such as Christian Dior's imagery of Alain Delon, used to relaunch its classic men's fragrance *Eau Sauvage* in 2009. The following year, Italian eyewear brand Persol reissued a limited edition of its iconic PO 714 sunglasses, made famous by Hollywood star Steve McQueen following their onscreen appearance in *The Thomas Crown Affair* (Norman Jewison, 1968). In 2011, the brand released an ad campaign using stills of McQueen shot by William Claxton in the early 1960s to accompany the item's reappearance as a contemporary classic. The campaign supported the brand's wider investment in screen culture, including its sponsorship of the Venice International Film Festival and a peripatetic exhibition tracing the parallel histories of craftsmanship in film and design.

The 1960s occupy a symbolic place in the layering of past styles in what Simon Reynolds has termed contemporary pop culture's "retromania."[1] Indeed, it was the 1960s that gave birth to the idea of fashion as not only the material object itself but also a whole "regime of visibility" articulated through the conjunction of design, image, and label.[2] This chapter explores the legacy of 1960s cinema through the stylistic lens of "vintage," defined as an aesthetic strategy that reads history through attention to tone, mood, and sensibility, as much as through the standard categories of costume, accessory, or dress. The iconographic hold of 1960s cinema over contemporary filmmaking raises important critical questions of lineage, adaptation, and heritage. This chapter aims to go beyond a routine discussion of period costume or pastiche design that references simply the visual clichés of the 1960s (such as the surface gloss of iconic consumables) to consider a more complex handling of cinematic memory, evoking the diffuse sensibilities of the period, particularly in relation to the aesthetics of masculinity. The chapter also argues for critical debate concerning fashion in film to consider a more capacious understanding of the heritage of men's style in the context of contemporary cinema. Drawing on a number of European films—including Joachim Trier's *Reprise* (2006) and *Oslo August 31st* (2011), the latter of which updates Louis Malle's *Le Feu Follet/The Fire Within* (1963)—I focus specifically on the forms of masculinity and their cinematic inscription within urban geography. The films under consideration all frame masculinity by dwelling on its formal shape and aesthetic design and mapping out the trajectories of the disaffected protagonists (the titular single men) as they traverse the cityscape.

While the film texts under discussion are European (with examples drawn from the cinemas of France, Norway, and the United Kingdom), the response to 60s aesthetics is more broadly international in nature. Popular cinema is persistently drawn to the decade through respectful remakes such as *The Thomas Crown Affair* (McTierney, 1999) with Pierce Brosnan taking on the McQueen mantle, or *Alfie* (Gilbert, 1966 and Shyer, 2004) in which Michael Caine's cockney man-about-town morphed into Jude Law's ironic Manhattan playboy. Other recent adaptations have cashed in on iconographic interest in the decade by purposefully shifting the timeframe to the 1960s for purely stylistic reasons: Rowan Joffe's *Brighton Rock* (2010) self-consciously draws on the contemporaneous mod revival in menswear design through the casting of Sam Riley as the male lead, an actor known at the time principally as the star of *Control* (2006), Anton Corbijn's ultra-cool biopic of postpunk band Joy Division, and as the face of Burberry menswear.

Vintage Cinema

Critical suspicion of fashion on film has historically focused on the perceived over-investment in artifice and surface. Pamela Church Gibson has noted the entrenched elitism in much academic film scholarship that leaves the study of costume design for fashion historians or journalists, thereby diminishing its disciplinary legitimacy.[3] The target of such critical suspicion of fashion and costume is the sort of production design that submerges the narrative in a stagnant aesthetic coding that relies on the clichéd look of the still fashion image.

Fashion designer Tom Ford's 2010 directorial debut, *A Single Man*, is instructive in this respect, for it self-consciously straddles the codes of advertising, branding, and art cinema, pointing to the surface perfectionism involved in the channelling of past styles. The film raises pertinent questions around the value of film authorship in the revised visual landscape of screen and consumer culture. What does the fashion designer bring to the creative and collaborative process of directing? Is the film simply part of a broader self-promotional strategy, with the product rolled out along with fashion and fragrance to promote the nominal brand? Church Gibson traces Ford's strategic positioning of his self-financed film within the new consumer culture of fashion branding and celebrity that he helped to forge as creative director of the Italian label Gucci in the 1990s.[4]

Following in the footsteps of the celebrated US television series *Mad Men*, Ford's glossy adaptation of Christopher Isherwood's 1964 novel was criticized for its contrived shots of designed interiors and its overinsistence on immaculate garments.[5] Isherwood's cruel realism was replaced by Ford's luxury aesthetic, the elegant clichés of which served to neutralize the existential angst and affective allure of the original narrative. However, the main criticism of *A Single Man*—that it is an artistic project wholly conceived under the sign of affectation—might not have been levelled quite so vehemently had the director's background not been in fashion.

Mad Men is an influential example of vintage stylization within contemporary screen culture. The impact of Matthew Weiner's dark and sexy series on current revisions of 1960s glamour is that it animates the look of fashion photography and the superficial packaging of consumer culture with its sparkling surfaces by conceiving of them as transparent metaphors for the characters' hidden depths and deceits. The series is also notable for its fetishistic investment in the range of consumables (cigarettes, alcohol, clothing, furniture, and gadgets) that we now casually associate with the lifestyle and technology of the period. As Prudence Black and Catherine Driscoll argue, *Mad Men*'s "embrace of period detail . . . is at once loving and fetishistic and it belongs, as in all period film and television, to the politics of the present." The series uses period detail to flag the radical difference between contemporary social values and those of the 1960s. "What that difference *looks like* is crucial to the way *Mad Men* represents history."[6] Casting aside a realist mode of representation, *Mad Men* imagines the past through the gaze of the adman, self-consciously channelling history through style.

In her seminal dissection of 1960s late-modernist culture, Susan Sontag distinguished between style and stylization, defining the latter as "creative mistreatment" occurring "when style and subject are . . . played off against one another."[7] The cinematic foregrounding of stylization is not a recent phenomenon. It was the cause of critical hostility toward the French *cinéma du look* of the 1980s with its aesthetic transfer of advertising, particularly the impact of the music video on narrative film. Fredric Jameson famously defined this tendency as the postmodern cultural sensibility knowingly assembling contemporary images from pop culture, fashion, and advertising alongside those from high culture and modernist art.[8] This pop sensibility forms part of the overall postmodern look of the work of contemporary directors attempting to stylize their subject matter not simply through surface design (such as the superficial rendition of 1960s fashion and interior design perceived in Ford's film), but rather through a more programmatic authorial strategy involving the intentionally jarring juxtaposition of subject with form. Examples drawn from contemporary cinema include Quebecois director Xavier Dolan's stylized melodramas *Heartbeats* (2010), *Laurence Anyways* (2012), and *Mommy* (2014), with their hybrid nods to pop music and video art, and Danish director Nicolas Winding Refn's mannered neonoir thrillers *Drive* (2011) and *Only God Forgives* (2013), both featuring Hollywood "it-boy" Ryan Gosling figured as a cross between a model and a performer. Gosling's physical allure and nonchalant technique hark back to Alain Delon's feline presence in Jean-Pierre Melville's classic crime film *Le Samouraï* (1967).

These questions of style and stylization, of affect and affectation, of the fashionable pleasure of certain films that are valued as much for their mood or tone as for their actual costume designs, suggest a more capacious understanding of vintage as an aesthetic sensibility in contemporary cinema. Emiliano Morreale defines vintage cinema as one that fabricates nostalgia generationally as a form of imagery attached to the so-called generations X (born between 1965 and 1980) and Y (digital natives born roughly after 1980) whose postcollective identities are made up entirely of the memories of spectator consumers.[9] Taking his theoretical cue from Jameson, Morreale argues that the difference between the 1970s visual nostalgia for previous decades—manifested in US films of the era such as *American Graffiti* (Lucas, 1973) and *The Way We Were* (Pollack, 1973)—and post-80s vintage is the construction of the past wholly through media representation, leading to the stalemate position of contemporary pop culture, in which past styles are eclectically positioned in an ahistorical mash-up to ensure maximal emotional engagement on the part of consumer audiences.

This conceptualization of vintage as an interrelationship between cinema, fashion, and consumption, as an aesthetic space rather than a predominantly temporal structure, follows theories propounded by philosopher Michel Foucault from the mid-1960s that charted the epistemological transition from a focus on history, development, and temporal cycles (found in both nineteenth-century realism and twentieth-century modernism) to the spatial realm of juxtaposition, heterotopias, and simultaneity.[10] Vintage cinema therefore implies reading history through the lens of style (through attention to mood, affect, and sensibility, through structures of feeling such as gloom, melancholy, or nostalgia) as much as through accessory, costume, or dress. The fabrication of vintage space on screen does not merely equate to narrative masquerading as advertising, with production designers raiding image banks in the way the modern styles and designs of *Mad Men* quite clearly translate the narrative's underlying sexiness into visual terms. Vintage cinema can also read history against the grain.

The legacy of early 1960s European art cinema (specifically the French New Wave and the Italian New Cinema) and its iconographic hold over certain artistic forms of contemporary cinema is particularly relevant to this discussion for the issues of lineage, adaptation, and heritage it raises. Some of Christophe Honoré's recent cinema, for example, has toyed with forms of knowing imitation, quoting the films of Jacques Demy, Jean-Luc Godard, and François Truffaut. *Love Songs* (*Les Chansons d'amour,* 2007) employs pastiche dialogue, song, movement, design, casting, and performance style; Louis Garrel pays imitative homage to Jean-Pierre Léaud's skittish performance as Antoine Doisnel, the iconic dandy in Truffaut's *Stolen Kisses*, (*Baisers volés*, 1968). However, Honoré has expressed reservations about the issue of generational transmission, refuting the normative nomenclature of legacy, filiation, and lineage, preferring instead to talk of his output in terms of cinematic memory.[11] Film scholar Pam Cook has argued that the distinction between memory, history, and nostalgia has become blurred in academic discussions of film. "Where traditional approaches prefer to emphasise the differences between them, in order to sanction the legitimacy of history as a means of explaining the world," argues Cook, "it is equally possible to see them as a continuum, with history at one end, nostalgia at the other and memory as a bridge or transition between them."[12] Rather than simply positioning nostalgia as a reactionary formation, Cook emphasizes how it foregrounds the role of fantasy in the re-presentation of the past. The more critically self-reflexive nostalgic memory film, therefore, plays on "the gap between representations of the past and actual past events, and the desire to overcome that gap and recover what has been lost."[13]

Honoré's critical manipulation of mnemonic imagery is further developed through the temporal and stylistic framework of his later film *Beloved* (*Les Bien-aimés*, 2011), which continued the pastiche tribute to Jacques Demy through the familiar motifs of love and loss, and through the casting of film star Catherine Deneuve. Ludivine Sagnier plays Deneuve's younger self, Madeleine, a shop assistant and call girl in the late 1960s. *Beloved* goes beyond straightforward pastiche, however, rubbing the colorful idealization of Parisian youthfulness up against the backdrop of epoch-defining historical events (the "Prague spring" of 1968 and 9/11 in the US) and the emotional displacement of unrequited love, missing home, and feeling lost. Alex Beaupain's score evokes the melancholy of the present by punctuating the fragmented narrative. Music is skilfully used in counterpoint to the neonostalgic recreation of sixties Paris playfully sketched out through attention to iconic objects and fashions of the period. These include shiny vintage cars and Sagnier's coquettish look, with her bottle-blond wig, cutesy frocks, and emblematic Roger Vivier buckled heels, which echo Deneuve's iconic role as *Belle de Jour* (Buñuel, 1967), symbolically showcased in the opening title sequence and the poignant final close-up.

Mood and Modernity

The final shot of *Beloved* focuses on the emblematic Roger Vivier heels and consolidates the film's affectionate investment in commodity fetishism. Honoré's calculated attempt to intertwine personal and public histories through the stylistic lens of vintage foregrounds a contemporary strategy that goes beyond a routine pastiche of stylistic clichés from past moments in film history and toward a more complex handling of cinematic memory, a treatment that uses it to evoke sensibilities, affects, and moods such as nostalgia and melancholy rather than to simply reproduce the surface gloss of the 1960s through the fetishistic allure of consumables.

Critical accounts of European art cinema of the period, such as Mark Betz's provocative reformulation of the body of work in terms of coproduction and the contextual politics of gender, race, and decolonization, draw considerable attention to the aesthetic elements that define modernist films, what David Bordwell termed their parametric stylistic features, particularly the lingering slowness so routinely associated with Michelangelo Antonioni's cycle of films of the period—*L'avventura* (1960), *La notte* (1961), *L'eclisse* (1962), and *Red Desert* (*Il deserto rosso*, 1964), or the fragmented subjectivity of Alain Resnais's *Last Year at Marienbad* (*L'Année dernière à Marienbad*, 1961).[14] Sontag's early criticism of the deep style of European art cinema of the period included an extended essay assessing Ingmar Bergman's *Persona* (1966), making parallel reference to the "abstract evocativeness" of the château in *Marienbad*, its complex mental universe, its discordant internal relations, and its opaque fusion of reality with fantasy.[15] Sontag also admired the "anti-romantic, cool, mundane, clinical (in one sense, literally so), and bourgeois-modern" tone and design of *Persona*, which functioned to locate time in a perpetual present tense.[16]

Like Sontag's appreciation of Bergman's design aesthetic, Giuliana Bruno reads Antonioni as an "architectural filmmaker." She observes that "unlike early modernism, which was more interested in speed, velocity, and acceleration, the late modernism that emerged in the postwar period conceived of modernity as inhabiting different, extended temporal zones, and it set out to explore this new shape of modern times." Antonioni's articulation of filmic space dwelt, Bruno argues, "on the architectonics of time," privileging scenic description over action, "an aesthetic of *temps mort*, absorbed in framing and mapping (interior) landscapes, and drawn to the time of non-action, a time when actors stop acting and space tells its story."[17] Bruno's analysis takes in the contemporary slow cinema of both Chantal Ackerman and Tsai Ming-liang, evidence that the late-modern artistic preference for slowness and stillness has come back into fashion—giving space to time, in Bruno's formulation.

The aesthetic influence of 1960s modernism is particularly apparent in a number of contemporary films that do not seek to replicate the particular looks or styles of the era (in the sense of the heritage or period film) but rather pay nostalgic attention to the mood, tone, and feeling—the affective pull—of 60s modernist cinema. An example of this type of tonal influence is Andrew Haigh's bleak gay romance *Weekend* (2011). Accompanying a shoot for the October 2011 edition of *L'Uomo Vogue*, photographer Bruce Weber pointed to the influence of the New British Cinema of the 1960s on his own aesthetic trajectory in both still and moving image.[18] The model chosen for the photo shoot was Tom Cullen, a British actor noted for his performance in *Weekend*, set in the postindustrial city of Nottingham, the same location used for Karel Reisz's kitchen-sink classic *Saturday Night and Sunday Morning* (1960). Haigh's low-key depiction of an aborted relationship over the course of a single weekend points to the film's roots in part in the British tradition of social-realist filmmaking, but also in the European modernist tradition. Haigh references the quiet, urban bleakness of Antonioni's cinema of the early 1960s through the subtle focus on the relationship's intimate and public spaces, together with the condensed timeframe lifted from *Cléo de 5 à 7* (Varda, 1962).[19]

Norwegian director Joachim Trier's films *Reprise* (2006) and *Oslo August 31st* (2011) similarly echo the mood and tone of the modernist European cinema through particular reference to films by Louis Malle, Eric Rohmer, and Agnès Varda. Trier's two films, in which hyperindividualized male protagonists navigate the spaces of contemporary Oslo, echo the framing of Paris of the 1960s, drawing on a number of visual intertexts, and as it was for Haigh's *Weekend*, the structure of Varda's *Cléo de 5 à 7* is a key reference point, as are Malle's *The Fire Within* (*Le Feu follet*, 1963), Rohmer's *The Sign of Leo* (*Le Signe du lion*, 1959), and Georges Perec and Bernard Queysanne's later film *A Sleeping Man* (*Un homme qui dort*, 1974). Trier's films self-consciously bind questions of style, design, and masculinity to those of place, space, and topography.

Malle's earlier film *Elevator to the Gallows* (*Ascenseur pour l'échafaud*, 1958) with its memorable sequence following Jeanne Moreau as she wanders the streets of Paris, influenced Antonioni's remapping of Milan in *La notte* using the same nomadic actress to highlight the dehumanizing space of the city.[20] The mere allusion to wandering and the nomadism associated with the style of the French New Wave protagonists situates contemporary films such as *Reprise* and *Oslo* quite clearly within the cultural heritage of the Western dandy and the attendant connotations of an affected Parisian melancholy, a nostalgic history Betz glosses by tracing the prototype of the *flâneur* back to Charles Baudelaire's Second-Empire Paris and Walter Benjamin's Weimar Berlin. The *flâneur*'s body, expressed through attitude, pose, and style, is captured through the posture of melancholy, the essential condition of life within capitalist modernity: "Since there is no escape from the melancholy that attends modern urban existence, the *flâneur* focuses his attention on the precise perception of its environs and spaces. He goes through life with eyes open."[21] Anders, the suicidal protagonist of Trier's *Oslo*, much like his predecessor Alain Leroy in Malle's *Le Feu follet*, carries with him the attitude of the melancholic *flâneur*, although not excessively dandified in the style of Jean-Pierre Léaud's signature silk scarves and tweed suit jackets.

Anne Friedberg traces the *flâneur* back to Baudelaire's original conception of the artist and dandy (types used to focus questions of beauty, artifice and fashion and their correlation to happiness) at the definitional core of modernity in his 1863 *The Painter of Modern Life*.[22] Indeed, the ephemeral nature of happiness underscores much of the playfulness associated with the 1960s New Wave brand of fecklessness, youth, and daring, particularly the freedoms enjoyed by its male protagonists (although not exclusively male, with Varda's *Cléo* being an important exception). Friedberg makes the crucial link between the aesthetic pose, attitude, and image of the urban dandy and the foundational emergence of commodity culture through the nineteenth century, with its creation of "new illusions of spatial and temporal mobility."[23] Unlike Honoré's bittersweet homages to Demy, Godard, and Truffaut, Trier's films remember the form of late-modern existential solitude, expressed through the somber tone and visual architecture of that certain type of 1960s modernist European cinema, a style associated in shorthand with much of 1960s Antonioni and echoed in the portraits of loneliness and unhappiness in other celebrated films of the period by Bergman, Malle, Rohmer, and Varda. This aesthetic of masculine melancholy extended into the early 1970s with the example of Perec and Queysanne's *Un homme qui dort*, a monochromatic portrait of depression with a modernist patchwork design and behavioral attempt to map out a young man's personal alienation and affective retreat through his real and imagined navigations across Paris.

Jonathan Flatley situates melancholy as an affective practice as much as a psychological state of mind. He defines the term as "longing for lost loves, brooding over absent objects and changed environments, reflecting on unmet desires, and lingering on events from the past. It is a practice that might, in fact, produce its own kind of knowledge."[24] Flatley's formulation of affective mapping is concerned with the urban topography of melancholy conceived as an affect, an emotion, or a mood, as a relational state of being as much as a clinical condition. He turns to Benjamin's labyrinthine investigation into the material experience of urban living in determining "one's way of being in the world."[25] "Mood" is precisely the term used to articulate the structuring role of history on our affective lives. Benjamin famously used fashion as an example of our scavenging approach to memory and history, a "temporally disjunctive evocation of the past,"[26] and his metaphor of history as a tiger's leap was used to describe the symbolic meanings of fashion within modernity. Fashion historian Caroline Evans also turns to Benjamin's writings from the 1930s as a method of inquiry to analyze contemporary fashion's tendency to segue between past and present. Drawing on his historical metaphor to juxtapose contemporary and past styles, "to illuminate the way that the past can resonate in the present to articulate modern anxieties and experiences,"[27] Evans employs the topographical metaphor of the labyrinth to allude to fashion's own doubling back on itself to reveal the memory traces in those styles and trends that appear most modern.

Cold Wave

Trier's dialogue with European cinema of the early 1960s channels imagery from across the arts through the layering of visual and sonic effects from the music, literature, and fashions of the period with those of the decades since, particularly new wave and postpunk pop music from the early 1980s. Much like the historical scavenging Evans detects in contemporary fashion's relaying of the past, the melancholic mood and acoustic design of Trier's cinema capture the disjunctive tones of the "new waves" of the 1960s (cinema) and the 1980s (music). The 2006 *Reprise* traces the artistic and sentimental adventures of two twenty-something aspiring novelists, Erik and Phillip, as they negotiate success, failure, rivalry, and depression. Whilst the film's study of the artist as a young man makes playful gestures to French New Wave cinema (particularly to Godard's temporal and spatial disorientation through jump-cutting), it also blends in references to postwar modernist fiction (including archive footage of Marguérite Duras and the radical heritage of the *nouveau roman*), juxtaposed with a soundtrack of later British new wave pop of the early 1980s.

Writing in *The New Yorker*, Richard Brody took issue with this flaunting of vintage styles, dismissing the film as a "pseudo-intellectual, faux-modernist pastiche of New Wave moods and tricks [lacking] any trace of spontaneity, the cinematic savvy, or the self-revealing emotional openness of the French New Wave's masterworks."[28] But in fact, the point of the prologue is to show off its pastiche affectation through the use of a future anterior tense, the hypothetical "what if" scenario used to fracture the narrative's dominant psychological realism. After Erik and Phillip post their finished manuscripts, the film toys with multiple possibilities of success figured predominantly as recognition by Parisian literary culture. The remainder of the film avoids the initial trickery, favoring a more controlled use of stylistic influence to trace both writers' personal insecurities and fractured relationships with women. The initial impression of glibness is carefully contrived to situate the film's opening flourish as an homage to the New Wave: close-ups of the pretentious book jackets, the use of ellipsis, disjuncture between image and sound, fast motion, black and white clichés of Parisian cafés, and an overlaid soundtrack borrowing the somber theme from Godard's *Contempt* (*Le Mépris*, 1963).

The acoustic effect of *Reprise*, however, points to the film's more ambitious formal composition. Laying down tracks from English postpunk and new wave pop music of the 1980s (the rhythmic patterns of Joy Division and New Order's *Substance* albums) onto the visual heritage of French New Wave cinema of the 1960s works to situate the film within a contemporary pop sensibility that layers its musical memories as part of a broader vintage style. Trier's creative mix of artefacts from across highbrow and popular cultural forms (skateboarding alongside Maurice Blanchot) certainly situates *Reprise* within a vintage cinema of self-referential allusion and surface chic. Philip (played by Anders Danielson Lie) even sports a T-shirt of The Smiths' *The Queen Is Dead* album cover showing a portrait of Alain Delon.

This actually works to frame a more probing account of the futility of middle-class aspirations. The extreme close-ups of the photogenic actors Anders Danielson Lie and Espen Klouman Høiner certainly resemble the anguished realism of 1990s fashion photography. But the Scandinavian style of monochromatic formal attire mixed with pieces from sportswear such as band T-shirts or hoodies (a style particularly associated with the emergence of fashion-forward Scandinavian labels such as Acne, Tiger or Our Legacy) serves to establish the film's social milieu, tonal sensibility, and cultural frame of reference.[29] The young men's creative ambitions are framed by their hipster milieu, the style of which combines low-key streetwear with minimal ornamentation, the transfer of countercultural symbolism (associated with the impact of Belgian designer Raf Simons on contemporary menswear since the mid-1990s), and a local adaptation of the classic postwar US iconography of anticonformism (T-shirts, leather jackets, and jeans). Trier aimed "to make a film that focused on the poetic details of boy culture."[30] His portrait of masculinity gestures to the familiar dandy figure (updated to the less obviously affected metrosexual male) and to the characters' immaturity and pretentions. The men are shown at times to be crass and sexist. The passing intrusion of a female editor into the all-male company serves to underscore their laddish insecurities.

Trier's insistent focus on posing and style—visual, literary, and acoustic—is purposefully used to sketch out a portrait of postadolescent ennui and aborted professional ambition leading to depression, madness, and suicide: Phillip finally accepts that his writing merely recycled the styles of the great Norwegian writers. Alongside the more familiar references to the modernist fiction of Duras or the literary philosophy of Blanchot, there is the inclusion of a fictional literary idol, Sten Egil Dahl, said to have retreated from public life and renounced a literary career through his self-imposed silence. The character is modelled on Tor Ulven, an experimental verse poet who committed suicide in 1995, like his fictional counterpart, whose death is registered at the end of the film. In a creative parallel, the spectral figure of Joy Division's suicidal front man Ian Curtis looms large over the film's interrogation of psychological fragility and artistic originality, and the rhythmic structures and mechanical loops of the band's music provide the transition between *Reprise* and *Oslo*, which in turn focuses on the final day in the life of a suicidal heroin addict who returns to the city in a failed attempt at redemption.

Unlike the ironic prologue to *Reprise*, *Oslo* begins with documentary snapshots showing the city as it was, remembered as a provincial backwater before the oil boom. The film ends with an elegiac long take of protagonist Anders's fatal overdose. Both the gesture to the subjective nature of memory (the reprise of Georges Perec's inventory invocation "I remember . . . I remember" relayed in voice-over) and the character study of intense loneliness indicate a careful elaboration of spatial design that is reminiscent of Antonioni's static shots documenting the cityscape. They also point to the influence of Perec's visual articulation of alienation through the topography of Paris, the sleeping man passing from one space to another.[31]

Trier's portrait draws attention to Anders' psychological state early on through drowning, showing his failed suicide attempt through total immersion. Like Varda's *Cléo*, a similarly moving portrait of a life in flux that unravels in almost real time on a single day in Paris from 5 pm to 7 pm, the temporal and spatial dynamics of Trier's film become themes in themselves, part of the film's contemplative structure. Trier's title, with its concise factual focus framing the narrative in both time and space (*Oslo, August 31st*), similarly underscores the protagonist's numbered days. Adrian Martin has described the effect of Varda's similar multiperspective approach as "the sense that it's not one person's story but a story that belongs to everyone who passes in and out of its frame."[32]

The elegance of Trier's film derives less from any obvious fashion sense or contrived aesthetic design than from the simple tracking of Danielson Lie's nonchalant movements through the city and his ability to capture the character's existential implosion through subtle physical expression. The dandy-rock style of *Reprise* morphs into a more neutral, monochromatic nonfashion: Anders's black leather bomber jacket is worn throughout to emphasize his ordinariness as much as his sexiness. Trier avoids the social realism prototype of the drug addict, instead focusing on Anders's concerted effort to overcome his addiction, to hang on to life.

The fleeting shot of him clinging on to a girl on the back of a bicycle as he is whisked away is intensely moving because it provides a striking contrast with the film's extended sequence depicting Anders' alienation through sensory perception. Seated in a glass-lined café, he observes the surrounding customers whose snatches of conversation become increasingly intrusive, disjointed and disorientating, allowing Trier to transpose into visual terms "the ways in which we perceive being alive."[33] This ontological sequence illustrates the character's psychological fracture through perception, through vocal inflection, and through extreme close-ups of Anders's drawn face, paying attention to his nose, mouth, and ears, rather than through the standard tropes of social realism more often used to stage an addict's decline through dramatic exaggeration.

This delicate attention to perception situates Trier under the influence of Varda, whose own more fluid sequence filmed at *Le Dôme* café followed Corinne Marchand as *Cléo* drifting in and out of conversations, cruising the outdoor

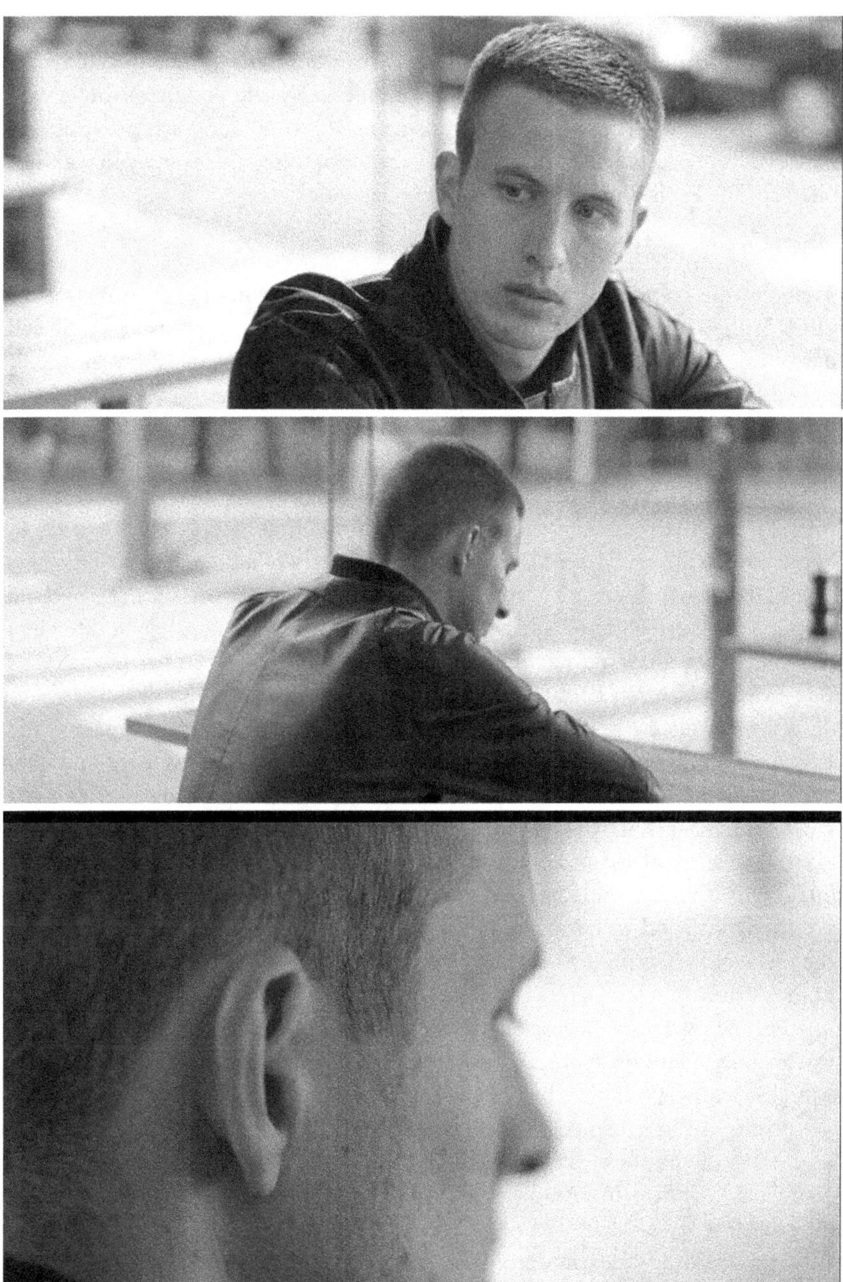

Figs. 11.1, 11.2, and 11.3 Design and perception: Anders (Anders Danielson Lie) in *Oslo, August 31st* (Joachim Trier, 2011).

tables, gracefully circling the bar inside. Varda's continuous long take allows for the fluidity of movement to be maintained, unlike Trier's more truncated series of static shots of spatial perception. The modern Nordic design aesthetic, with its transparent surfaces and geometric shapes, its wood and glass, its simplicity and structure, stands in stark contrast to the animation, the promiscuity, and the bustle of the Parisian public space of the early 1960s.

Ode to a Dying Hipster

Trier's ironic tribute to Pierre Drieu la Rochelle's original novel from 1931 and Louis Malle's screen adaptation from 1963 (an "ode to a dying hipster," as he calls it[34]) masks his sincere admiration for both source texts, which drew on the life story of the decadent Dadaist poet Jacques Rigaut, who shot himself in Paris in 1929. Man Ray memorably filmed the impeccably dressed dandy for his short "ciné-poem" *Emak-Bakia* (*Leave Me Alone*) in 1926, making use of his sharp sense of style by filming his starched shirt collars through revolving, deforming mirrors. He later remembered Rigaut in his autobiographical *Self-Portrait* as "the handsomest, the best dressed of the group—my idea of a French dandy."[35]

Malle's own interest in Drieu la Rochelle's fictional account of Rigaut was inspired by the feeling of passivity following the suicide of a friend. He channelled this personal trauma into Maurice Ronet's visceral portrayal of the recovering alcoholic Alain Leroy, whose demise is charted through a film that Malle described as austere and antidecorative.[36] The haunting piano refrain taken from Erik Satie's ambient *Gymnopédies* (1888) accompanies the slow pace and somber tone, heightened only by the pointed emphasis on appearance. Malle provided Ronet with articles of clothing from his own wardrobe of formal suits, glasses, ties, sweaters, and even the pistol used to stage the fatal climax. While *The Fire Within* is an intense character study of existential angst, it also includes polished black and white photography of the left-bank café society, documenting the scene at St. Germain-des-Prés, a concentration of Parisian intellectual styles of the period.

Following Drieu la Rochelle's preoccupation with artistic creativity and wasted talent, Malle pictured his protagonist, Alain Leroy, as a drifter who was politically apathetic (the film references the extremist French paramilitary organisation OAS formed to prevent Algerian independence) and unlucky in love (as in the novel, he has left his American lover Dorothy and returned from New York). Underlying Alain's inability to become a responsible adult is a nagging anxiety about being ordinary, his life perceived as a form of gilded mediocrity by his middle-class academic friend Dubourg. Trier's contemporary version includes touches of humor as Thomas (Hans Olav Brenner), a Proust scholar, exposes the reassuring banality of his petit bourgeois lifestyle, a safety net that Anders discards in his self-imposed failure to find employment as a journalist in Trier's film. Malle's vision of artistic creativity as a palliative to life's hardships in *The Fire Within* echoed an earlier film by Eric Rohmer, *The Sign of Leo* (1959), which traced the fortunes of Pierre Wesselrin, an unaccomplished American musician in Paris whose bohemian good life is upturned when he is disinherited. The middle section of the film charts his physical decline from stylish artist to drunken bum across the Parisian public stage, a section of the film without dialogue apart from ironic snatches of overheard conversations that compound his alienation. Rohmer's pointed questioning of Wesselrin's wasted potential as an artist and musician is manifested through his outward appearance: his physical disintegration is presented as a symptom of his moral putrefaction.[37]

This focus on the male body as more than a site for superficial investment in appearance, as an index of prevailing moral and social values, points to a critical understanding of masculinity and style in conjunction with space and topography, underlining the basic centrality of corporeal display to filmic mise-en-scène.[38] From a theoretical perspective, Foucault's radio broadcasts from the mid-1960s articulated the productive tensions between space and the body, anticipating the philosopher's later reconfiguration of both from the vantage point of sexuality, bio-power, and the technologies of the self.[39] There has been a substantial critical relaying of Foucault's concept of "heterotopia" (spaces containing multiple layers of meaning, functioning in nonhegemonic ways) in cultural geography and architectural theory.[40]

Although the spatial turn has impacted analysis of film art of the 1960s, the dialogue between Foucault's early writing on the body and the contextual culture of the period has not received the same attention. In "The Utopian Body," Foucault situated the body's mirror image at the centre of heterotopia. The body is perceived as the ultimate place of confinement, the utopian image of which is expressed through attempts at cosmetic disguise and modification such as masks, makeup, and tattoos. The mirror image and the corpse are figured as the only mechanisms by which the body can escape pure utopia.[41]

Malle operates in a similar thematic territory in *The Fire Within* (with the ghostly transience of its original title, *Le Feu follet*, meaning "Will o' the wisp") particularly in his filming of Maurice Ronet, encasing the suicidal man (originally described in the novel as a naïve, splenetic dandy in the Baudelairean vein) within a disturbing artificial interior and a larger canvas of sex, decadence, and death.[42] There is an insistent focus throughout on the maudlin array of esoteric objects in Alain's room, an emphasis on his fading beauty and on the elaborate display of his accessories and suits, one of which falls from its hanger like a collapsing ghost of a man. Jeanne Moreau's striking cameo as Eva begins with the foreboding line "You look like a corpse," and Alain later comments to Dubourg that it was only when making love to women that he felt he had some hold on life.

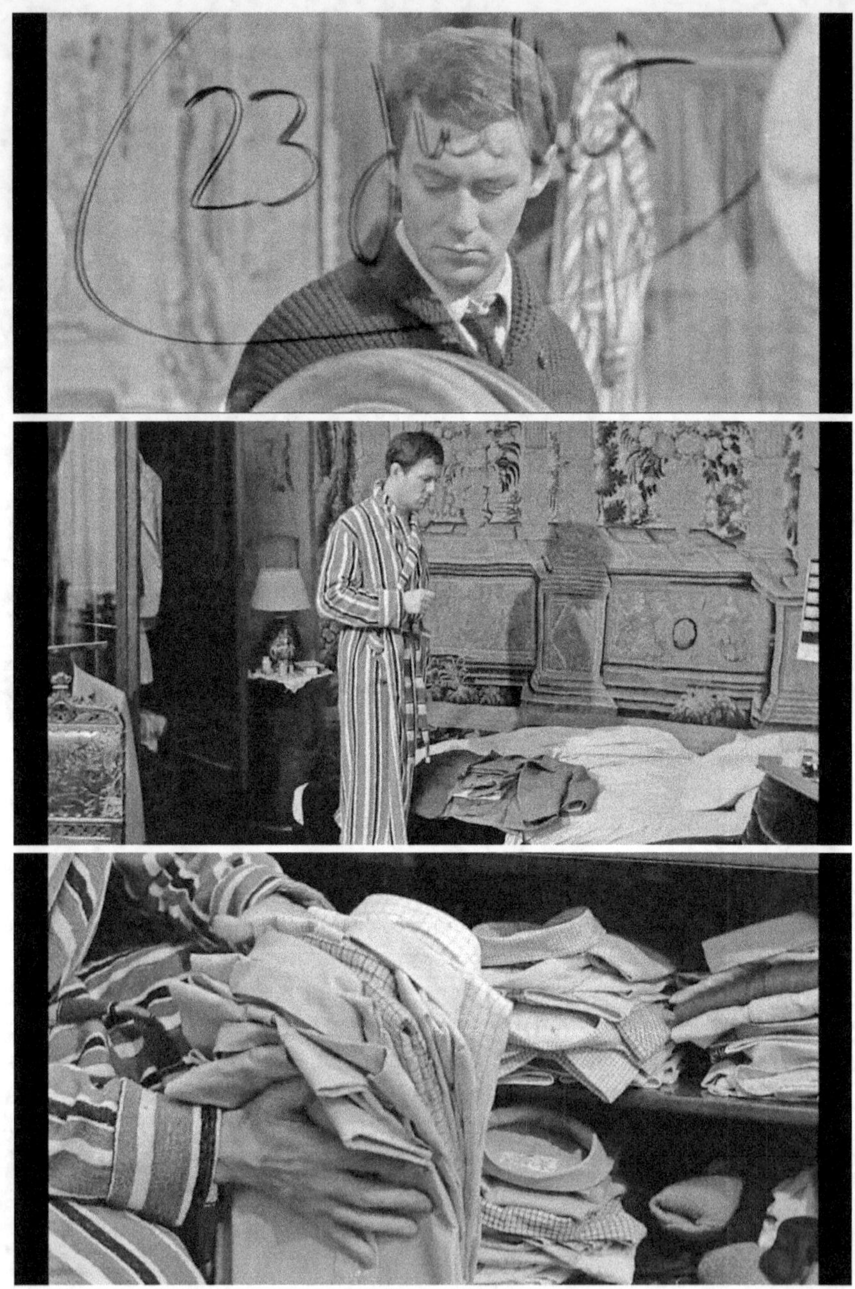

Figs. 11.4, 11.5, and 11.6 Style and death: Alain (Maurice Ronet) in *The Fire Within / Le Feu Follet* (Louis Malle, 1963).

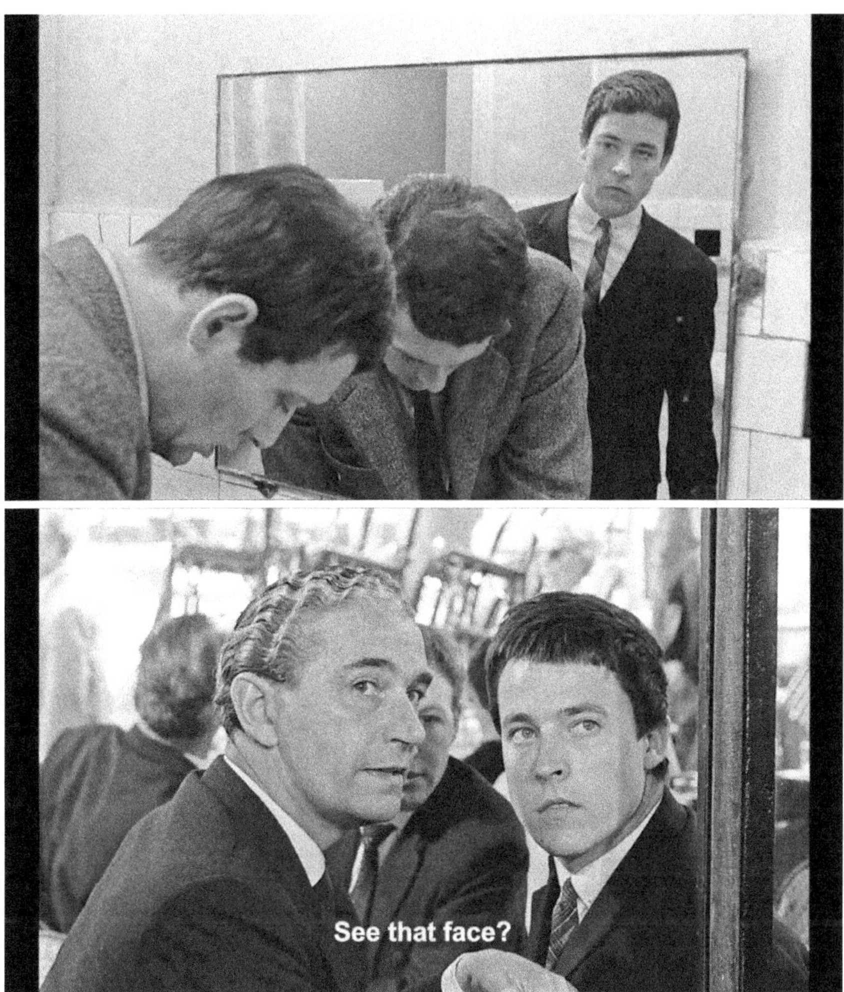

Figs. 11.7, 11.8, 11.9, and 11.10 Queerness and disavowal: despite his fading looks, Alain (Maurice Ronet) still receives attention from other men (*The Fire Within* / *Le Feu Follet* (Louis Malle, 1963).

In short, Alain is out of place and out of time, anachronistic in the context of the emerging youth culture of the decade.

This idea of bodies being out of joint occurs elsewhere in Malle's cinema. Discussing Malle's earlier *Elevator to the Gallows*, with its prototypical rebellious teenage boy whose fierce leather jacket (the iconic symbol of 1950s anticonformism) is ridiculed in passing, Betz comments that it is a "film largely about modern

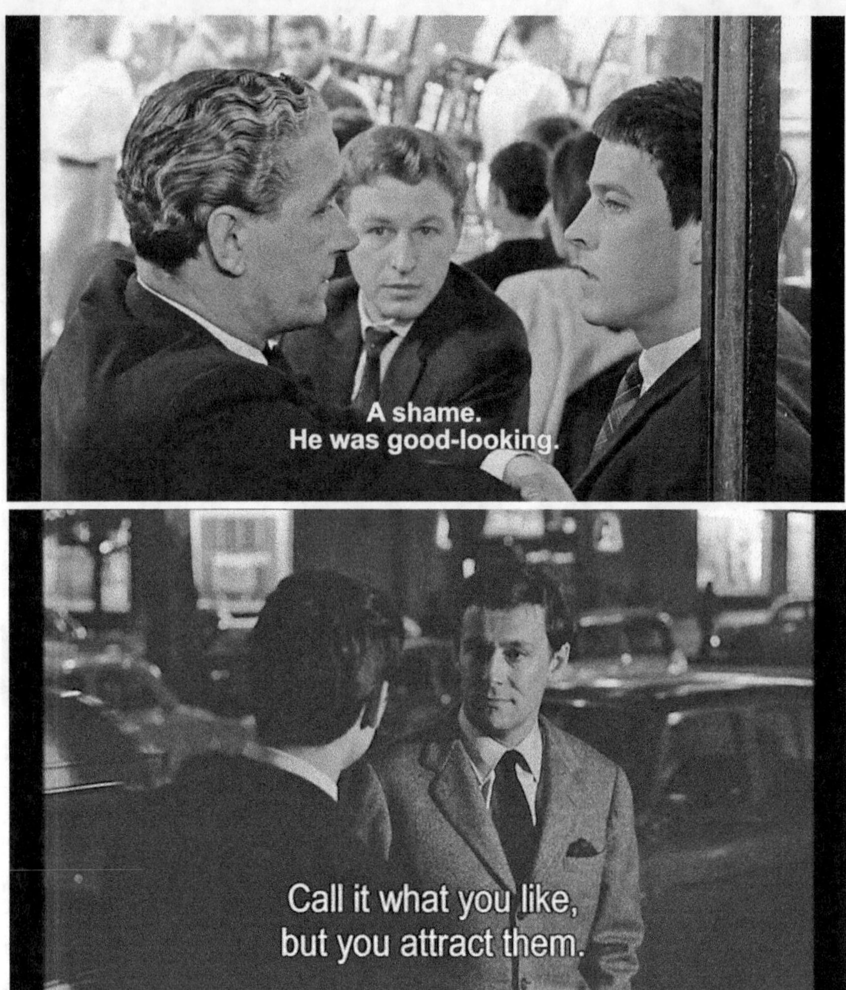

Figs. 11.9, and 11.10 *Continued*

time and the way it entraps characters who are either past their time (Tavernier, the ex-soldier) or before it (the teenagers), in either case never fully *of* it."[43] While Dubourg's daughter in *The Fire Within* is a fan of 1960s pop singer Sylvie Vartan, Alain is out of step with cultural change. Maurice Ronet's body is shown to move awkwardly and to age visibly through the course of the film.[44]

This coincidence of male beauty and aging also indicates the disavowed homonarcissism lurking in both the original novel and Malle's film adaptation. It is also suggestive of the type of same-sex look now more readily associated with fashion and advertising imagery. The novel contains recondite passages describing a peculiar aversion to the female form, an expressive over investment in antique objects, and a pronounced disgust at male homosexuals. An allusive sequence in the film in which Alain exchanges glances with an attractive young man in the cloakroom of a café captures this sexual ambiguity through the use of a mirror to frame their communion. The handsome homosexual scrutinizes the fading Alain with an ambiguous blend of curiosity, desire, and disgust. Alain's solitude and distance from other men is said to be linked to his absence of goals, the dandy's aimless cruising of the city suggestive of not only the history of gay male occupation of urban space but also of a queer rejection of the normative regulation of time, with its coherent categories of adulthood and youth and its linear narratives of progress and accomplishment.[45]

Like Malle's *The Fire Within*, Trier's films *Reprise* and *Oslo August 31st* subtly interrogate the form, shape, and feel of masculinity by charting the movement of the male body through urban space, suggestive of how masculinity can be articulated through cinematic mood and tonal design as much as through costume or style. Trier's cinema gestures to ways of remembering not just the superficial aesthetic codes of 1960s European art cinema but also its affective sensibility without recourse to the more obvious excesses of pastiche reproduction. His films instead reinterpret the allure of the urban loner, the disaffected single man. They also echo Christophe Honoré's layering of cinematic memory (as opposed to mere visual quotation) as a means of capturing the more complex coincidence of tonal influence and creative design. This approach to evoking the 1960s moves critical debate of film, fashion, and costume beyond a one-dimensional vintage aesthetic and toward a more complex handling and understanding of heritage, masculinity, and style in contemporary European cinema.

NICK REES-ROBERTS is Professor of Media and Cultural Studies at the Université Sorbonne Nouvelle--Paris III, France. He is the author of *French Queer Cinema*, and coeditor of *Alain Delon: Style, Stardom and Masculinity*.

Notes

1. Simon Reynolds, *Retromania: Pop Culture's Addictions to its Own Past* (London: Faber & Faber, 2011).
2. Bruno Remaury, "Rituel de mode et objet de consummation," in *La Mode des sixties: L'entrée dans la modernité*, ed. Dominique Veillon and Michele Ruffat (Paris: Les Editions Autrement, 2007), 155–62, at 159.
3. Pamela Church Gibson, "Film Costume," in *Film Studies: Critical Approaches*, ed. John Hill and Pamela Church Gibson (Oxford: Oxford University Press, 2000), 34–40, at 35.

4. Pamela Church Gibson, *Fashion and Celebrity Culture* (London: Berg, 2011), 95–102.

5. Ben Walters, "The Trouble with Perfume," *Film Quarterly* 63, no. 4 (2010): 14–17.

6. Prudence Black and Catherine Driscoll, "Don, Betty and Jackie Kennedy: On *Mad Men* and Periodisation," *Cultural Studies Review* 18, no. 2 (2012): 188–206, at 188–189.

7. Susan Sontag, *Against Interpretation and Other Essays* (London: Penguin Books, 1966).

8. Fredric Jameson, "Postmodernism and Consumer Society," in *The Anti-Aesthetic: Essays on Postmodern Culture*, ed. Hal Foster (Seattle: Bay Press, 1983), 111–25.

9. Emiliano Morreale, *L'invenzione della nostalgia: Il vintage nel cinema italiano e dintorni* (Rome: Donzelli, 2009); Emiliano Morreale, "Le Cinéma vintage," *Cahiers du cinéma* 673 (2011): 16–19.

10. Antony Easthope, "Cinecities in the Sixties," in *The Cinematic City*, ed. David B. Clarke (London: Routledge, 1997), 129–39.

11. Isabelle Vanderschelden, "The 'Beautiful People' of Christophe Honoré: New Wave Legacies and New Directions in French Auteur Cinema," *Studies in European Cinema* 7.2 (2010): 135–48, at 136.

12. Pam Cook, *Screening the Past: Memory and Nostalgia in Cinema* (London: Routledge, 2005), 3.

13. Cook, *Screening the Past*, 4.

14. Mark Betz, *Beyond the Subtitle: Remapping European Art Cinema* (Minneapolis: University of Minnesota Press, 2009).

15. Susan Sontag, *Styles of Radical Will* (London: Penguin Books, 1967), 125.

16. Sontag, *Styles of Radical Will*, 125.

17. Giuliana Bruno, *Public Intimacy: Architecture and the Visual Arts* (Cambridge, MA: MIT Press, 2007), 199–200.

18. Leonardo Clausi, "Tom Cullen by Bruce Weber," *L'Uomo Vogue* 424 (October 2011): 152–57; Kin Woo, "Bruce Weber Selects Andrew Haigh: Gay Film Gets a Very Modern Makeover," in *Dazed and Confused*, October, 2011, 78.

19. The 1960s inspiration for Haigh's cinema, including references to both Reisz and Varda, was documented in Dennis Lim, "Romance and Reflection, Hand in Hand," *New York Times*, September 22, 2011, AR8. For extensive coverage of women's fashion in Antonioni's cinema, see Eugenia Paulicelli, "Framing the Self: Staging Identity: Clothing and Italian style in the Films of Michelangelo Antonioni (1950–1964)," in *The Fabric of Cultures: Fashion, Identity and Globalization*, ed. Eugenia Paulicelli and Hazel Clark (New York: Routledge, 2008), 53–72.

20. *Malle on Malle*, ed. Philip French (London: Faber and Faber, 1993), 44.

21. Betz, *Beyond the Subtitle*, 133.

22. Charles Baudelaire, *The Painter of Modern Life and Other Essays* (London: Phaidon, 1995).

23. Anne Friedberg, *Window Shopping: Cinema and the Postmodern* (Berkeley: University of California Press, 1993), 37.

24. Jonathan Flatley, *Affective Mapping: Melancholia and the Politics of Modernism* (Cambridge, MA: Harvard University Press, 2008), 2.

25. Flatley, *Affective Mapping*, 19.

26. Flatley, *Affective Mapping*, 75.

27. Caroline Evans, *Fashion at the Edge: Spectacle, Modernity and Deathliness* (London: Yale University Press, 2003), 9.

28. Richard Brody, "Film File: *Reprise*," *The New Yorker*, June 2, 2008.

29. Dorothea Gundtoft, *Fashion Scandinavia: Contemporary Cool* (London: Thames and Hudson, 2013).

30. Dennis Lim, "Cinematic Life in Oslo (Where Else?)," *New York Times*, May 11, 2008.
31. Georges Perec, *Species of Spaces and Other Pieces* (London: Penguin Books, 1974), 5.
32. Adrian Martin, "Passionate Time," sleeve notes to *4 by Agnès Varda*, DVD, The Criterion Collection.
33. Dominique Païni, "La Forme d'une ville," *Cahiers du cinéma* 676 (2012): 52–53, at 53.
34. Joachim Trier, quoted in Julien Gester, "Oslo périlleux," *Libération*, February 29, 2012, http://next.liberation.fr/cinema/2012/02/29/oslo-perilleux_799384, accessed 30 March 2017.
35. Man Ray, *Self-Portrait* (London: Penguin Books, 1963), 108.
36. Louis Malle, "Cinq à la zero," *Cahiers du cinéma* 146 (1963): 33.
37. Pascal Bonitzer, *Eric Rohmer* (Paris: Cahiers du cinéma, 1999), 84.
38. In the case of Hollywood cinema, Stella Bruzzi has analyzed the mise-en-scène of masculinity through aesthetics and form rather than through representation (*Men's Cinema: Masculinity and Mise-en-Scene in Hollywood* [Edinburgh: Edinburgh University Press, 2013]).
39. Michel Foucault, *Histoire de la sexualité 1: La Volonté de savoir* (Paris: Gallimard, 1976), translated as *The History of Sexuality: The Will to Knowledge*, trans. R. Hurley (London: Allen Lane, 1978).
40. Daniel Defert, "'Hétérotopie': Tribulations d'un concept entre Venise, Berlin et Los Angeles," in Michel Foucault, *Le Corps utopique, Les Hétérotopies* (Paris: Nouvelles Editions Lignes, 2009); Edward W. Soja, *Thirdspace: Journeys to Los Angeles and Other Real-and-Imagined Places* (Oxford: Wiley-Blackwell, 1996).
41. Michel Foucault, "Utopian Body," in *Sensorium: Embodied Experience, Technology and Contemporary Art*, ed. Caroline E. Jones (Cambridge MA: The MIT Press, 2006), 229–34. "Le Corps utopique" was first broadcast by *France-Culture* on December 7, 1966.
42. Pierre Drieu la Rochelle, *Le Feu follet* (Paris: Gallimard, 1931), 41, 132.
43. Betz, *Beyond the Subtitle*, 156.
44. Malle, "Cinq à la zero," 33.
45. Judith Halberstam, *In a Queer Time and Place: Transgender Bodies, Subcultural Lives* (New York: New York University Press, 2005).

PART IV
Epilogue

12 Adriana Berselli: Costume Designer for Film and Theater

Eugenia Paulicelli

My first contact with Adriana Berselli was on the telephone in December 2007. At that time I was completing an essay on Michelangelo Antonioni's films and the impact that clothing and fashion had on his cinematic language and Italy's process of modernization. The essay was to be published in the volume *The Fabric of Culture. Fashion, Identity, Globalization* that Hazel Clark and I coedited (Routledge 2009).[1] Adriana had been the costume designer for Antonioni's *L' Avventura*, and I had been trying to connect with her for some time when I found some information at the Biblioteca "Luigi Chiarini" in the Centro Sperimentale di Cinematografia in Rome. As I had a number of questions about details to do with the film, I decided to call the biblioteca. I was passed on to Laura Ceccarelli, who, without even knowing me, was gracious enough to give me Adriana's phone number.[2] As it happened, Laura had recently completed a book on Adriana Berselli, which she had coedited with Marina Cipriani.

I called Adriana and had a long conversation on the phone. I also arranged a meeting for the following January so I could interview her in person in her apartment in Rome. After that, we stayed in contact, and when Louise Wallenberg and I organized the conference on *The 1960s: Fashion and Film*, we both agreed to invite Adriana to New York to take part in the conversation with film scholars. The talk she gave is now part of this volume. Some of her sketches for *L' Avventura* were also on view in the exhibition at the James Gallery in The Graduate Center of the City University of New York during the time of the conference and thereafter for three months.

In this short note here, let me offer some background about Adriana's career so that readers can contextualize her short memoir. She was born to a family of musicians in 1937 in Ferrara, where Antonioni was also born. She recalls the talent of her mother, a pianist who, at sixteen years of age, was invited to play in a "futurist concert" presented by the poet Filippo Tommaso Marinetti at the Teatro Comunale in Ferrara. When the family moved to Rome after her high school years, she attended the Accademia delle Belle Arti (an arts college) before applying to and being accepted by the Centro Sperimentale di Cinematografia.

Here she received a fellowship and spent beautiful and intense years at the School of Cinematography. She graduated in 1951 and started to work in the world of cinema with Georg Wilhelm Pabst, Alessandro Blasetti, Dino Risi, Luigi Comencini, Michelangelo Antonioni, and the other filmmakers and actors and actresses she mentions in her memoir (Sophia Loren, Marcello Mastroianni, Peter Sellers, and others). After working in Italy for some years, she moved to Venezuela, where she abandoned cinema for a while to be close to her husband. She dedicated herself to costuming for theatre, teaching costume design, and writing about fashion for a South American magazine.

She firmly believes that a costume designer must have a high-quality education not only to develop the practical skills necessary to execute a dress but also to acquire the knowledge and understanding of the culture and history of a specific period. She believes that, without having the cultural foundations necessary to interpret a costume, it is almost impossible to do a good job in costume design. In addition, she stresses that it is not only the style, the cut, and the colors that determine the feel of an epoch, but also the movements of the body: the way one walks or puts on a veil, a hat, or a glove, and so on.[3] She also thinks that drawing and sketching the character is a very important part of the process of working on costumes. Her own sketches are very detailed. Indeed, while at the Conference in New York in the spring of 2010, she spent a great deal of time drawing, not only the speakers (drawings that she gave us and that we now cherish), but also the people she saw in the street. Observing street fashion in New York was a great pleasure for her and instead of a camera, she carried a sketch pad and a pencil.

As our book is focused on the 1960s, it is natural to think of Adriana and the work she did with Antonioni on one of his most groundbreaking films, one that is still making waves as a watershed in the invention of filmic language. Adriana recalls that when Piero Poletto, the set designer for the film (and her friend from the time they were both students at the Centro Sperimentale di Cinematografia), invited her to work on *L'Avventura*, he warned her that it would be a difficult film with a complicated and demanding director. And to make things even more difficult, he told her that the film had not received much funding. Nevertheless, it was a great opportunity for Adriana.

As she found out, Antonioni was the most meticulous of directors. He liked to control every single detail of costumes, fabric, color, and patterns. Most of the time, he liked solid colors, often black and white. Differently from other directors, he wanted to see quite a lot of fabric, to touch it and then figure out the chromatic effect on screen. Antonioni was also the kind of director who used to explain exactly what he wanted, and he had long conversations with Adriana before she embarked on the costume sketches and designs for the film. She received precise and copious instructions and worked with set designers and assistant directors, such as Franco Indovina and Gianni Arduini, who were also former students at the CSC.

She recalled a specific episode in *L'Avventura* that amounted to a declaration of independence by Monica Vitti.[4] In the sequence shot in the Sicilian town of Noto (with Gabriele Ferzetti as Sandro), Vitti wanted (as Claudia) to wear a suit and a string of pearls, and while Adriana was away, she bought the suit for herself in a boutique. Adriana did not agree with Vitti's choice, as she thought the suit and the pearls were a deviation from the bohemian type of character she was playing at the beginning of the film when she acts as the outsider, even to her friend Anna (played by Lea Massari), who gets lost on the Sicilian island and is never found.

Who knows who was right? What we can say is that Vitti's black and white suit with minuscule polka dots and her beautiful and distressed mane of blond hair look stunning against the backdrop of Noto's baroque cathedral. And although, typically, the suit with a string of pearls is the uniform of a bourgeois lady, on Monica Vitti, with her hair and the nontraditional kind of Italian beauty she conveyed in the scene, the suit takes on different meanings. On her body and persona, it loses its uniformity to become part of the innovation that is Antonioni's cinematic language. This episode points to what Barthes called the "obtuse," by which he means a detail that is able to interrupt the expectations not only of viewers, but even of those working on the making of the film, such as Berselli, whose only concern is to do their job well.[5] Even an apparent "philological" mistake, narrative deviations, and neurotic characters become what Sam Rohdie beautifully described, "opportunities for film."[6]

EUGENIA PAULICELLI is Professor of Italian, Comparative Literature and, Women's Studies at Queens College and The Graduate Center of the City University of New York (CUNY). She is author of *Fashion under Fascism. Beyond the Black Shirt; Writing Fashion in Early Modern Italy: From Sprezzatura to Satire*; *Fashion is a Serious Business: Rosa Genoni, Milan Expo 1906 and the Great War*; and *Italian Style: Fashion & Film from Early Cinema to the Digital Age.*

Notes

1. Eugenia Paulicelli, "Framing the Self, Staging Identity: Clothing and Italian Style in the Films of Michelangelo Antonioni (1950–1964)", in *The Fabric of Cultures: Fashion, Identity, Globalization*, ed. Paulicelli and Hazel Clark (London and New York: Routledge, 2009), 53–72. See also Paulicelli, "*Cronaca di un amore*: Fashion and Italian Cinema in Michelangelo Antonioni's Films (1949–1955)", in *New Perspectives in Italian Cultural Studies*, vol. 2, *The Arts and History*, ed. Graziella Parati, (Madison, NJ: Farleigh Dickinson University Press, 2013), 107–30.

A longer version of this text is contained in my book *Italian Style: Fashion & Film from Early Cinema to the Digital Age* (London and New York: Bloomsbury Academics, 2016).

2. The most detailed publication on Adriana Berselli are the recently published *Adriana Berselli. L'avventura del costume. Cinema, teatro, television, moda,* design by Caratazzolo Caterina and Tarquini Silvia (Dublin: Artdigiland, 2016) and *Carte, colori e tessuti: Ritratto di una costumista: Adriana Berselli,* ed. Laura Ceccarelli and Marina Cipriani, Quaderni della Biblioteca "Luigi Chiarini" (Rome: Centro Sperimentale di Cinematografia, 2005). The book contains an interview, detailed information regarding her film and theatre activities, and extensive information on the Fondo Berselli that the costume designer donated to Centro Sperimentale di Cinematografia in 2005, and Domenico Monetti's interview with Berselli at the opening of the book. See also http://siusa.archivi.beniculturali.it/cgi-bin/pagina.pl?TuttoAperto=1&TipoPag=comparc&ChiaveRadice=351534&ChiaveAlbero=351534&Chiave=351623&RicSez=fondi&RicVM=indice&ApriNodo=0&RicTipoScheda=ca, accessed June 15, 2015.

3. Domenico Monetti, "Conversazione con Adriana Berselli," in Ceccarelli and Cipriani, *Carte, colori e tessuti*, 13.

4. Interview by the author with Adriana Berselli, 2011.

5. Roland Barthes, "The Third Meaning: Research Notes on Several Eisenstein Stills," in *The Responsibility of Forms: Critical Essays on Music, Art and Representation*, trans. Richard Howard (Berkley: University of California Press, 1970).

6. Sam Rohdie, *Antonioni* (London: BFI, 1990).

13 Souvenir of a Costume Designer

Adriana Berselli

I started to practice my craft in the movies (and later in the theater, fashion, and TV industries) after having studied at the Centro Sperimentale di Cinematografia, the school of cinema in Rome, at the end of the 1950s.

If I have a strong point, it's my experience that has been built through extensive study, attendance at specialist courses, and endless work on film sets. In the end, however, I'd say my natural curiosity and a keen eye for observation have provided the driving force that has enabled me to gain all this priceless experience.

I've designed for some interesting historical films, but I've preferred working on those set in contemporary times, which are more complicated perhaps but, to my mind, more intriguing (tricky), with a role's characterization being particularly dependent on the costume designer, personal taste, interpretation of the script, and the ability to translate it into an effective cinematographic image.

Having chosen this profession, my main interest has always been centered around the actors, not only their personality but also, and above all, their physical characteristics. So, the material with which one starts out is the body, which is not being decorated with what suits it best, but rather cancelled out in order to build a new one according to the type of cinematographic image that best suits the story, bearing in mind the requirements of the director and the producer and in harmony with the set designer and the director of photography. A film represents a team effort where a shared overall vision is essential.

We know that the garment dresses us up and, so, represents the outer surface through which we present ourselves to society. The film costume has to communicate this and has to represent the character's skin, in which the actors will move around the set as if they were wearing an outfit taken straight from their own wardrobe. According to the French director Jean Delannony, the contribution of the costume designer to the film's narrative is essential because a character on the screen is much more easily defined by means of clothing detail than by the ten lines of dialogue that are supposed to provide us all the insight into a character.

One thing to point out is that, in modern films, it's not advisable to take too much inspiration from the fashion of the time or you run the risk of having a "mannequin-actor," as happened in the film *Breakfast at Tiffany's*, of 1961, in which Audrey Hepburn's elegant clothes' parade, designed by the French couterier Hubert De Givenchy, doesn't contribute at all to the correct description of her cinematographic character.

To keep to our context, however, in the 1950s and 60s there was a radical change in the way people dressed that revealed the political and economic influences, the poverty that followed the war, and the various moments of recovery, as well as the feminist movement, the advent of pop art, new industrial techniques, and jeans, which (together with the miniskirt) represented youth protest movements.

My work in that period concerned the very successful films called *commedie all'Italiana*, shot, as well as many American historical movies, in the Cinecittà Studios of Rome, known as "Hollywood on the Tiber."

The directors of those comedies, which represent the problems, the unhappiness, and the fun had by families of a working class background (yet with a certain amount of economic affluence) were Luigi Comencini, Dino Risi, Steno, Mario Camerini, and others.

The female characters, often selected from beauty competitions, such as Sylva Koshina, Sophia Loren, Silvana Mangano, and Gina Lollobrigida had very pronounced physical attributes heightened by waspies and padding, unlike the women who were less showy but more influenced by the styles like "balloon," "boustier," "tulip," and "bell-shaped" that high fashion was launching through the much cheaper *prêt-à-porter.*

Among the male actors of that time, I designed for the great Totò, Vittorio De Sica, Edoardo and Peppino De Filippo, Aldo Fabrizi, and Walter Chiari, who successfully performed both comic and dramatic roles. They wore the "Borsalino" hat, the wide trousers and jacket in checkered wool material, double-breasted suit in large white striped fabric, and white shirts—with a lit cigarette in their hand.

The meeting with Michelangelo Antonioni represented a turning point in my work because the characters of the film *L'Avventura* are part of a psychological thriller set, for the most part, in locations dominated by a wild natural habitat. The story required very simple "visual screens" in which sometimes the clothing was required to blend in with, sometimes to disappear into, and sometimes to stand out against a very mysterious and dramatic world. The initial outfits of the two leading female characters, who are about to leave for a trip on a friend's yacht, are very important for presenting their respective social standing at first glance.

Claudia (played by Monica Vitti) is a middle-class girl who has been invited by her friend Anna (played by Lea Massari), who is rich and spoiled. Claudia represents the external and odd element that enters a world that is not her own, so she had to be dressed differently from Anna and the other female roles. Claudia, in fact, wears a simple checkered cotton skirt and a plain monochromatic sweater, while Anna wears a white shantung silk-pleated dress and carries a classic Gucci bamboo handbag.

Among the other female roles, the eccentric Patrizia (played by Esmeralda Ruspoli) is always covered in jewellery, inappropriately dressed in all places and circumstances, and with her little dog always in tow, and Giulia (played by Dominique Blachar) is an unhappy, beautiful, and boring woman whom I clad in "printed" fabric, some bows on her shoulders, large collars, and fluttering skirts to make her a little "dollish."

Michelangelo Antonioni was a very meticulous director who took particular care regarding the wardrobe of his female characters, and sometimes he liked to use the same details of a dress in many of his films. The thin shoulder straps that I added in Claudia's black evening dress, for example, represent an important element of the identical attire of Monica Vitti and Jeanne Moreau in the film *La notte*. Even the actress Dorian Gray in the film *Il Grido* wears a black petticoat with shoulder straps as do the female characters in *Deserto Rosso* (*Red Desert*) and *Identificazione di una donna* (*Identity of a Woman*).

In the course of the 1960s and the 1970s, I had the chance to work for some directors whose films' characters required eccentric outfits in a variety of styles (including revivals of the 30s and 40s). For films such as *Pussycat, Pussycat, I Love You* by Rod Amateau, *Three Bites of the Apple* by Alvin Ganzer, *The Bobo* by Robert Parrish, *The Battle of Villa Fiorita* by Dalmer Daves, and *L'Invasion* by Yves Allégret, I sketched mini- and maxiskirts, hot pants, minibrocade dresses with plastic tops, elegant evening suits in silver and golden and creased materials, plain or curled hairstyles, wide hats, little picked cups, highlegs boots, ballerian shoes, and so on.

All the material was made by a staff of clever film artisans, like Pompei and Arditi for the boots, and costume houses such as Anna Mode, Mayer, and Farani for the clothes. They worked at the side of famous shoemakers like Ferragamo and Dalcò, with the famous hat maker Cleo Romagnoli, and with fashion houses De Luca, Antonelli, Schuberth, Gattinoni, Carosa, Balestra, Piattelli, Brioni, and Angelo Palazzi, who lent their work enthusiastically to meet our frenetic cinematographic rhythms.

At the end of the 70s, the "couturiers" in the middle of a big stylistic confusion had started to adjust their product to the cultural transformation and to the market. The "casual style," the "blousons noir," the overall, and the wearing of jeans all over the world had created more spontaneity in social life and an easier way to dress during the day and in different circumstances. The movies reflect all of that, and my work at that time with directors like Carlo Lizzani, Vittorio Sindoni, and Duccio Tessari tell stories that hinge on existential factors that some of us had lived firsthand or known through family photos.

In the following years, I also worked on some interesting historical films, for TV and talk shows, and for the theatre, especially in South America, where I lived for many years.

In the films set in contemporary times, my directors have been Alberto Bevilacqua, George Pan Cosmatos, Carlo Di Palma, and Roman Polanski, and among the actors and actresses I have dressed are Sophia Loren, Richard Harris, Burt Lancaster, Ava Gardner, Sydney Rome, Marcello Mastroianni, Vittoria Gasman, Monica Vitti, Claudia Cardinale, Harvey Keitel, Margaux Hemingway, Virna Lisi, Karen Black, Brian Denney, and many other people who have given to me some moments of great satisfaction.

ADRIANA BERSELLI has worked as a costume designer on more than eighty films, including *L'avventura* (Michelangelo Antonioni), *Teresa la ladra* (Carlo Di Palma); *Le rose di Danzica* (Alberto Bevilacqua); *What?* (Roman Polansky); *L'Invasion* (Yves Allegret); and *Caro Gorbaciov* (Carlo Lizzani). She has researched and lectured internationally on the history of costume.

Index

www.ingramcontent.com/pod-product-compliance
Lightning Source LLC
LaVergne TN
LVHW020438080826
844660LV00033B/1319

* 9 7 8 0 2 5 3 0 2 6 1 0 1 *